Most Quoted
SCRIPTURES

Most Quoted SCRIPTURES

**of the
Standard Works
of
The Church of Jesus Christ of Latter-day Saints**

Compiled by Kay Briggs

RANDALL PUBLISHERS

SPECIAL FIRST PRINT EDITION
Commemorating the 150th Anniversary of
The Church of Jesus Christ of Latter-day Saints

Randall Publishers
462 North 150 East
Orem, Utah 84057

Acknowledgements

Thanks to Pauline Burnett, Sherrie Johnson, and Marge Taylor
for patiently editing and typing the manuscript.

Table of Contents

Gospel Topics (continued)

Preface

How To Use This Book

Most Quoted Scriptures is a collection of the scriptures most frequently quoted in General and Area Conferences, Church manuals and magazines, Seminary and Institute materials, and other Church programs during the past 150 years since the organization of the Church of Jesus Christ of Latter-day Saints. The four standard works of the Church contain over 40,000 scriptural verses. However, most of these verses are rarely quoted in talks or manuals. This selection contains the 1,000 scriptures most frequently quoted.

Most Quoted Scriptures is not meant to replace the scriptures, but to be used as a companion volume to improve your study of the Gospel. As a companion to your gospel study, this work may be used in several ways:

•Topical Index To the Scriptures

Most Quoted Scriptures is a topical index to the scriptures. The scriptures are arranged into 100 gospel topics from America to Zion. Since only the most popular scriptures are used, it is much easier to find that ideal scriptural reference for talks, family discussions, quiet reading, etc. Other scriptural references use a small line of the scripture and must have the "topic-word" in the phrase before it can be located. *Most Quoted Scriptures* uses the sense of the scripture, as well as the "topic-word." For example, under the topic "Attitude," a very popular scripture is "For as he thinketh in his heart, so is he. . ." (Proverbs 23:7). In other reference books, this phrase must be located under "heart" where it is one of many scriptures referring to "heart" as an organ of the body, etc.

•Quote Book Of Scriptures

Most Quoted Scriptures contains only approved scriptures from the four standard works of the Church. There are no "philosophies of men" to baffle the reader. Every teacher or speaker will appreciate the simple arrangement and easy referencing. Each scripture is prefaced, with brief background information concerning who is speaking, the time, place, and/or situation, etc.

•Aid For Marking The Scriptures

Most Quoted Scriptures is arranged to help gospel students mark their scriptures in three ways:

•Index By Book

In the back of the book, there is an index reference by book in the following order: Old Testament, New Testament, Book of Mormon, Doctrine and Covenants, Pearl of Great Price. This enables you to mark the most popular scriptures book by book, chapter by chapter, or section by section as they are found in the standard works.

•By Priority of Popularity

There is, in addition to the reference by book index, an index of the "100 Most Quoted Scriptures" in order of their popularity. Thus, if you prefer, you can mark only the most frequently used.

•By Gospel Topic

Many people prefer to mark in the margins the topical reference (title) so they can know why a scripture has been marked. The scriptural references listed by gospel topic in this book are as accurate as any available.

•Aid To Scripture Memorization

Many people would like to start a scripture memorization program in their family. However, they can't decide where to start. Why not use the list of the "100 Most Quoted Scriptures" as a start, then add additional scriptures as wanted by topical interest? The entire book contains approximately 1,000 scriptures.

•Positive Thinking Guide and Leadership Manual

Every year literally billions of dollars are spent on positive thinking books, "get rich quick" ideas, and manuals to improve business leadership and family relations. Jesus Christ is the greatest example of success the world has ever known. The scriptures can be used as guides for successful living both at home and at work. As President Kimball said to the Young Presidents Conference in 1977:

> "We forget that the scriptures present us with centuries of experience in leadership and, even more importantly, the fixed principles upon which real leadership must operate if it is to succeed."

• Good Reading Material

Many people want to have available a good book to read in their spare minutes, but don't have time to get involved in a novel. Spending some free moments reading *Most Quoted Scriptures* is a positive mental experience that doesn't have the plot interrupted by a phone call or child.

Happy reading!

ᕮMERICA

(See Patriotism)

A CHOICE LAND, PRESERVED FOR THE RIGHTEOUS

1 Nephi 2:20 *(Lord's Promise to Nephi — 600 BC)*

And inasmuch as ye shall keep my commandments, ye shall prosper, and shall be led to a land of promise; yea, even a land which I have prepared for you; yea, a land which is choice above all other lands.

Ether 2:7 *(The Lord's promise to the Brother of Jared — 1500 BC)*

And the Lord would not suffer that they should stop beyond the sea in the wilderness, but he would that they should come forth even unto the land of promise, which was choice above all other lands, which the Lord God had preserved for a righteous people.

AMERICAN HISTORY FORETOLD

1 Nephi 13:10-12 *(Nephi's vision of Columbus — 600 BC)*

10. And it came to pass that I looked and beheld many waters; and they divided the Gentiles from the seed of my brethren.

11. And it came to pass that the angel said unto me: Behold the wrath of God is upon the seed of thy brethren.

12. And I looked and beheld a man among the Gentiles, who was separated from the seed of my

brethren by the many waters; and I beheld the Spirit of God, that it came down and wrought upon the man; and he went forth upon the many waters, even unto the seed of my brethren, who were in the promised land.

1 Nephi 13:17-19 *(Nephi's vision of the Revolutionary War — 600 BC)*

17.   And I beheld that their mother Gentiles were gathered together upon the waters, and upon the land also, to battle against them.

18.   And I beheld that the power of God was with them, and also that the wrath of God was upon all those that were gathered together against them to battle.

19.   And I, Nephi, beheld that the Gentiles that had gone out of captivity were delivered by the power of God out of the hands of all other nations.

LORD WILL LEAD THE RIGHTEOUS TO AMERICA

2 Nephi 1:5 *(Lord's promise to Lehi — 588 BC)*

. . .Yea, the Lord hath covenanted this land unto me, and to my children forever, and also all those who should be led out of other countries by the hand of the Lord.

AMERICA WILL BE FREE AS LONG AS THE PEOPLE SERVE GOD

2 Nephi 1:7,9 *(Lord's promise to Lehi — 588 BC)*

7.   Wherefore, this Land is consecrated unto him whom he shall bring. And if it so be that they shall serve him according to the commandments which he

hath given, it shall be a land of liberty unto them; wherefore, they shall never be brought down into captivity; if so, it shall be because of iniquity; for if iniquity shall abound cursed shall be the land for their sakes, but unto the righteous it shall be blessed forever.

9.   . . .And if it so be that they shall keep his commandments they shall be blessed upon the face of this land, and there shall be none to molest them, nor to take away the land of their inheritance; and they shall dwell safely forever.

Ether 2:9,12 *(Lord's warning to the Brother of Jared — 1500 BC)*

9.   And now, we can behold the decrees of God concerning this land, that it is a land of promise; and whatsoever nation shall possess it shall serve God, or they shall be swept off when the fulness of his wrath shall come upon them. And the fulness of his wrath cometh upon them when they are ripened in iniquity.

12.   Behold, this is a choice land, and whatsoever nation shall possess it shall be free from bondage, and from captivity, and from all other nations under heaven, if they will but serve the God of the land, who is Jesus Christ, who hath been manifested by the things which we have written.

LAND OF LIBERTY, NO KING EXCEPT GOD, HIMSELF

2 Nephi 10:11-14 *(Jacob's teachings to the Nephites — 559 BC)*

11.   And this land shall be a land of liberty unto the Gentiles, and there shall be no kings upon the land, who shall raise up unto the Gentiles.

12.   And I will fortify this land against all other nations.

13.   And he that fighteth against Zion shall perish, saith God.

14.   For he that raiseth up a king against me shall perish, for I, the Lord, the king of heaven, will be their king, and I will be a light unto them forever, that hear my words.

PROPHECY ABOUT CIVIL WAR

D & C 87:1-3 *(Prophecy by Joseph Smith — December, 1832)*

(Note: The Civil War started on April 12, 1861, 29 years after this prophecy, when the Southern artillery shelled Fort Sumter in the harbor of Charleston, South Carolina.)

1.   Verily, thus saith the Lord concerning the wars that will shortly come to pass, beginning at the rebellion of South Carolina, which will eventually terminate in the death and misery of many souls;

2.   And the time will come that war will be poured out upon all nations, beginning at this place.

3.   For behold, the Southern States shall be divided against the Northern States, and the Southern States will call on other nations, even the nation of Great Britain, as it is called, and they shall also call upon other nations, in order to defend themselves against other nations; and then war shall be poured out upon all nations.

THE SAINTS ADMONISHED TO SUPPORT THE CONSTITUTION

D & C 98:4-10 *(Revelation to Joseph Smith — August, 1833)*

4. And now, verily I say unto you concerning the laws of the land, it is my will that my people should observe to do all things whatsoever I command them.

5. And that law of the land which is constitutional, supporting that principle of freedom in maintaining rights and privileges, belongs to all mankind, and is justifiable before me.

6. Therefore, I, the Lord, justify you, and your brethren of my church, in befriending that law which is the constitutional law of the land;

7. And as pertaining to law of man, whatsoever is more or less than this, cometh of evil.

8. I, the Lord God, make you free, therefore ye are free indeed; and the law also maketh you free.

9. Nevertheless, when the wicked rule the people mourn.

10. Wherefore, honest men and wise men should be sought for diligently, and good men and wise men ye should observe to uphold; otherwise whatsoever is less than these cometh of evil.

CONSTITUTION OF THE UNITED STATES WAS DIRECTED BY THE LORD

D & C 101:80 *(Revelation to Joseph Smith — December, 1833)*

And for this purpose have I established the Constitution of this land, by the hands of wise men whom I raised up unto this very purpose, and redeemed the land by the shedding of blood.

NGER

BE SLOW TO ANGER

Proverbs 16:32 *(Proverb of Solomon, King of Israel)*

He that is slow to anger is better than the mighty; and he that ruleth his spirit than he that taketh a city.

NOTHING ACCOMPLISHED BY ANGER

Jonah 4:4 *(When the people of Nineveh repented, the Lord refused to destroy them. This made Jonah angry.)*

Then said the Lord,
Doest thou well to be angry?

IT IS A SIN TO BE ANGRY WITHOUT JUST CAUSE

Matthew 5:22 *(also 3 Nephi 12:22) (Jesus Christ in the Sermon on the Mount)*

But I say unto you, That whosoever is angry with his brother without a cause shall be in danger of the judgment: and whosoever shall say to his brother, Raca, shall be in danger of the council: but whosoever shall say, Thou fool, shall be in danger of hell fire.

DEALING WITH THE ANGER OF OTHERS

Matthew 5:38-39 *(also 3 Nephi 12:38-39) (Jesus Christ in the Sermon on the Mount)*

38.   Ye have heard that it hath been said, An eye for an eye, and a tooth for a tooth:

39.   But I say unto you, That ye resist not evil: but whosoever shall smite thee on thy right cheek, turn to him the other also.

CONTENTION IS OF THE DEVIL

3 Nephi 11:29 *(The resurrected Jesus Christ teaches the Nephites, 34 AD)*

For verily, verily I say unto you, he that hath the spirit of contention is not of me, but is of the devil, who is the father of contention, and he stirreth up the hearts of men to contend with anger, one with another.

APOSTASY

A FAMINE OF THE GOSPEL

Amos 8:11-12 *(Amos prophesies to Israel)*

11.   Behold, the days come, saith the Lord God, that I will send a famine in the land, not a famine of bread, nor a thirst for water, but of hearing the words of the Lord:

12.   And they shall wander from sea to sea, and from the north even to the east, they shall run to and fro to seek the word of the Lord, and shall not find it.

CHRIST PREDICTS THE APOSTASY

Matthew 24:24 *(Jesus Christ teaches his disciples)*

For there shall arise false Christs, and false prophets, and shall shew great signs and wonders; insomuch that, if it were possible, they shall deceive the very elect.

A RESTITUTION OF THE GOSPEL

Acts 3:20-21 *(Peter and John preach in the temple)*

20.   And he shall send Jesus Christ, which before was preached unto you:

21.   Whom the heaven must receive until the times of restitution of all things, which God hath spoken by the mouth of all his holy prophets since the world began.

APOSTASY COMES FROM WITHIN

Acts 20:30 *(Paul to the elders of Ephesus)*

Also, of your own selves shall men arise, speaking perverse things, to draw away disciples after them.

CHANGES MADE IN THE BIBLE

1 Nephi 13:28 *(Nephi's vision — 592 BC)*

Wherefore, thou seest that after the book hath gone forth through the hands of the great and abominable church, that there are many plain and precious things taken away from the book, which is the book of the Lamb of God.

FATE OF CHURCHES BUILT BY MEN

1 Nephi 22:23 *(Nephi's predictions of the last days — 588 BC)*

For the time speedily shall come that all churches which are built up to get gain, and all those who are built up to get power over the flesh, and those who are built up to become popular in the eyes of the world, and those who seek the lusts of the flesh and the things of the world, and to do all manner of iniquity; yea, in fine, all those who belong to the kingdom of the devil are they who need fear, and tremble, and quake; they are those who must be brought low in the dust; they are those who must be consumed as stubble; and this is according to the words of the prophet.

CONSEQUENCES OF BAD EXAMPLE

Alma 4:10 *(Alma tells of the growth of the church — 84 BC)*

. . . and the wickedness of the church was a great stumbling-block to those who did not belong to the church; and thus the Church began to fail in its progress.

FATE OF THOSE WHO FALL AWAY

Alma 24:30 *(Alma tells of the wickedness of the Nephites who left the church — 90 BC)*

And thus we can plainly discern, that after a people have been once enlightened by the Spirit of God, and have had great knowledge of things pertaining to righteousness, and then have fallen away into sin and transgression, they become more hardened, and thus their state becomes worse than though they had never known these things.

ATONEMENT

ALL SHALL BE MADE ALIVE IN CHRIST

1 Corinthians 15:22 *(Paul to the Corinthians)*

For as in Adam all die, even so in Christ shall all be made alive.

VICTORY OVER DEATH COMES THROUGH JESUS CHRIST

1 Corinthians 15:55,57 *(Paul to the Corinthians)*

55. O death, where is thy sting? O grave, where is thy victory?

57. But thanks be to God, which giveth us the victory through our Lord Jesus Christ.

DEATH HAS NO CONTROL

Romans 6:9-10 *(Paul to the Romans)*

9. Knowing that Christ being raised from the death dieth no more; death hath no more dominion over him.

10. For in that he died, he died unto sin once: but in that he liveth, he liveth unto God.

REDEMPTION COMES THROUGH CHRIST

2 Nephi 2:6-7 *(Lehi to his son, Jacob — 588 BC)*

6. Wherefore, redemption cometh in and through the Holy Messiah; for he is full of grace and truth.

7. Behold, he offereth himself a sacrifice for sin, to answer the ends of the law, unto all those who have a broken heart and a contrite spirit; and unto none else can the ends of the law be answered.

NEED FOR THE INFINITE ATONEMENT

2 Nephi 9:6-9 *(Jacob's teachings to the Nephites — 559 BC)*

6. For as death hath passed upon all men, to fulfil the merciful plan of the great Creator, there must needs be a power of resurrection, and the resurrection must needs come unto man by reason of the fall; and the fall came by reason of transgression; and because man became fallen they were cut off from the presence of the Lord.

7. Wherefore, it must needs be an infinite atonement — save it should be an infinite atonement this corruption could not put on incorruption. Wherefore, the first judgment which came upon man must needs have remained to an endless duration. And if so, this flesh must have laid down to rot and to crumble to its mother earth, to rise no more.

8. O the wisdom of God, his mercy and grace! For behold, if the flesh should rise no more our spirits must become subject to that angel who fell from before the presence of the Eternal God, and became the devil, to rise no more.

9. And our spirits must have become like unto him, and we become devils, angels to a devil, to be shut out from the presence of our God, and to remain with the father of lies, in misery, like unto himself; yea, to that being who beguiled our first parents, who transformeth himself nigh unto an angel of light, and

stirreth up the children of men unto secret combinations of murder and all manner of secret works of darkness.

SALVATION COMES ONLY THROUGH THE ATONEMENT OF JESUS CHRIST

Mosiah 3:17-19 *(King Benjamin's final address to the Nephites — 124 BC)*

17.   And moreover, I say unto you, that there shall be no other name given nor any other way nor means whereby salvation can come unto the children of men, only in and through the name of Christ, the Lord Omnipotent.

18.   For behold he judgeth, and his judgment is just; and the infant perisheth not that dieth in his infancy; but men drink damnation to their own souls except they humble themselves and become as little children, and believe that salvation was, and is, and is to come, in and through the atoning blood of Christ, the Lord Omnipotent.

19.   For the natural man is an enemy to God, and has been from the fall of Adam, and will be, forever and ever, unless he yields to the enticings of the Holy Spirit, and putteth off the natural man and becometh a saint through the atonement of Christ the Lord, and becometh as a child, submissive, meek, humble, patient, full of love, willing to submit to all things which the Lord seeth fit to inflict upon him, even as a child doth submit to his father.

ATONEMENT OF CHRIST

Third Article of Faith

We believe that through the Atonement of Christ, all mankind may be saved, by obedience to the laws and ordinances of the Gospel.

ATTITUDE

INTENTIONS ARE IMPORTANT

Genesis 4:7 *(The Lord's comment to Cain after he offered the sacrifice according to Satan's instructions rather than those prescribed by the Lord.)*

If thou doest well, shalt thou not be accepted? And if thou doest not well, sin lieth at the door. . .

THE LORD LOOKS AT PEOPLE'S HEARTS

1 Samuel 16:7 *(The Lord tells the prophet Samuel how to pick a new king. David, although young, is picked to replace Saul as the King of Israel.)*

. . .Look not on his countenance, or on the height of his stature. . .man looketh on the outward appearance, but the Lord looketh on the heart.

RESULTS OF ATTITUDES

Proverbs 23:7 *(Proverb of Solomon, King of Israel)*

For as he thinketh in his heart, so is he. . .

Matthew 6:21 *(also Luke 12:34, 3 Nephi 13:21) (Jesus in the Sermon on the Mount)*

For where your treasure is, there will your heart be also.

THE THOUGHT MATTERS

Matthew 5:27-28 *(also 3 Nephi 12:27-28) (Jesus Christ in the Sermon on the Mount)*

27. Ye have heard that it was said by them of old time, Thou salt not commit adultery:

28. But I say unto you, That whosoever looketh on a woman to lust after her hath committed adultery with her already in his heart.

APTISM

BAPTISM OF CHRIST

Matthew 3:13-17 *(Matthew's account of Christ's baptism)*

13.   Then cometh Jesus from Galilee to Jordan unto John, to be baptized of him.

14.   But John forbad him, saying, I have need to be baptized of thee, and comest thou to me?

15.   And Jesus answering said unto him, Suffer it to be so now: for thus it becometh us to fulfil all righteousness. Then he suffered him.

16.   And Jesus, when he was baptized, went up straightway out of the water: and, lo, the heavens were opened unto him, and he saw the Spirit of God descending like a dove, and lighting upon him:

17.   And lo a voice from heaven, saying, This is my beloved Son, in whom I am well pleased.

IMPORTANCE OF BAPTISM

John 3:3-5 *(Jesus Christ to Nicodemus, a ruler of the Jews)*

3.   Jesus answered and said unto him, Verily, verily, I say unto thee, Except a man be born again, he cannot see the kingdom of God.

4.   Nicodemus saith unto him, How can a man be born when he is old? can he enter the second time into his mother's womb, and be born?

5.   Jesus answered, Verily, verily, I say unto thee, Except a man be born of water and of the Spirit, he cannot enter into the kingdom of God.

2 Nephi 31:5 *(Nephi's testimony about Christ, 545 BC)*

And now, if the Lamb of God, he being holy, should have need to be baptized by water, to fulfil all righteousness, O then, how much more need have we, being unholy, to be baptized, yea, even by water!

PETER COMMANDS THE MULTITUDE TO BE BAPTIZED

Acts 2:37-38 *(Peter baptizes 3000 on the day of Pentecost)*

37.   Now when they heard this, they were pricked in their heart, and said unto Peter and to the rest of the apostles, Men and brethren, what shall we do?

38.   Then Peter said unto them, Repent, and be baptized every one of you in the name of Jesus Christ for the remission of sins, and ye shall receive the gift of the Holy Ghost.

BAPTISM FOR THE DEAD

1 Corinthians 15:29 *(Paul to the Saints in Corinth)*

Else what shall they do which are baptized for the dead, if the dead rise not at all? Why are they then baptized for the dead?

COVENANTS MADE AT BAPTISM

Mosiah 18:8-10 *(Alma teaching his followers at the waters of Mormon)*

8.   . . .as ye are desirous to come into the fold of God, and to be called his people, and are willing to

bear one another's burdens, that they may be light;

9. Yea, and are willing to mourn with those that mourn; yea, and comfort those that stand in need of comfort, and to stand as witnesses of God at all times and in all things, and in all places that ye may be in, even until death, that ye may be redeemed of God, and be numbered with those of the first resurrection, that ye may have eternal life —

10. Now I say unto you, if this be the desire of your hearts, what have you against being baptized in the name of the Lord, as a witness before him that ye have entered into a covenant with him, that ye will serve him and keep his commandments, that he may pour out his Spirit more abundantly upon you?

D & C 20:37 *(Revelation on Church organization and government — April, 1830)*

And again, by way of commandment to the church concerning the manner of baptism — All those who humble themselves before God, and desire to be baptized, and come forth with broken hearts and contrite spirits, and witness before the church that they have truly repented of all their sins, and are willing to take upon them the name of Jesus Christ, having a determination to serve him to the end, and truly manifest by their works that they have received of the Spirit of Christ unto the remission of their sins, shall be received by baptism into his church.

REPENTANCE FOLLOWED BY BAPTISM WASHES AWAY SIN

Alma 7:14 *(The words of Alma to the people of Gideon — 83 BC)*

Now I say unto you that ye must repent, and be born again; for the Spirit saith if ye are not born again ye cannot inherit the kingdom of heaven; therefore come and be baptized unto repentance, that ye may be washed from your sins, that ye may have faith on the Lamb of God, who taketh away the sins of the world, who is mighty to save and to cleanse from all unrighteousness.

LITTLE CHILDREN HAVE NO NEED OF BAPTISM

Moroni 8:9-12 *(Mormon's Epistle to his son Moroni, 400 AD)*

9. . . .it is solemn mockery before God, that ye should baptize little children.

10. Behold I say unto you that this thing shall ye teach — repentance and baptism unto those who are accountable and capable of committing sin; yea, teach parents that they must repent and be baptized, and humble themselves as their little children, and they shall all be saved with their little children.

11. And their little children need no repentance, neither baptism. Behold, baptism is unto repentance to the fulfilling the commandments unto the remission of sins.

12. But little children are alive in Christ, even from the foundation of the world. . .

D & C 29:46-47 *(Revelation to Joseph Smith — September, 1830)*

46. But behold, I say unto you, that little children are redeemed from the foundation of the world through mine Only Begotten;

47. Wherefore, they cannot sin, for power is not given unto Satan to tempt little children, until they begin to become accountable before me;

BAPTISMAL PRAYER

D & C 20:73 *(Revelation of Church organization and government given to Joseph Smith — April, 1830)*

The person who is called of God and has authority from Jesus Christ to baptize, shall go down into the water with the person who has presented himself or herself for baptism, and shall say, calling him or her by name:

Having been commissioned of Jesus Christ, I baptize you in the name of the Father, and of the Son, and of the Holy Ghost. Amen.

SYMBOLISM OF BAPTISM

D & C 128:12 *(also Romans 6:3-5) (Epistle of Joseph Smith to the Nauvoo saints — September, 1842)*

Herein is glory and honor, and immortality and eternal life — The ordinance of baptism by water. . . to be immersed in the water and come forth out of the water is in the likeness of the resurrection of the dead in coming forth out of their graves, . . .

Moses 6:53, 59-60 *(Adam and the Lord converse regarding baptism)*

53. And our father Adam spake unto the Lord, and said: Why is it that men must repent and be baptized in water? And the Lord said unto Adam: Behold I have forgiven thee thy transgression in the Garden of Eden.

59. That by reason of transgression cometh the fall, which fall bringeth death, and inasmuch as ye were born into the world by water, and blood, and the spirit, which I have made, and so became of dust a living soul, even so ye must be born again into the kingdom of heaven, of water, and of the Spirit, and be cleansed by blood, even the blood of mine Only Begotten; that ye might be sanctified from all sin, and enjoy the words of eternal life in this world, and eternal life in the world to come, even immortal glory.

60. For by the water ye keep the commandment; by the Spirit ye are justified, and by the blood ye are sanctified;

ADAM'S BAPTISM AND CONFIRMATION

Moses 6:64-65 *(Moses records the baptism of Adam)*

64. And it came to pass, when the Lord had spoken with Adam, our father, that Adam cried unto the Lord, and he was caught away by the Spirit of the Lord, and was carried down into the water, and was laid under the water, and was brought forth out of the water.

65. And thus he was baptized, and the Spirit of God descended upon him, and thus he was born of the Spirit, and became quickened in the inner man.

BAPTISM IS A SAVING ORDINANCE

Fourth Article of Faith

We believe that the first principles and ordinances of the Gospel are: first, Faith in the Lord Jesus Christ; second, Repentance; third, Baptism by immersion for the remission of sins; fourth, Laying on of hands for the gift of the Holy Ghost.

ⒷIBLE

THE PURPOSE OF THE BIBLE

John 20:31 *(John tells the purpose of his writings)*

But these are written, that ye might believe that Jesus is the Christ, the Son of God; and that believing ye might have life through his name.

THE BIBLE IS NOT COMPLETE

John 21:24-25 *(John's last comments in the Gospel of John about Jesus Christ)*

24. This is the disciple which testifieth of these things, and wrote these things: and we know that his testimony is true.

25. And there are also many other things which Jesus did, the which, if they should be written every one, I suppose that even the world itself could not contain the books that should be written.

REACTION OF GENTILES TO THE BOOK OF MORMON

2 Nephi 29:3,4,10 *(Nephi predicts what the Gentiles' reaction will be toward the Book of Mormon being declared as a second witness to Jesus Christ — 559 BC)*

3. And because my words shall hiss forth — many of the Gentiles shall say: A Bible! A Bible! We have got a Bible, and there cannot be any more Bible.

4. But thus saith the Lord God: O fools, they shall

have a Bible; and it shall proceed forth from the Jews, mine ancient covenant people. . .

10.   Wherefore, because that ye have a Bible ye need not suppose that it contains all my words; neither need ye suppose that I have not caused more to be written.

THE BIBLE IS THE WORD OF GOD

Eighth Article of Faith

We believe the Bible to be the word of God as far as it is translated correctly; we also believe the Book of Mormon to be the word of God.

BOOK OF MORMON

(See Scriptures)

THE BOOKS OF JUDAH AND OF JOSEPH SHALL BE JOINED

Ezekiel 37:16-17 *(The prophet Ezekiel's vision of the last days)*

16. Moreover, thou son of man, take thee one stick, and write upon it, For Judah, and for the children of Israel his companions: then take another stick, and write upon it, For Joseph, the stick of Ephraim, and for all the house of Israel his companions:

17. And join them one to another into one stick; and they shall become one in thine hand.

(The stick of Judah is the Bible, and the stick of Joseph is the Book of Mormon.)

OTHER SHEEP I HAVE WHICH ARE NOT OF THIS FOLD

John 10:16 *(Jesus Christ testifies of people on the American continent)*

And other sheep I have, which are not of this fold: them also I must bring, and they shall hear my voice; and there shall be one fold, and one shepherd.

3 Nephi 15:21,24 *(The resurrected Christ explains John 10:16 to the Nephites — 34 AD)*

21. And verily I say unto you, that ye are they of whom I said: Other sheep I have which are not of this fold; them also I must bring, and they shall hear my

voice; and there shall be one fold, and one shepherd.

24.   But behold, ye have both heard my voice, and seen me; and ye are my sheep, and ye are numbered among those whom the Father hath given me.

PURPOSES OF THE BOOK OF MORMON

The title page of the Book of Mormon

. . .to the convincing of the Jew and Gentile that JESUS is the CHRIST, the ETERNAL GOD, manifesting himself unto all nations.

IMPORTANCE OF RECORDS

1 Nephi 4:13 *(Nephi explains why the Lord had him kill Laban when he went back for the plates of brass — 600 BC)*

Behold the Lord slayeth the wicked to bring forth his righteous purposes. It is better that one man should perish than that a nation should dwindle and perish in unbelief.

1 Nephi 6:4 *(Nephi states his reason for writing the record — 600 BC)*

For the fulness of my intent is that I may persuade men to come unto the God of Abraham, and the God of Isaac, and the God of Jacob, and be saved.

2 Nephi 25:26 *(Nephi's predictions of the coming of Christ — 545 BC)*

And we talk of Christ, we rejoice in Christ, we preach of Christ, we prophesy of Christ, and we write according to our prophecies, that our children may know to what source they may look for a remission of their sins.

Moroni 9:31 *(Moroni's testimony why he compiled the Book of Mormon — 421 AD)*

. . .give thanks unto God that he hath made manifest unto you our imperfections, that ye may learn to be more wise than we have been.

MORONI'S PROMISE TO THOSE WHO READ THE BOOK OF MORMON

Moroni 10:4-5 *(Moroni's last testimony before he hid the gold plates in the Hill Cumorah — 421 AD)*

4. And when ye shall receive these things, I would exhort you that ye would ask God, the Eternal Father, in the name of Christ, if these things are not true; and if ye shall ask with a sincere heart, with real intent, having faith in Christ, he will manifest the truth of it unto you, by the power of the Holy Ghost.

5. And by the power of the Holy Ghost ye may know the truth of all things.

BOOK OF MORMON WRITTEN FOR THE LAMANITES

D & C 3:19-20 *(Jesus Christ explains to Joseph Smith the importance of the book to the Lamanites — July, 1825)*

19. And for this very purpose are these plates preserved, which contain these records — that the promises of the Lord might be fulfilled, which he made to his people;

20. And that the Lamanites might come to the knowledge of their fathers, and that they might know the promises of the Lord, and that they may believe the gospel and rely upon the merits of Jesus Christ,

and be glorified through faith in his name, and that through their repentance they might be saved. Amen.

BOOK OF MORMON CONTAINS THE FULNESS OF THE GOSPEL

D & C 42:12 *(Revelation to Joseph Smith — February, 1831)*

And again, the elders, priests, and teachers of this church shall teach the principles of my gospel, which are in the Bible and the Book of Mormon, in the which is the fulness of the gospel.

THE BOOK OF MORMON IS THE WORD OF GOD

Eighth Article of Faith

We believe the Bible to be the word of God as far as it is translated correctly; we also believe the Book of Mormon to be the word of God.

CHARITY

(See Love, Gifts, Friendship)

FREELY GIVE

Matthew 10:8 *(Jesus Christ to his twelve apostles)*

. . .freely ye have received, freely give.

PAUL DEFINES CHARITY

1 Corinthians 13:3-8, 13 *(also Moroni 7:44-47) (Paul to the Corinthians)*

3. And though I bestow all my goods to feed the poor, and though I give my body to be burned, and have not charity, it profiteth me nothing.

4. Charity suffereth long, and is kind; charity envieth not; charity vaunteth not itself, is not puffed up.

5. Doth not behave itself unseemly, seeketh not her own, is not easily provoked, thinketh no evil;

6. Rejoiceth not in iniquity, but rejoiceth in the truth;

7. Beareth all things, believeth all things, hopeth all things, endureth all things.

8. Charity never faileth. . .

13. And now abideth faith, hope, charity, these three; but the greatest of these is charity.

CHARITY IS THE BOND OF PERFECTNESS

Colossians 3:14 *(Paul to the Colossians)*

And above all these things put on charity, which is the bond of perfectness.

CHARITY IS LOVE

2 Nephi 26:30 *(Nephi's predictions of the last day — 545 BC)*

. . .wherefore, the Lord God hath given a commandment that all men should have charity, which charity is love.

CHARITY NEVER FAILETH

Moroni 7:46-48 *(Mormon's teaching of faith, hope and charity — 400 AD)*

46.   Wherefore, my beloved brethren, if ye have not charity, ye are nothing, for charity never faileth. Wherefore, cleave unto charity, which is the greatest of all, for all things must fail —

47.   But charity is the pure love of Christ, and it endureth forever; and whoso is found possessed of it at the last day, it shall be well with him.

48.   Wherefore, my beloved brethren, pray unto the Father with all the energy of heart, that ye may be filled with this love, which he hath bestowed upon all who are true followers of his Son, Jesus Christ; that ye may become the sons of God; that when he shall appear we shall be like him, for we shall see him as he is; that we may have this hope; that we may be purified even as he is pure. Amen.

DISCIPLES OF CHRIST MUST SHOW CHARITY

D & C 52:40 *(Revelation to Joseph Smith — June, 1831)*

And remember in all things the poor and the needy, the sick and the afflicted, for he that doeth not these things, the same is not my disciple.

MAN MUST SHARE OF HIS ABUNDANCE

D & C 104:18 *(Revelation to Joseph Smith concerning the United Order — April, 1834)*

Therefore, if any man shall take of the abundance which I have made, and impart not his portion, according to the law of my gospel, unto the poor and the needy, he shall, with the wicked, lift up his eyes in hell, being in torment.

Chastity

SEVENTH COMMANDMENT

Exodus 20:14 *(Ten Commandments)*

Thou shalt not commit adultery.

THE ADULTERER DESTROYS HIS SOUL

Proverbs 6:32 *(Proverb of Solomon, King of Israel)*

But whoso committeth adultery with a woman lacketh understanding: he that doeth it destroyeth his own soul.

CONSEQUENCES OF LUST

Matthew 5:27-28 *(Jesus Christ during the Sermon on the Mount)*

27.   Ye have heard that it was said by them of old time, Thou shalt not commit adultery:

28.   But I say unto you, That whosoever looketh on a woman to lust after her hath committed adultery with her already in his heart.

WEAKNESS OF THE FLESH – STRENGTH OF THE SPIRIT

Galatians 5:19-22 *(Paul's epistle to the Galatians)*

19.   Now the works of the flesh are manifest, which are these; Adultery, fornication, uncleanness, lasciviousness,

20. Idolatry, witchcraft, hatred, variance, emulations, wrath, strife, seditions, heresies,

21. Envyings, murders, drunkenness, revellings, and such like: of the which I tell you before, as I have also told you in time past, that they which do such things shall not inherit the kingdom of God.

22. But the fruit of the Spirit is love, joy, peace, longsuffering, gentleness, goodness, faith, . . .

LORD DELIGHTS IN CHASTITY

Jacob 2:28 *(Jacob speaking to the Nephites — between 544 and 421 BC)*

For I, the Lord God, delight in the chastity of women. And whoredoms are an abomination before me; thus saith the Lord of Hosts.

ADULTERY IS THE THIRD GREATEST SIN

Alma 39:5 *(Alma to his son Corianton after his sins with Isabel, the harlot — 73 BC)*

Know ye not, my son, that these things are an abomination in the sight of the Lord; yea, most abominable above all sins save it be the shedding of innocent blood or denying the Holy Ghost?

CHASTITY AND VIRTUE ARE DEAR AND PRECIOUS ABOVE ALL THINGS

Moroni 9:9 *(The second epistle of Mormon to his son Moroni — 400 AD)*

. . .that which was most dear and precious above all things, which is chastity and virtue.

LOVE THY WIFE

D & C 42:22 *(Revelation to Joseph Smith — February, 1831)*

Thou shalt love thy wife with all thy heart, and shalt cleave unto her and none else.

THE ADULTERER CAN REPENT

D & C 42:25 *(Revelation to Joseph Smith — February 1831)*

But he that has committed adultery and repents with all his heart, and forsaketh it, and doeth it no more, thou shalt forgive.

CHILDREN

(See Family)

LOVE THE LORD AND TEACH THE COMMANDMENTS TO YOUR CHILDREN

Deuteronomy 6:5-7 *(The Lord to Moses after he received the ten commandments)*

5. And thou shalt love the Lord thy God with all thine heart, and with all thy soul, and with all thy might.

6. And these words, which I command thee this day, shall be in thine heart:

7. And thou shalt teach them diligently unto thy children, . . .

CHILDREN SHOULD OBEY

Proverbs 6:20-22 *(Proverb of Solomon, King of Israel)*

20. My son, keep thy father's commandment, and forsake not the law of thy mother:

21. Bind them continually upon thine heart, and tie them about thy neck.

22. When thou goest, it shall lead thee; when thou sleepest, it shall keep thee; and when thou awakest, it shall talk with thee

A WISE SON LISTENS

Proverbs 10:1 *(Proverb of Solomon, King of Israel)*

...A wise son maketh a glad father: but a foolish son is the heaviness of his mother.

Proverbs 13:1 *(Proverb of Solomon, King of Israel)*

A wise son heareth his father's instruction. . . .

TRAIN UP A CHILD

Proverbs 22:6 *(Proverb of Solomon, King of Israel)*

Train up a child in the way he should go: and when he is old, he will not depart from it.

BECOME AS A LITTLE CHILD

Matthew 18:1-6 *(Jesus Christ to his disciples)*

1.   At the same time came the disciples unto Jesus, saying, Who is the greatest in the kingdom of heaven?

2.   And Jesus called a little child unto him, and set him in the midst of them,

3.   And said, Verily I say unto you, Except ye be converted, and become as little children, ye shall not enter into the kingdom of heaven.

4.   Whosoever therefore shall humble himself as this little child, the same is greatest in the kingdom of heaven.

5.   And whoso shall receive one such little child in my name receiveth me.

6.   But whoso shall offend one of these little ones which believe in me, it were better for him that a

millstone were hanged about his neck, and that he were drowned in the depth of the sea.

3 Nephi 9:22 *(Jesus Christ to the Nephites — 34 AD)*

Therefore, whoso repenteth and cometh unto me as a little child, him will I receive, for of such is the kingdom of God. Behold, for such I have laid down my life, and have taken it up again. . .

CHRIST BLESSED THE LITTLE CHILDREN

Matthew 19:13-14 *(Jesus to his disciples)*

13. Then were there brought unto him little children, that he should put his hands on them, and pray: and the disciples rebuked them.

14. But Jesus said, Suffer little children, and forbid them not, to come unto me: for of such is the kingdom of heaven.

3 Nephi 17:21 *(The resurrected Jesus Christ teaches the Nephites — 34 AD)*

And when he had said these words, he wept, and the multitude bare record of it, and he took their little children, one by one, and blessed them, and prayed to the Father for them.

THE FIRST COMMANDMENT WITH A PROMISE

Ephesians 6:1-3 *(Paul to the Ephesians)*

1. Children, obey your parents in the Lord: for this is right.

2. Honour thy father and mother; (which is the first commandment with promise;)

3.   That it may be well with thee, and thou mayest live long on the earth.

PROVOKE NOT YOUR CHILDREN

Colossians 3:20-21 *(also Ephesians 6:4) (Paul to the Colossians)*

20.   Children, obey your parents in all things: for this is well pleasing unto the Lord.

21.   Fathers, provoke not your children to anger, lest they be discouraged.

CHILDREN ARE FREE FROM SIN

D & C 29:46-47 *(Revelation to Joseph Smith — September, 1830)*

46.   . . .little children are redeemed from the foundation of the world through mine Only Begotten.

47.   Wherefore, they cannot sin, for power is not given unto Satan to tempt little children, until they begin to become accountable before me;

PARENTS SHOULD TEACH CHILDREN

D & C 68:25, 27-28 *(Revelation to Joseph Smith — November, 1831)*

25.   And again, inasmuch as parents have children in Zion, or in any of her stakes which are organized, that teach them not to understand the doctrine of repentance, faith in Christ the Son of the living God, and of baptism and the gift of the Holy Ghost by the laying on of the hands, when eight years old, the sin be upon the heads of the parents.

27. And their children shall be baptized for the remission of their sins when eight years old, and receive the laying on of the hands.

28. And they shall also teach their children to pray, and to walk uprightly before the Lord.

COMMANDMENTS

(See Diligence, Obedience, Revelation)

GOD HELPS US LIVE THE COMMANDMENTS

Genesis 18:14 *(Comments of an angel to Abraham, because his wife Sarah had laughed at the prophecy that she would have a child in her old age [approx. 90]).*

Is any thing too hard for the Lord? At the time appointed I will return unto thee, according to the time of life, and Sarah shall have a son.

Matthew 19:26 *(Jesus to his disciples)*

But Jesus beheld them, and said unto them, With men this is impossible; but with God all things are possible.

Luke 1:37 *(The Angel Gabriel to Mary when she questioned how a virgin could have the Christ child)*

. . .With God nothing shall be impossible.

1 Nephi 3:7 *(Nephi speaking to his father, Lehi — 600 BC)*

. . .I will go and do the things which the Lord hath commanded, for I know that the Lord giveth no commandments unto the children of men, save he shall prepare a way for them that they may accomplish the thing which he commandeth them.

TEN COMMANDMENTS

Exodus 20:3-4, 7-8, 12-17 *(Also Mosiah 13 and Deuteronomy 5) (Given to Moses on Mt. Sinai)*

3. Thou shalt have no other gods before me.

4. Thou shalt not make unto thee any graven image. . .

7. Thou shalt not take the name of the Lord thy God in vain. . .

8. Remember the sabbath day, to keep it holy.

12. Honour thy father and thy mother: that thy days may be long upon the land which the Lord thy God giveth thee.

13. Thou shalt not kill.

14. Thou shalt not commit adultery.

15. Thou shalt not steal.

16. Thou shalt not bear false witness against thy neighbour.

17. Thou shalt not covet thy neighbour's house, thou shalt not covet thy neighbour's wife. . .nor any thing that is thy neighbour's.

BLESSINGS OF KEEPING THE COMMANDMENTS

Deuteronomy 5:29 *(The Lord to Moses after he received the Ten Commandments)*

O that there were such an heart in them, that they would fear me, and keep all my commandments always, that it might be well with them, and with their children forever!

THE WISE WILL RECEIVE COMMANDMENTS

Proverbs 10:8 *(Proverb of Solomon, King of Israel)*

The wise in heart will receive commandments: but a prating fool shall fall.

PEOPLE PROFESS CHRIST, BUT TEACH THE COMMANDMENTS OF MEN

Matthew 15:8-9 *(Jesus to the Pharisees and Scribes)*

8. This people draweth nigh unto me with their mouth, and honoureth me with their lips; but their heart is far from me.

9. But in vain they do worship me, teaching for doctrines the commandments of men.

SEARCH THE COMMANDMENTS

D & C 1:37 *(Revelation to Joseph Smith — November, 1831)*

Search these commandments, for they are true and faithful, and the prophecies and promises which are in them shall all be fulfilled.

GOD WILL NOT COMMAND US IN ALL THINGS

D & C 58:26-29 *(The Lord to Edward Partridge — August, 1831)*

26. For behold, it is not meet that I should command in all things; for he that is compelled in all things, the same is a slothful and not a wise servant; wherefore he receiveth no reward.

27. Verily I say, men should be anxiously engaged in a good cause, and do many things of their own free will, and bring to pass much righteousness;

28. For the power is in them, wherein they are agents unto themselves. And inasmuch as men do good they shall in nowise lose their reward.

29. But he that doeth not anything until he is commanded, and receiveth a commandment with doubtful heart, and keepeth it with slothfulness, the same is damned.

CONTENTMENT

BE CONTENT WITH YOUR SITUATIONS IN LIFE

Philippians 4:11 *(Paul to the Philippians)*

Not that I speak in respect of want: for I have learned, in whatsoever state I am, therewith to be content.

GODLINESS WITH CONTENTMENT

1 Timothy 6:6 *(Paul to Timothy)*

But godliness with contentment is great gain.

COURAGE

(See Fear)

THE COURAGE OF SHADRACH, MESHACH AND ABEDNEGO

Daniel 3:17-18 *(The three young men answer Nebuchadnezzar's threat to throw them in the fiery furnace)*

17. . . .our God whom we serve is able to deliver us from the burning fiery furnace, and he will deliver us out of thine hand, O king.

18. But if not, be it known unto thee, O king, that we will not serve thy gods, nor worship the golden image which thou hast set up.

BE NOT ASHAMED OF THE GOSPEL OF JESUS CHRIST

Romans 1:16 *(Paul to the Romans)*

For I am not ashamed of the gospel of Christ: for it is the power of God unto Salvation to every one that believeth; . . .

PUT ON THE WHOLE ARMOR OF GOD

2 Nephi 1:23 *(Lehi exorts Laman and Lemuel — 575 BC)*

Awake, my sons; put on the armor of righteousness. Shake off the chains with which ye are bound, and come forth out of obscurity, and arise from the dust.

D & C 27:15-18 *(also Ephesians 6:11-18, Paul's letter to the Ephesians) (Revelation to Joseph Smith, August, 1830)*

15. Wherefore, lift up your hearts and rejoice, and gird up your loins, and take upon you my whole

armor, that ye may be able to withstand the evil day, having done all, that ye may be able to stand.

16. Stand, therefore, having your loins girt about with truth, having on the breastplate of righteousness, and your feet shod with the preparation of the gospel of peace, which I have sent mine angels to commit unto you;

17. Taking the shield of faith wherewith ye shall be able to quench all the fiery darts of the wicked;

18. And take the helmet of salvation, and the sword of my Spirit, which I will pour out upon you, and my word which I reveal unto you, and be agreed as touching all things whatsoever ye ask of me, and be faithful until I come, and ye shall be caught up, that where I am ye shall be also. Amen.

HELAMAN DESCRIBES THE 2000 STRIPLING WARRIORS

Alma 53:20-21 *(Helaman lead 2000 young Lamanite warriors into battle and to his surprise not one was killed, although more than 1000 of his regular troops died — 64 BC)*

20. And they were all young men, and they were exceedingly valiant for courage and also for strength and activity; but behold, this was not all — they were men who were true at all times in whatsoever thing they were entrusted.

21. Yea, they were men of truth and soberness, for they had been taught to keep the commandments of God and to walk uprightly before him.

Alma 56:45,47 *(Helaman's letter to Moroni — 64 BC)*

45. And now I say unto you, my beloved brother Moroni, that never had I seen so great courage, not amongst all the Nephites.

47. Now they never had fought, yet they did not fear death; and they did think more upon the liberty of their fathers than they did upon their lives; yea, they had been taught by their mothers, that if they did not doubt, God would deliver them.

NO FEAR WITH THE LORD

D & C 68:6 *(Revelation through Joseph Smith to Orson Hyde, Luke S. Johnson, Lyman E. Johnson, and William E. M'Lellin — November, 1831)*

Wherefore, be of good cheer, and do not fear, for I the Lord am with you, and will stand by you; . . .

COVENANTS

(See Baptism, Commandments, Marriage)

ABRAHAM'S COVENANT

Genesis 12:2-3 *(The Lord speaking to Abraham)*

2. And I will make of thee a great nation, and I will bless thee, and make thy name great; and thou shalt be a blessing:

3. And I will bless them that bless thee, and curse him that curseth thee: and in thee shall all families of the earth be blessed.

Genesis 22:17-18 *(The Lord speaking to Abraham)*

17. That in blessing I will bless thee, and in multiplying I will multiply thy seed as the stars of the heaven, and as the sand which is upon the sea shore; and thy seed shall possess the gate of his enemies;

18. And in thy seed shall all the nations of the earth be blessed; because thou hast obeyed my voice.

Abraham 2:9-11 *(The Lord speaking to Abraham)*

9. And I will make of thee a great nation, and I will bless thee above measure, and make thy name great among all nations, and thou shalt be a blessing unto thy seed after thee, that in their hands they shall bear this ministry and Priesthood unto all nations;

10. And I will bless them through thy name; for as many as receive this Gospel shall be called after thy name, and shall be accounted thy seed, and shall rise up and bless thee, as their father;

11. And I will bless them that bless thee, and curse them that curse thee; and in thee (that is, in thy Priesthood) and in thy seed (that is, thy Priesthood), for I give unto thee a promise that this right shall continue in thee, and in thy seed after thee (that is to say, the literal seed, or the seed of the body) shall all the families of the earth be blessed, even with the blessings of the Gospel, which are the blessings of salvation, even of life eternal.

IF YOU OBEY THE COVENANTS, YOU'LL BECOME A PECULIAR PEOPLE

Exodus 19:5-6 *(The Lord's covenant to Moses)*

5. Now therefore, if ye will obey my voice indeed, and keep my covenant, then ye shall be a peculiar treasure unto me above all people: for all the earth is mine:

6. And ye shall be unto me a kingdom of priests, and an holy nation. These are the words which thou shalt speak unto the children of Israel.

SERIOUSNESS OF BREAKING COVENANTS

Ecclesiastes 5:4-5 *(Teachings of Ecclesiastes, son of King David)*

4. When thou vowest a vow unto God, defer not to pay it; for he hath no pleasure in fools: pay that which thou has vowed.

5. Better is it that thou shouldest not vow, than that thou shouldest vow and not pay.

MY SOUL DELIGHTETH IN THE COVENANTS

2 Nephi 11:5 *(Jacob's teachings to the Nephites — 545 BC)*

And also my soul delighteth in the covenants of the Lord which he hath made to our fathers. . .

THOSE WHO ACCEPT THE COVENANTS OF GOD BECOME HIS CHILDREN

Mosiah 5:7 *(King Benjamin's farewell address to the Nephites — 124 BC)*

And now, because of the covenant which ye have made ye shall be called the children of Christ, his sons, and his daughters; for behold, this day he hath spiritually begotten you; for ye say that your hearts are changed through faith on his name; therefore, ye are born of him and have become his sons and his daughters.

THE TEMPLE COVENANT IS A STANDARD FOR THE LORD'S PEOPLE

D & C 45:9 *(Revelation to Joseph Smith — March, 1831)*

And even so I have sent mine everlasting covenant into the world, to be a light to the world, and to be a standard for my people, and for the Gentiles to seek to it, and to be a messenger before my face to prepare the way before me.

CONSEQUENCES OF OBEDIENCE

D & C 82:10 *(Revelation to Joseph Smith — January, 1832)*

I, the Lord, am bound when ye do what I say; but when ye do not what I say, ye have no promise.

THE LORD'S FORMULA FOR SUCCESS

D & C 90:24 *(Revelation to Joseph Smith — March, 1833)*

Search diligently, pray always, and be believing, and all things shall work together for your good, if ye walk uprightly and remember the covenant wherewith ye have covenanted one with another.

CONSEQUENCES OF NOT KEEPING THE COVENANTS

D & C 98:15 *(Revelation to Joseph Smith — August, 1833)*

For if ye will not abide in my covenant ye are not worthy of me.

COVENANTS TO BE SEALED BY HOLY SPIRIT OF PROMISE

D & C 131:1-3 *(Revelation on temple marriage — May, 1843)*

1. In the celestial glory there are three heavens or degrees;

2. And in order to obtain the highest, a man must enter into this order of the priesthood (meaning the new and everlasting covenant of marriage);

3. And if he does not, he cannot obtain it.

CREATION

THE BEGINNING

Genesis 1:1 *(Moses writes about the creation)*

In the beginning God created the heaven and the earth.

MAN CREATED IN GOD'S IMAGE

Genesis 1:26-27 *(Moses writes about the creation)*

26.   And God said, Let us make man in our image, after our likeness: and let them have dominion over the fish of the sea, and over the fowl of air, over the cattle, and over all the earth, and over every creeping thing that creepeth upon the earth.

27.   So God created man in his own image, in the image of God created he him; male and female created he them.

Genesis 5:1 *(Moses writes about the creation)*

. . .In the day that God created man, in the likeness of God made he him.

MAN GIVEN DOMINION

Psalms 8:4-6 *(Psalm of David, King of Israel)*

4.   What is man, that thou art mindful of him? and the son of man, that thou visitest him?

5.   For thou hast made him a little lower than the angels, and hast crowned him with glory and honour.

6. Thou madest him to have dominion over the works of thy hands; thou hast put all things under his feet.

EARTH IS GOD'S HANDYWORK

Psalms 19:1 *(A Psalm of David)*

The heavens declare the glory of God; and the firmament sheweth his handywork.

THE EARTH CREATED BY WISDOM

Proverbs 3:19 *(Proverb of Solomon, King of Israel)*

The Lord by wisdom hath founded the earth; by understanding hath he established the heavens.

CHRIST CREATED THE WORLD

John 1:1-5 *(John's account of the creation)*

1. In the beginning was the Word, and the Word was with God, and the Word was God.

2. The same was in the beginning with God.

3. All things were made by him; (Jesus Christ) and without him was not any thing made that was made.

4. In him was life; and the life was the light of men.

5. And the light shineth in darkness; and the darkness comprehended it not.

Ephesians 3:9 *(Paul to the people in Ephesus)*

And to make all men see . . . the mystery, which from the beginning of the world hath been hid in God, who created all things by Jesus Christ:

3 Nephi 9:15 *(Christ's testimony to the Nephites — 34 AD)*

Behold, I am Jesus Christ the Son of God. I created the heavens and the earth, and all things that in them are. I was with the Father from the beginning. I am in the Father, and the Father in me; and in me hath the Father glorified his name.

MAN WAS IN THE BEGINNING WITH GOD

D & C 93:29 *(Revelation to Joseph Smith — May, 1833)*

Man was also in the beginning with God. Intelligence or the light of truth, was not created or made, neither indeed can be.

WORLDS WITHOUT NUMBER HAVE BEEN CREATED

Moses 1:33 *(The Lord Jesus Christ speaks to Moses)*

And worlds without number have I created; and I also created them for mine own purpose; and by the Son I created them, which is mine Only Begotten.

ALL THINGS WERE ORGANIZED SPIRITUALLY BEFORE PHYSICALLY

Moses 3:5,7 *(The Lord to Moses)*

5. . . . For I, the Lord God, created all things, of which I have spoken, spiritually, before they were naturally upon the face of the earth. . . . for in heaven created I them; and there was not yet flesh upon the earth, neither in the water, neither in the air;

7. . . .and man became a living soul, the first flesh upon the earth, the first man also; nevertheless, all things were before created; but spiritually were they created and made according to my word.

CHRIST TOOK THE SPIRITS AND MADE THE EARTH

Abraham 3:24 *(Translation of the ancient records of Abraham)*

And there stood one among them that was like unto God, and he said unto those who were with him: We will go down, for there is space there, and we will take of these materials, and we will make an earth whereon these may dwell;

DEATH

(See Resurrection, Funeral Messages)

UNTO DUST WE RETURN

Genesis 3:19 *(The Lord speaking to Adam)*

In the sweat of thy face shalt thou eat bread, till thou return unto the ground; for out of it wast thou taken: for dust thou art, and unto dust shalt thou return.

FEAR NOT THOSE WHO KILL THE BODY

Matthew 10:28 *(Christ to the disciples)*

And fear not them which kill the body, but are not able to kill the soul: but rather fear him which is able to destroy both soul and body in hell.

VICTORY OVER DEATH

1 Corinthians 15:55,57 *(Paul to the Corinthians)*

55. O death, where is thy sting? O grave, where is thy victory?

57. But thanks be to God, which giveth us the victory through our Lord Jesus Christ.

WE TAKE NOTHING WHEN WE DIE

1 Timothy 6:7 *(Paul to Timothy)*

For we brought nothing into this world, and it is certain we can carry nothing out.

PAUL'S TESTIMONY OF WHAT DEATH HOLDS

2 Timothy 4:7-8 *(Paul's testimony to Timothy)*

7. I have fought a good fight, I have finished my course, I have kept the faith:

8. Henceforth there is laid up for me a crown of righteousness, which the Lord, the righteous judge, shall give me at that day: and not to me only, but unto all them also that love his appearing.

WE SHALL SEE GOD

2 Nephi 9:4 *(Jacob's teachings to the Nephites — 559 BC)*

. . .our flesh must waste away and die; nevertheless, in our bodies we shall see God.

SPIRITUAL AND TEMPORAL DEATH EXPLAINED

2 Nephi 9:10-13 *(Jacob's teachings to the Nephites — 559 BC)*

10. O how great the goodness of our God, who prepareth a way for our escape from the grasp of this awful monster; yea, that monster, death and hell, which I call the death of the body, and also the death of the spirit.

11. And because of the way of deliverance of our God, the Holy One of Israel, this death, of which I have spoken, which is the temporal, shall deliver up its dead; which death is the grave.

12. And this death of which I have spoken, which is the spiritual death, shall deliver up its dead; which spiritual death is hell; wherefore, death and hell must deliver up their dead, and hell must deliver up its captive spirits and the grave must deliver up its

captive bodies, and the bodies and the spirits of men
will be restored one to the other; and it is by the
power of the resurrection of the Holy One of Israel.

13.   O how great the plan of our God! For on the
other hand, the paradise of God must deliver up the
spirits of the righteous, and the grave deliver up the
body of the righteous; and the spirit and the body is
restored to itself again, and all men become
incorruptible, and immortal, and they are living
souls, having a perfect knowledge like unto us in the
flesh, save it be that our knowledge shall be perfect.

SPIRITUAL DEATH IS THE SECOND DEATH

Alma 12:16 *(Alma's teachings — 82 BC)*

And now behold, I say unto you then cometh a death,
even a second death, which is a spiritual death; then is
a time that whosoever dieth in his sins, as to a
temporal death, shall also die a spiritual death; yea he
shall die as to things pertaining unto righteousness.

LITTLE CHILDREN ARE REDEEMED BY JESUS CHRIST

D & C 29:46 *(Revelation to Joseph Smith — September, 1830)*

But behold, I say unto you, that little children are
redeemed from the foundation of the world through
mine Only Begotten;

D & C 74:7 *(Revelation to Joseph Smith — January, 1832)*

But little children are holy, being sanctified through
the atonement of Jesus Christ. . . .

BLESSINGS TO THE DYING

D & C 42:44,46,48 *(Revelation to Joseph Smith — February, 1831)*

44. And the elders of the church, two or more, shall be called, and shall pray for and lay their hands upon them in my name; and if they die they shall die unto me, and if they live they shall live unto me.

46. And it shall come to pass that those that die in me shall not taste of death, for it shall be sweet unto them;

48. And again, it shall come to pass that he that hath faith in me to be healed, and is not appointed unto death, shall be healed.

DEBT

DO NOT ENTER INTO DEBT

Romans 13:8 *(Paul to the Romans)*

Owe no man any thing, but to love one another:

WE ARE IN GOD'S DEBT

Mosiah 4:19 *(King Benjamin's address — 124 BC)*

For behold, are we not all beggars? Do we not all depend upon the same Being, even God, for all the substance which we have, for both food and raiment, and for gold, and for silver, and for all the riches which we have of every kind?

RETURN WHATEVER YOU BORROW

Mosiah 4:28 *(King Benjamins address — 124 BC)*

. . .whosoever among you borroweth of his neighbor should return the thing that he borroweth, according as he doth agree, or else thou shalt commit sin; and perhaps thou shalt cause thy neighbor to commit sin also.

IT IS GOD'S WILL THAT WE PAY ALL OUR DEBTS

D & C 104:78 *(Revelation to Joseph Smith — April, 1834)*

. . .concerning your debts — behold it is my will that you shall pay all your debts.

DELEGATION

(See Stewardship)

JETHRO TEACHES MOSES HOW TO DELEGATE

Exodus 18:13-14, 17-18, 20-21 *(Jethro, Moses' father-in-law, counsels Moses)*

13. . . .Moses sat to judge the people: and the people stood by Moses from the morning unto the evening.

14. And when Moses' father in law saw all that he did to the people, he said, What is this thing that thou doest to the people? why sittest thou thyself alone, and all the people stand by thee from morning unto even?

17. . . .The thing that thou doest is not good.

18. Thou wilt surely wear away, both thou, and this people that is with thee: for this thing is too heavy for thee; thou art not able to perform it thyself alone.

20. And thou shalt teach them ordinances and laws, and shalt shew them the way wherein they must walk, and the work that they must do.

21. Moreover thou shalt provide out of all the people able men, such as fear God, men of truth, hating covetousness; and place such over them, to be rulers of thousands, and rulers of hundreds, rulers of fifties, and rulers of tens:

THE LORD DELEGATES WORK TO PEOPLE

D & C 64:29-30 *(Revelation concerning those of Zion's camp — September, 1831)*

29. Wherefore, as ye are agents, ye are on the Lord's errand; and whatever ye do according to the will of the Lord is the Lord's business.

30. And he hath set you to provide for his saints in these last days, that they may obtain an inheritance in the land of Zion.

DELEGATION REQUIRES EVALUATION AND PERFORMANCE

D & C 82:3 *(Revelation to Joseph Smith — April, 1832)*

For of him unto whom much is given much is required; . . .

THE LORD DELEGATED THE WORK IN THE SPIRIT WORLD

D & C 138:29-30 *(Vision to Joseph F. Smith of the Spirit World — October, 1918)*

29. And as I wondered, my eyes were opened, and my understanding quickened, and I perceived that the Lord went not in person among the wicked and the disobedient who had rejected the truth, to teach them;

30. But behold, from among the righteous, he organized his forces and appointed messengers, clothed with power and authority, and commissioned them to go forth and carry the light of the gospel to them that were in darkness, even to all the spirits of men; and thus was the gospel preached to the dead.

DILIGENCE

(See Stewardship, Tribulation)

LORD VISITS MEN ACCORDING TO THEIR DILIGENCE

Enos 1:10 *(The Lord speaks to Enos after a day and night prayer — 544 BC)*

And while I was thus struggling in the spirit, behold, the voice of the Lord came into my mind again, saying: I will visit thy brethren according to their diligence in keeping my commandments. I have given unto them this land, and it is a holy land; and I curse it not save it be for the cause of iniquity; wherefore, I will visit thy brethren according as I have said; and their transgressions will I bring down with sorrow upon their own heads.

MAN SHOULD BE DILIGENT

Mosiah 4:27 *(King Benjamin's address — 124 BC)*

And see that all these things are done in wisdom and order; for it is not requisite that a man should run faster than he has strength. And again, it is expedient that he should be diligent, that thereby he might win the prize; therefore, all things must be done in order.

AFTER MUCH TRIBULATION COME BLESSINGS

D & C 58:4 *(Revelation to Joseph Smith — August, 1831)*

For after much tribulation come the blessings. Wherefore the day cometh that ye shall be crowned with much glory; the hour is not yet, but is nigh at hand.

OUT OF SMALL THINGS COME GREAT ACHIEVEMENT

D & C 64:33 *(Revelations for the Elders at Kirtland, Ohio — September, 1831)*

Wherefore, be not weary in well-doing, for ye are laying the foundation of a great work. And out of small things proceedeth that which is great.

LET MEN BE DILIGENT IN ALL THINGS

D & C 75:29 *(Revelation to Joseph Smith — January, 1832)*

Let every man be diligent in all things. And the idler shall not have place in the church, except he repent and mend his ways.

GIVE DILIGENT HEED TO THE WORDS OF ETERNAL LIFE

D & C 84:43-44 *(Revelation on the priesthood — September, 1832)*

43. And I now give unto you a commandment to beware concerning yourselves, to give diligent heed to the words of eternal life.

44. For you shall live by every word that proceedeth forth from the mouth of God.

CONSEQUENCE OF DILIGENCE

D & C 127:4 *(An epistle from Joseph Smith to the Saints in Nauvoo — September, 1842)*

. . .let your diligence, and your perseverance, and patience, and your works be redoubled, and you shall in nowise lose your reward, saith the Lord of Hosts. . . .

DISCIPLINE

(See Diligence, Family, and Obedience)

FATHERS SHOULD DISCIPLINE THEIR CHILDREN

Deuteronomy 8:5 *(Moses exhorts the children of Israel to be obedient)*

Thou shalt also consider in thine heart, that, as a man chasteneth his son, so the Lord thy God chasteneth thee.

THE LORD CORRECTS THOSE HE LOVES

Proverbs 3:11-12 *(Proverb of Solomon, King of Israel)*

11.   My son, despise not the chastening of the Lord; neither be weary of his correction:

12.   For whom the Lord loveth he correcteth; even as a father the son in whom he delighteth.

TRAIN CHILDREN IN THEIR YOUTH

Proverbs 22:6 *(Proverb of Solomon, King of Israel)*

Train up a child in the way he should go: and when he is old, he will not depart from it.

IS SPANKING ACCEPTABLE?

Proverbs 23:13-14 *(Proverb of Solomon, King of Israel)*

13.   Withold not correction from the child: for if thou beatest him with the rod, he shall not die.

14.   Thou shalt beat him with the rod, and shalt deliver his soul from hell.

ENDURE TO THE END

Matthew 24:13 *(Jesus Christ to his disciples)*

But he that shall endure unto the end, the same shall be saved.

DISCIPLINE MUST NOT DISCOURAGE OR PROVOKE ANGER

Ephesians 6:1-4 *(Paul's epistle to the saints at Ephesus)*

1.   Children, obey your parents in the Lord: for this is right.

2.   Honour thy father and mother; (which is the first commandment with promise;)

3.   That it may be well with thee, and thou mayest live long on the earth.

4.   And, ye fathers, provoke not your children to wrath: but bring them up in the nurture and admonition of the Lord.

Colossians 3:20-21 *(Paul's epistle to the Colossians)*

20.   Children, obey your parents in all things: for this is well pleasing unto the Lord.

21.   Fathers, provoke not your children to anger, lest they be discouraged.

OBEY GOD AS YOU DO YOUR FATHERS

Hebrews 12:9 *(Paul's epistle to the Hebrews)*

Furthermore we have had fathers of our flesh which corrected us, and we gave them reverence: shall we not much rather be in subjection unto the Father of spirits, and live?

MEN MUST DISCIPLINE THEMSELVES

Mosiah 4:27 *(King Benjamin's address — 124 BC)*

And see that all these things are done in wisdom and order; for it is not requisite that a man should run faster than he has strength. And again, it is expedient that he should be diligent, that thereby he might win the prize; therefore, all things must be done in order.

LOVE IS AN IMPORTANT PART OF DISCIPLINE

D & C 121:43 *(Writings of Joseph Smith from the jail at Liberty, Missouri — March, 1839)*

Reproving betimes with sharpness, when moved upon by the Holy Ghost; and then showing forth afterwards an increase of love toward him whom thou hast reproved, lest he esteem thee to be his enemy;

ᴇᴛERNAL LIFE

(See God, Jesus Christ)

BE YE THEREFORE PERFECT

Matthew 5:48 *(Jesus Christ in the Sermon on the Mount)*

Be ye therefore perfect, even as your Father which is in heaven is perfect.

THE GATE AND THE WAY TO ETERNAL LIFE

Matthew 7:13-14 *(Jesus Christ in the Sermon on the Mount)*

13. Enter ye in at the strait gate: for wide is the gate, and broad is the way, that leadeth to destruction, and many there be which go in thereat:

14. Because strait is the gate, and narrow is the way, which leadeth unto life, and few there be that find it.

WHAT SHOULD WE DO TO OBTAIN ETERNAL LIFE

Matthew 19:16-22 *(The young man talks with Jesus Christ)*

16. And, behold, one came and said unto him, Good Master, what good thing shall I do, that I may have eternal life?

17. And he said unto him, Why callest thou me good? there is none good but one, that is, God: but if thou wilt enter into life, keep the commandments.

18. He saith unto him, Which? Jesus said, Thou shalt do no murder, Thou shalt not commit adultery,

Thou shalt not steal, Thou shalt not bear false witness,

19.   Honour thy father and thy mother: and, Thou shalt love they neighbour as thyself.

20.   The young man saith unto him, All these things have I kept from my youth up: what lack I yet?

21.   Jesus said unto him, If thou wilt be perfect, go and sell that thou hast, and give to the poor, and thou shalt have treasure in heaven: and come and follow me.

A KINGDOM HAS BEEN PREPARED FOR THE ELECT FROM THE BEGINNING

Matthew 25:34 *(Jesus Christ to his disciples)*

Then shall the King say unto them on his right hand, Come, ye blessed of my Father, inherit the kingdom prepared for you from the foundation of the world:

HE THAT DRINKS OF THE GOSPEL SHALL NEVER THIRST

John 4:13-14 *(Jesus Christ talks to the Samaritan woman at Jacob's well)*

13.   . . .Whosoever drinketh of this water shall thirst again:

14.   But whosoever drinketh of the water that I shall give him shall never thirst; but the water that I shall give him shall be in him a well of water springing up into everlasting life.

IN MY FATHER'S HOUSE ARE MANY MANSIONS

John 14:1-4 *(Jesus Christ to his disciples)*

1. Let not your heart be troubled: ye believe in God, believe also in me.

2. In my Father's house are many mansions: if it were not so, I would have told you. I go to prepare a place for you.

3. And if I go and prepare a place for you, I will come again, and receive you unto myself; that where I am, there ye may be also.

4. And whither I go ye know, and the way ye know.

ETERNAL LIFE IS TO KNOW GOD

John 17:3 *(Christ's prayer to God the Father)*

And this is life eternal, that they might know thee the only true God, and Jesus Christ, whom thou hast sent.

ETERNAL LIFE IS A GIFT OF GOD

Romans 6:23 *(Paul to the Romans)*

For the wages of sin is death; but the gift of God is eternal life through Jesus Christ our Lord.

WE ARE THE CHILDREN AND HEIRS OF GOD

Romans 8:16-17 *(Paul to the Romans)*

16. The Spirit itself beareth witness with our spirit, that we are the children of God:

17. And if children, then heirs; heirs of God, and

joint-heirs with Christ; if so be that we suffer with him, that we may be also glorified together.

THREE DEGREES OF GLORY

1 Corinthians 15:40-42 *(Paul to the Corinthians)*

40. There are also celestial bodies, and bodies terrestrial: but the glory of the celestial is one, and the glory of the terrestrial is another.

41. There is one glory of the sun, and another glory of the moon, and another glory of the stars: for one star differeth from another star in glory.

42. So also is the resurrection of the dead. It is sown in corruption; it is raised in incorruption:

CHRIST'S PROMISE

1 John 2:25 *(Epistle of John the Beloved)*

And this is the promise that he hath promised us, even eternal life.

THE GATE TO ETERNAL LIFE

2 Nephi 31:17, 19-20 *(Nephi's prediction of the last days, 545 BC)*

17. . . .the gate by which ye should enter is repentance and baptism by water; and then cometh a remission of your sins by fire and by the Holy Ghost.

19. And now, my beloved brethren, after ye have gotten into this straight and narrow path, I would ask if all is done? Behold, I say unto you, Nay; for ye have not come thus far save it were by the word of Christ with unshaken faith in him, relying wholly upon the merits of him who is mighty to save.

20. Wherefore, ye must press forward with a steadfastness in Christ, having a perfect brightness of hope, and a love of God and of all men. Wherefore, if ye shall press forward, feasting upon the word of Christ, and endure to the end, behold, thus saith the Father: Ye shall have eternal life.

HE THAT HATH ETERNAL LIFE IS RICH

D & C 6:7 *(Revelation to Joseph Smith and Oliver Cowery — April, 1829)*

Seek not for riches but for wisdom, and behold, the mysteries of God shall be unfolded unto you, and then shall you be made rich. Behold, he that hath eternal life is rich.

CHRIST GAVE MEN THE POWER TO OBTAIN ETERNAL LIFE

D & C 45:8 *(Revelation to Joseph Smith — March, 1831)*

I came unto mine own, and mine own received me not; but unto as many as received me gave I power to do many miracles, and to become the sons of God; and even unto them that believed on my name gave I power to obtain eternal life.

REWARDS OF RIGHTEOUSNESS

D & C 59:23 *(Revelation to Joseph Smith — August, 1831)*

But learn that he who doeth the works of righteousness shall receive his reward, even peace in this world, and eternal life in the world to come.

GOD'S WORK AND GLORY

Moses 1:39 *(The Lord to Moses)*

For behold, this is my work and my glory — to bring to pass the immortality and eternal life of man.

ℰXAMPLE

LET YOUR LIGHT SHINE

Matthew 5:14-16 *(also 3 Nephi 12:15-16) (Jesus Christ in the Sermon on the Mount)*

14.   Ye are the light of the world. A city that is set on an hill cannot be hid.

15.   Neither do men light a candle, and put it under a bushel, but on a candlestick; and it giveth light unto all that are in the house.

16.   Let your light so shine before men, that they may see your good works, and glorify your Father which is in heaven.

BY THEIR FRUITS YE SHALL KNOW THEM

Matthew 7:20 *(Jesus Christ in the Sermon on the Mount)*

Wherefore by their fruits ye shall know them.

THE BLIND LEAD THE BLIND

Matthew 15:14 *(Jesus Christ talks about the Pharisees to his apostles)*

Let them alone: they be blind leaders of the blind. And if the blind lead the blind, both shall fall into the ditch.

Luke 6:39 *(Jesus preaching to his disciples)*

And he spake a parable unto them, Can the blind lead the blind? Shall they not both fall into the ditch?

THEY THAT PREACH THE GOSPEL MUST LIVE IT

1 Corinthians 9:14 *(Paul to the Corinthians)*

Even so hath the Lord ordained that they which preach the gospel should live of the gospel:

TO BE AN EXAMPLE, YOU MUST BE UNDERSTOOD

1 Corinthians 14:8 *(Paul to the Corinthians)*

For if the trumpet give an uncertain sound, who shall prepare himself to the battle?

YOUTH SHOULD BE AN EXAMPLE

1 Timothy 4:12 *(Paul's epistle to Timothy)*

Let no man despise thy youth; but be thou an example of the believers, in word, in conversation, in charity, in spirit, in faith, in purity.

FATHERS BE A GOOD EXAMPLE TO YOUR FAMILY

Jacob 2:35 *(Jacob's teachings to the Nephites — 421 BC)*

Behold, ye have done greater iniquities than the Lamanites, our brethren. Ye have broken the hearts of your tender wives, and lost the confidence of your children, because of your bad examples before them. . .

Jacob 3:10 *(Jacob's teachings to the Nephites — 421 BC)*

Wherefore, ye shall remember your children, how that ye have grieved their hearts because of the example that ye have set before them; and also, remember that ye may, because of your filthiness, bring your children unto destruction, and their sins be heaped upon your heads at the last day.

Example 79

CONSEQUENCES OF BAD EXAMPLE

Alma 4:10 *(Alma tells of the growth of the Church — 84 BC)*

. . .And the wickedness of the Church was a great stumbling block to those who did not belong to the Church; and thus the Church began to fail in its progress.

Alma 48:11,17 *(Alma describes Moroni, the general of righteous Nephites — 72 BC)*

11.   And Moroni was a strong and a mighty man; he was a man of a perfect understanding; yea, a man that did not delight in bloodshed; a man whose soul did joy in the liberty and the freedom of his country, and his brethren from bondage and slavery;

17.   . . .if all men had been, and were, and ever would be, like unto Moroni, behold, the very powers of hell would have been shaken forever; yea, the devil would never have power over the hearts of the children of men.

BE LIKE CHRIST

3 Nephi 27:27 *(Jesus Christ to the Nephite 12 — 34 AD)*

. . .What manner of men ought ye to be? Verily I say unto you, even as I am.

ҒAITH

DOUBT IS OPPOSITE OF FAITH

Matthew 14:31 *(Jesus Christ to Peter when Peter sank as he tried to walk on the water)*

And immediately Jesus stretched forth his hand, and caught him, and said unto him, O thou of little faith, wherefore didst thou doubt?

THE FAITH OF THE CANAANITE WOMAN

Matthew 15:28 *(Jesus Christ to the Canaanite woman when he healed her daughter)*

O woman, great is thy faith: be it unto thee even as thou wilt. And her daughter was made whole from that very hour.

FAITH AS A GRAIN OF MUSTARD SEED

Matthew 17:20 *(Jesus Christ to his apostles after they failed to cure the lunatic child)*

. . .If ye have faith as a grain of mustard seed, ye shall say unto this mountain, Remove hence to yonder place; and it shall remove; and nothing shall be impossible unto you.

REWARDS FOR THE FAITHFUL SERVANT

Matthew 25:21 *(Jesus Christ tells the parable of the talents)*

His lord said unto him, Well done, thou good and faithful servant: thou hast been faithful over a few things, I will make thee ruler over many things: enter thou into the joy of thy lord.

FAITH COMES BY HEARING

Romans 10:17 *(Paul to the Romans)*

So then faith cometh by hearing, and hearing by the word of God.

FAITH SHOULD BE IN GOD

1 Corinthians 2:5 *(Paul to the church at Corinth)*

. . .your faith should not stand in the wisdom of men, but in the power of God.

FIGHT TO RETAIN FAITH

1 Timothy 6:12 *(Paul to Timothy)*

Fight the good fight of faith, lay hold on eternal life. . .

PROMISE TO THOSE WHO KEEP THE FAITH

2 Timothy 4:7-8 *(Paul to Timothy)*

7.   I have fought a good fight, I have finished my course; I have kept the faith:

8.   Henceforth there is laid up for me a crown of righteousness, which the Lord, the righteous judge, shall give me at that day; and not to me only, but unto all them also that love his appearing.

PAUL DEFINES FAITH

Hebrews 11:1 *(Paul to the Hebrews)*

Now faith is the substance of things hoped for, the evidence of things not seen.

JESUS IS THE AUTHOR OF FAITH

Hebrews 12:2 *(Paul to the Hebrews)*

Looking unto Jesus the author and finisher of our faith; who for the joy that was set before him endured the cross, despising the shame, and is set down at the right hand of the throne of God.

FAITH WITHOUT WORKS IS DEAD

James 2:14, 17-18, 20,26 *(Epistle of James the brother of Christ)*

14.   What doth it profit, my brethren, though a man say he hath faith, and have not works? can faith save him?

17.   Even so faith, if it hath not works, is dead, being alone.

18.   Yea, a man may say, Thou hast faith, and I have works: shew me thy faith without thy works, and I will shew thee my faith by my works.

20.   But wilt thou know, O vain man, that faith without works it dead?

26.   For as the body without the spirit is dead, so faith without works is dead also.

FAITH IS NOT KNOWLEDGE

Alma 32:21 *(Alma's discourse on faith — 74 BC)*

And now as I said concerning faith — faith is not to have a perfect knowledge of things; therefore if ye have faith ye hope for things which are not seen, which are true.

THE BEGINNING OF FAITH IS A DESIRE TO BELIEVE

Alma 32:27 *(Alma's discourse on faith — 74 BC)*

But behold, if ye will awake and arouse your faculties, even to an experiment upon my words, and exercise a particle of faith, yea, even if ye can no more than desire to believe, let this desire work in you, even until ye believe in a manner that ye can give place for a portion of my words.

ALMA'S PARABLE ON FAITH

Alma 32:28 *(also Alma 32:28-43) (Alma's discourse on faith — 74 BC)*

Now, we will compare the word unto a seed. Now, if ye give place, that a seed may be planted in your heart, behold, if it be a true seed, or a good seed, if ye do not cast it out by your unbelief, that ye will resist the Spirit of the Lord, behold, it will begin to swell within your breasts; and when you feel these swelling motions, ye will begin to say within yourselves — It must needs be that this is a good seed, or that the word is good, for it beginneth to enlarge my soul; yea, it beginneth to enlighten my understanding, yea, it beginneth to be delicious to me.

THE FAITH OF THE 2000 STRIPLING WARRIORS

Alma 56:47 *(Epistle of Helaman to General Moroni — 64 BC)*

Now they never had fought, yet they did not fear death; and they did think more upon the liberty of their fathers than they did upon their lives; yea, they had been taught by their mothers, that if they did not doubt, God would deliver them.

THE BROTHER OF JARED'S FAITH LET HIM SEE GOD

Ether 3:9 *(Jesus Christ talks to the Brother of Jared — 1500 BC)*

And the Lord said unto him: Because of thy faith thou hast seen that I shall take upon me flesh and blood; and never has man come before me with such exceeding faith as thou hast; for were it not so ye could not have seen my finger. Sawest thou more than this?

A WITNESS OF THE TRUTH COMES AFTER A TRIAL OF FAITH

Ether 12:6 *(Moroni's comments about the destruction of the Jaredites, 420 AD)*

. . .I would show unto the world that faith is things which are hoped for and not seen; wherefore, dispute not because ye see not, for ye receive no witness until after the trial of your faith.

FAITH TO BE HEALED

D & C 42:48 *(Revelation to Joseph Smith — February, 1831)*

And again, it shall come to pass that he that hath faith in me to be healed, and is not appointed unto death, shall be healed.

THE FIRST PRINCIPLE OF THE GOSPEL

Fourth Article of Faith

We believe that the first principles and ordinances of the Gospel are: first, Faith in the Lord Jesus Christ; second, Repentance; third, Baptism by immersion for the remission of sins; fourth, Laying on of hands for the gift of the Holy Ghost.

FAMILY: RESPONSIBILITY OF PARENTS

(See Discipline, Fathers, Mothers)

MULTIPLY AND REPLENISH THE EARTH

Genesis 1:28 *(Moses' account of the creation)*

> And God blessed them, and God said unto them, Be fruitful, and multiply, and replenish the earth, and subdue it: and have dominion over the fish of the sea, and over the fowls of the air, and over every living thing that moveth upon the earth.

MAN SHOULD NOT BE ALONE

Genesis 2:18,24 *(Moses' account of the creation)*

> 18.   And the Lord God said, It is not good that the man should be alone; I will make him an help meet for him.

> 24.   Therefore shall a man leave his father and his mother, and shall cleave unto his wife; and they shall be one flesh.

THE LORD CORRECTS THOSE WHOM HE LOVES

Proverbs 3:11-12 *(Proverb of Solomon, King of Israel)*

> 11.   My son, despise not the chastening of the Lord; neither be weary of his correction:

> 12.   For whom the Lord loveth he correceth; even as a father the son in whom he delighteth.

THE VALUE OF A GOOD NAME

Proverbs 22:1 *(Proverb of Solomon, King of Israel)*

A good name is rather to be chosen than great riches, and loving favour rather than silver and gold.

TRAIN YOUR CHILD

Proverbs 22:6 *(Proverb of Solomon, King of Israel)*

Train up a child in the way he should go: and when he is old, he will not depart from it.

MEN WITH STRONG FAMILIES SHOULD BE CALLED TO LEAD THE CHURCH

1 Timothy 3:5 *(Paul to Timothy)*

For if a man know not how to rule his own house, how shall he take care of the Church of God.

FAMILIES SHOULD PROVIDE FOR FAMILY MEMBERS

1 Timothy 5:8 *(Paul to Timothy)*

But, if any provide not for his own, and specially for those of his own house, he hath denied the faith, and is worse than an infidel.

NEPHI BORN OF GOODLY PARENTS

1 Nephi 1:1 *(Nephi's first words in the Book of Mormon — 600 BC)*

I, Nephi, having been born of goodly parents. . .

PARENTS SHOULD SET THE EXAMPLE FOR THEIR CHILDREN

Jacob 2:35 *(Jacob's teachings to the Nephites — 421 BC)*

Behold, ye have done greater iniquities than the Lamanites, our brethren. Ye have broken the hearts of your tender wives, and lost the confidence of your children, because of your bad examples before them. . .

Jacob 3:10 *(Jacob's teachings to the Nephites — 421 BC)*

Wherefore, ye shall remember your children, how that ye have grieved their hearts because of the example that ye have set before them; and also, remember that ye may, because of your filthiness, bring your children unto destruction, and their sins be heaped upon your heads at the last day.

PARENTS MUST TEACH THEIR CHILDREN NOT TO QUARREL

Mosiah 4:14-15 *(King Benjamin's address — 124 BC)*

14.   And ye will not suffer your children that they go hungry, or naked; neither will ye suffer that they transgress the laws of God, and fight and quarrel one with another, and serve the devil. . .

15.   But ye will teach them to walk in the ways of truth and soberness; ye will teach them to love one another, and to serve one another.

MOTHERS TAUGHT THE 2000 STRIPLING WARRIORS

Alma 56:47-48 *(Epistle of Helaman to General Moroni — 64 BC)*

47.   . . .yea, they had been taught by their mothers, that if they did not doubt, God would deliver them.

48. And they rehearsed unto me the words of their mothers, saying: We do not doubt our mothers knew it.

FAMILY PRAYER ALWAYS

3 Nephi 18:21 *(The resurrected Jesus Christ to the Nephites — 34 AD)*

Pray in your families unto the Father, always in my name, that your wives and your children may be blessed.

MARRIAGE IS ORDAINED OF GOD

D & C 49:15 *(Revelation for Leman Copley, who was previously a Shaking Quaker — March, 1831)*

And again, verily I say unto you, that whoso forbiddeth to marry is not ordained of God, for marriage is ordained of God unto man.

PARENTS MUST TEACH THEIR CHILDREN

D & C 68:25,28 *(Revelation to Joseph Smith — November, 1831)*

25. And again, inasmuch as parents have children in Zion, or in any of her stakes which are organized, that teach them not to understand the doctrine of repentance, faith in Christ the Son of the living God, and of baptism and the gift of the Holy Ghost by the laying on of the hands, when eight years old, the sin be upon the heads of the parents.

28. And they shall also teach their children to pray, and to walk uprightly before the Lord.

D & C 93:40 *(Revelation to Joseph Smith — May, 1833)*

But I have commanded you to bring up your children in light and truth.

ORGANIZE YOURSELVES, PREPARE EVERY NEEDFUL THING

D & C 88:119 *(Revelation to Joseph Smith — December, 1832)*

Organize yourselves; prepare every needful thing; and establish a house, even a house of prayer, a house of fasting, a house of faith, a house of learning, a house of glory, a house of order, a house of God;

TEACH CHILDREN OF REPENTANCE AND BAPTISM

Moses 6:57 *(The Lord speaks to Adam)*

Wherefore teach it unto your children, that all men, everywhere, must repent, or they can in nowise inherit the kingdom of God, for no unclean thing can dwell there, or dwell in his presence. . .

FAMILY: RESPONSIBILITY OF CHILDREN

(See Children, Fathers, Mothers)

HONOR PARENTS

Exodus 20:12 *(also Mosiah 13:20, Deuteronomy 5:16)* *(The Fifth Commandment)*

Honour thy father and thy mother: that thy days may be long upon the land which the Lord thy God giveth thee.

THE LORD CORRECTS HIS CHILDREN

Deuteronomy 8:5 *(Moses exhorts the children of Israel to be obedient)*

Thou shalt also consider in thine heart, that, as a man chasteneth his son, so the Lord thy God chasteneth thee.

CHILDREN, OBEY PARENTS

Proverbs 6:20-22 *(Proverb of Solomon, King of Israel)*

20. My son, keep thy father's commandment, and forsake not the law of thy mother:

21. Bind them continually upon thine heart, and tie them about thy neck.

22. When thou goest, it shall lead thee; when thou sleepest, it shall keep thee; and when thou awakest, it shall talk with thee.

A WISE SON

Proverbs 10:1 *(Proverb of Solomon, King of Israel)*

. . .A wise son maketh a glad father: but a foolish son is the heaviness of his mother.

A WISE SON LISTENS TO HIS FATHER

Proverbs 13:1 *(Proverb of Solomon, King of Israel)*

A wise son heareth his father's instruction: but a scorner heareth not rebuke.

CHILDREN HONOR PARENTS — PARENTS DON'T PROVOKE CHILDREN

Ephesians 6:1-4 *(Paul to the Ephesians)*

1.   Children, obey your parents in the Lord: for this is right.

2.   Honour thy father and mother; (which is the first commandment with promise;)

3.   That it may be well with thee, and thou mayest live long on the earth.

4.   And, ye fathers, provoke not your children to wrath: but bring them up in the nurture and admonition of the Lord.

Colossians 3:20-21 *(Paul's epistle to the Colossians)*

20.   Children, obey your parents in all things: for this is well pleasing unto the Lord.

21.   Fathers, provoke not your children to anger, lest they be discouraged.

LEARN WISDOM WHILE YOUNG

Alma 37:35 *(Alma to his son, Helaman — 73 BC)*

O, remember, my son, and learn wisdom in thy youth; yea, learn in thy youth to keep the commandments of God.

FASHION

THE LORD LOOKS AT PEOPLE'S HEARTS

1 Samuel 16:7 *(The Lord tells the prophet Samuel how to pick a new king. David, although young, is picked to replace Saul as the King of Israel.)*

. . .Look not on his countenance, or on the height of his stature. . .man looketh on the outward appearance, but the Lord looketh on the heart.

COSTLY CLOTHING NOT IMPORTANT

Alma 1:27 *(Alma describes the saints — 90 BC)*

. . .they did not wear costly apparel, yet they were neat and comely.

THE FASHIONS OF THE ZORAMITES

Alma 31:24,28 *(Alma's prayer for the Zoramites — 74 BC)*

24.   Now when Alma saw this his heart was grieved; for he saw that they were a wicked and a perverse people; yea, he saw that their hearts were set upon gold, and upon silver, and upon all manner of fine goods.

28.   Behold, O my God, their costly apparel, and their ringlets, and their bracelets, and their ornaments of gold, and all their precious things which they are ornamented with; and behold, their hearts are set upon them, and yet they cry unto thee and say — We

thank thee, O God, for we are a chosen people unto thee, while others shall perish.

ADVICE FOR THOSE QUESTIONING CLOTHING STANDARDS

D & C 46:7 *(Revelation to Joseph Smith — March, 1831)*

But ye are commanded in all things to ask of God, who giveth liberally; and that which the Spirit testifies unto you even so I would that ye should do in all holiness of heart, walking uprightly before me, considering the end of your salvation, doing all things with prayer and thanksgiving, that ye may not be seduced by evil spirits, or doctrines of devils, or the commandments of men; for some are of men, and others of devils.

FASTING

ATTITUDE WHEN FASTING

Matthew 6:16-18 *(also 3 Nephi, 13:16-18) (Jesus Christ in the Sermon on the Mount)*

16. Moreover when ye fast, be not, as the hypocrites, of a sad countenance: for they disfigure their faces, that they may appear unto men to fast. Verily I say unto you, they have their reward.

17. But thou, when thou fastest, anoint thine head, and wash thy face;

18. That thou appear not unto men to fast, but unto thy Father which is in secret: and thy Father, which seeth in secret, shall reward thee openly.

D & C 59:14-16 *(Revelation to Joseph Smith — August, 1831)*

14. Verily, this is fasting and prayer, or in other words, rejoicing and prayer.

15. And inasmuch as ye do these things with thanksgiving, with cheerful hearts and countenances, not with much laughter, for this is sin, but with a glad heart and a cheerful countenance —

16. Verily I say, that inasmuch as ye do this, the fulness of the earth is yours, the beasts of the field and the fowls of the air, and that which climbeth upon the trees and walketh upon the earth;

HEALING THE SICK REQUIRES FASTING AND PRAYER

Matthew 17:21 *(Jesus Christ to his apostles after they failed to heal the lunatic child)*

Howbeit this kind goeth not out but by prayer and fasting.

UNDERSTANDING AND POWER COME THROUGH FASTING

Alma 17:2-3 *(Alma is reunited with the sons of Mosiah after their 14-year mission to the Lamanites — 91 BC)*

2. . . .Alma did rejoice exceedingly to see his brethren; and what added more to his joy, they were still his brethren in the Lord; yea, and they had waxed strong in the knowledge of the truth; for they were men of a sound understanding and they had searched the scriptures diligently, that they might know the word of God.

3. But this not all, they had given themselves to much prayer, and fasting; therefore they had the spirit of prophecy, and the spirit of revelation, and when they taught, they taught with power and authority of God.

⒡ATHERS

(See Marriage, Family, Mothers)

FATHER AND MOTHER SHOULD BECOME ONE

Genesis 2:24 *(Moses' record of the beginning of the world)*

Therefore shall a man leave his father and his mother, and shall cleave unto his wife: and they shall be one flesh.

CHILDREN SHOULD OBEY PARENTS

Exodus 20:12 *(also Mosiah 13:20, Deuteronomy 5:16) (Given to Moses on Mt. Sinai)*

Honour thy father and thy mother: that thy days may be long upon the land which the Lord thy God giveth thee.

Ephesians 6:1-4 *(Epistle of Paul to the people at Ephesus)*

1.   Children, obey your parents in the Lord: for this is right.

2.   Honour thy father and mother: (which is the first commandment with promise;)

3.   That it may be well with thee, and thou mayest live long on the earth.

4.   And, ye fathers, provoke not your children to wrath: but bring them up in the nurture and admonition of the Lord.

FATHERS SHOULD INSTRUCT THEIR CHILDREN

Proverbs 1:8 *(Proverb of Solomon, King of Israel)*

My son, hear the instruction of thy father, and forsake not the law of thy mother;

Proverbs 6:20 *(Proverb of Solomon, King of Israel)*

My son, keep thy father's commandment, and forsake not the law of thy mother:

Proverbs 10:1 *(Proverb of Solomon, King of Israel)*

. . .A wise son maketh a glad father: but a foolish son is the heaviness of his mother.

Proverbs 13:1 *(Proverb of Solomon, King of Israel)*

A wise son heareth his father's instruction:. . .

Proverbs 23:22 *(Proverb of Solomon, King of Israel)*

Hearken unto thy father that begat thee, and despise not thy mother when she is old.

GOD IS THE FATHER OF ALL

Malachi 2:10 *(Words of Malachi the prophet)*

Have we not all one father? hath not one God created us? why do we deal treacherously every man against his brother, by profaning the covenant of our fathers?

FATHER IN HEAVEN IS PERFECT

Matthew 5:48 *(Jesus Christ to his disciples)*

Be ye therefore perfect, even as your Father which is in heaven is perfect.

GOD THE FATHER BEARS TESTIMONY OF HIS SON

Matthew 16:17 *(Jesus Christ to Simon Peter)*

. . .Blessed art thou, Simon Barjona: for flesh and blood hath not revealed it unto thee, but my Father which is in heaven.

GOD IS THE FATHER OF CHRIST

John 20:17 *(Jesus Christ speaking to Mary after his resurrection)*

. . .Touch me not; for I am not yet ascended to my Father: but go to my brethren, and say unto them, I ascend unto my Father, and your Father; and to my God, and your God.

CHILDREN SHOULD LEARN GENEALOGY OF THEIR FATHERS

D & C 2:1-2 *(Revelation given to Joseph Smith — September, 1823)*

1.   Behold, I will reveal unto the Priesthood, by the hand of Elijah the prophet, before the coming of the great and dreadful day of the Lord.

2.   And he shall plant in the hearts of the children the promises made to the fathers, and the hearts of the children shall turn to their fathers.

ADAM IS MICHAEL, FATHER OF ALL

D & C 27:11 *(Revelation given to Joseph Smith — August, 1830)*

. . .With Michael, or Adam, the father of all, the prince of all, the ancient of days; . . .

FATHERS SHOULD PROVIDE FOR THEIR FAMILIES

D & C 75:28 *(Revelation given to Joseph Smith — January, 1832)*

And again, verily I say unto you, that every man who is obliged to provide for his own family, let him provide, and he shall in nowise lose his crown: and let him labor in the church.

GOD, THE FATHER, HAS A PHYSICAL BODY

D & C 130:22 *(Instructions given by Joseph Smith — April, 1843)*

The Father has a body of flesh and bones as tangible as man's;. . .

ABRAHAM SHALL BECOME FATHER OF THE FAITHFUL

Abraham 2:10 *(Blessing given to Abraham by the Lord)*

And I will bless them through thy name; for as many as receive this Gospel shall be called after thy name, and shall be accounted thy seed, and shall rise up and bless thee, as their father.

FEAR

FEAR NOT IF ON THE LORD'S SIDE

2 Kings 6:16 *(Elisha faces the charging Syrians. His servant asks what they should do. They are protected when the Lord blinds the Syrians, and they fight among themselves.)*

And he answered, Fear not: for they that be with us are more than they that be with them.

FEAR NO EVIL

Psalms 23:4 *(Psalm of David, King of Israel)*

Yea, though I walk through the valley of the shadow of death, I will fear no evil: for thou art with me; thy rod and thy staff they comfort me.

FEAR CAUSED BY LACK OF FAITH

Matthew 8:26 *(Jesus Christ to his apostles when they awakened him during a storm at sea)*

. . .Why are ye fearful, O ye of little faith?

FEAR NOT PHYSICAL HARM, BUT SPIRITUAL DESTRUCTION

Matthew 10:28 *(Jesus Christ's instruction to the twelve apostles)*

And fear not them which kill the body, but are not able to kill the soul: but rather fear him which is able to destroy both soul and body in hell.

FEAR NOT TO DO THE LORD'S COMMAND

Luke 1:30 *(The Angel Gabriel to Mary)*

And the angel said unto her, Fear not, Mary: for thou hast found favour with God.

JESUS ADMONISHES TO BE NOT AFRAID

John 14:27-28 *(Jesus to his disciples)*

27. Peace I leave with you, my peace I give unto you: not as the world giveth, give I unto you. Let not your heart be troubled, neither let it be afraid.

28. . . .I go unto the Father: for my Father is greater than I.

GOD DOES NOT GIVE US THE SPIRIT OF FEAR

2 Timothy 1:7 *(Paul to Timothy)*

For God hath not given us the spirit of fear; but of power, and of love, and of a sound mind.

LOVE CASTS OUT FEAR

1 John 4:18 *(John's Epistle on brotherly love)*

There is no fear in love; but perfect love casteth out fear: because fear hath torment. He that feareth is not made perfect in love.

Moroni 8:16 *(Mormon's epistle to Moroni — 400 AD)*

. . .for perfect love casteth out all fear.

THE RIGHTEOUS NEED NOT FEAR

1 Nephi 22:22 *(Nephi exhorts his people — 588 BC)*

. . .the righteous need not fear, for they are those who shall not be confounded. . .

THE RIGHTEOUS DO NOT FEAR WORDS OF TRUTH

2 Nephi 9:40 *(Jacob's teachings to the Nephites — 560 BC)*

. . .I know that the words of truth are hard against all uncleanness; but the righteous fear them not, for they love the truth and are not shaken.

THE 2000 STRIPLING WARRIORS OF HELAMAN HAD NO FEAR

Alma 56:47 *(Epistle of Helaman to General Moroni — 64 BC)*

Now they never had fought, yet they did not fear death; and they did think more upon the liberty of their fathers than they did upon their lives; yea, they had been taught by their mothers, that if they did not doubt, God would deliver them.

FEAR NOT TO DO GOOD

D & C 6:33,36 *(Revelation to Joseph Smith and Oliver Cowdery — April, 1829)*

33.　Fear not to do good, my sons, for whatsoever ye sow, that shall ye also reap; therefore, if ye sow good ye shall also reap good for your reward.

36.　Look unto me in every thought; doubt not, fear not.

THE PREPARED SHALL NOT FEAR

D & C 38:30 *(The Lord to Joseph Smith — January, 1831)*

. . .but if ye are prepared ye shall not fear.

MEN HIDE THEIR TALENTS BECAUSE OF FEAR

D & C 60:2 *(Revelation to Joseph Smith — August, 1831)*

But with some I am not well pleased, for they will not open their mouths, but they hide the talent which I have given unto them, because of the fear of man. Wo unto such, for mine anger is kindled against them.

FORGIVENESS

(See Repentance)

SINS CAN BE FORGIVEN

Isaiah 1:16,18 *(The vision of Isaiah)*

16.   Wash you, make you clean; put away the evil of your doings from before mine eyes; cease to do evil;

18.   Come now, and let us reason together, saith the Lord: though your sins be as scarlet, they shall be as white as snow; though they be red like crimson, they shall be as wool.

THE LORD PROMISES TO FORGET OUR SINS IF WE REPENT

Jeremiah 31:34 *(Prophecies of Jeremiah)*

. . .they shall all know me, from the least of them unto the greatest of them, saith the Lord: for I will forgive their iniquity, and I will remember their sin no more.

GOD WILL FORGIVE THOSE WHO FORGIVE OTHERS

Matthew 6:14-15 *(Jesus Christ in the Sermon on the Mount)*

14.   If ye forgive men their trespasses, your heavenly Father will also forgive you:

15.   But if ye forgive not men their trespasses, neither will your Father forgive your trespasses.

JESUS FORGAVE SINS

Matthew 9:2 *(Jesus Christ to the man sick of palsy)*

...Son, be of good cheer; thy sins be forgiven thee.

FORGIVE UNTIL SEVENTY TIMES SEVEN

Matthew 18:21-22 *(Jesus to Peter)*

21. Then came Peter to him, and said, Lord, how oft shall my brother sin against me, and I forgive him? till seven times?

22. Jesus saith unto him, I say not unto thee, Until seven times: but, Until seventy times seven.

JESUS FORGAVE

Luke 23:34 *(Christ on the Cross)*

...Father, forgive them; for they know not what they do.

HE WHO REPENTS AND OBEYS SHALL BE FORGIVEN

D & C 1:32 *(Revelation to Joseph Smith — November, 1831)*

Nevertheless, he that repents and does the commandments of the Lord shall be forgiven;

THE LORD FORGIVES THOSE WHO CONFESS

D & C 64:7 *(Revelation about Joseph Smith to the Elders of the Church — September, 1831)*

...he (Joseph Smith), has sinned; but verily I say unto you, I, the Lord, forgive sins unto those who confess their sins before me and ask forgiveness, who have not sinned unto death.

HE WHO FORGIVES NOT SINS

D & C 64:8-9 *(Revelation to the Elders of the Church — September, 1831)*

8.　My disciples, in days of old, sought occasion against one another and forgave not one another in their hearts; and for this evil they were afflicted and sorely chastened.

9.　Wherefore, I say unto you, that ye ought to forgive one another; for he that forgiveth not his brother his trespasses standeth condemned before the Lord; for there remaineth in him the greater sin.

WE MUST FORGIVE ALL MEN

D & C 64:10 *(Revelation to the Elders of the Church — September, 1831)*

I, the Lord, will forgive whom I will forgive, but of you it is required to forgive all men.

FREE AGENCY

THE SPIRIT OF THE LORD BRINGS LIBERTY

2 Corinthians 3:17 *(Paul to the Corinthians)*

. . .where the Spirit of the Lord is, there is liberty.

BE NOT ENTANGLED WITH BAD HABITS

Galatians 5:1 *(Paul to the Galatians)*

Stand fast therefore in the liberty wherewith Christ hath made us free, and be not entangled again with the yoke of bondage.

MEN CHOOSE THEIR ETERNAL STATION

2 Nephi 2:27 *(Lehi's teachings to his son Jacob — 570 BC)*

. . .they are free to choose liberty and eternal life, through the great mediation of all men, or to choose captivity and death, according to the captivity and power of the devil; for he seeketh that all men might be miserable like unto himself.

MEN ARE FREE TO ACT

2 Nephi 10:23 *(Jacob's teaching to the Nephites)*

Therefore, cheer up your hearts, and remember that ye are free to act for yourselves — to choose the way of everlasting death or the way of eternal life.

GOD WILL NOT COMMAND IN ALL THINGS

D & C 58:26-29 *(Revelation to Joseph Smith — August, 1831)*

26. For behold, it is not meet that I should command in all things; for he that is compelled in all things, the same is a slothful and not a wise servant; wherefore he receiveth no reward.

27. Verily I say, men should be anxiously engaged in a good cause, and do many things of their own free will, and bring to pass much righteousness;

28. For the power is in them, wherein they are agents unto themselves. And inasmuch as men do good they shall in nowise lose their reward.

29. But he that doeth not anything until he is commanded, and receiveth a commandment with doubtful heart, and keepeth it with slothfulness, the same is damned.

THE LAW MAKES MEN FREE

D & C 98:8 *(Revelation to Joseph Smith — August, 1833)*

I, the Lord God, make you free, therefore ye are free indeed; and the law also maketh you free.

WE CLAIM THE PRIVILEGE TO WORSHIP GOD

Eleventh Article of Faith

We claim the privilege of worshiping Almighty God according to the dictates of our own conscience, and allow all men the same privilege, let them worship how, where, or what they may.

FRIENDSHIP

(See Charity, Love, and Service)

LOVE YOUR NEIGHBOR AS YOURSELF

Leviticus 19:18 *(The Lord speaking to Moses)*

Thou shalt not avenge, nor bear any grudge against the children of thy people, but thou shalt love thy neighbor as thyself. . .

FRIENDS SHOW LOVE

Proverbs 17:17 *(Proverb of Solomon, King of Israel)*

A friend loveth at all times. . .

TO HAVE A FRIEND, YOU MUST BE A FRIEND

Proverbs 18:24 *(Proverb of Solomon, King of Israel)*

A man that hath friends must shew himself friendly: and there is a friend that sticketh closer than a brother.

PICK YOUR FRIENDS WISELY

Proverbs 22:24 *(Proverb of Solomon, King of Israel)*

Make no friendship with an angry man; and with a furious man thou shalt not go:

FRIENDS BUILD EACH OTHER

Proverbs 27:17 *(Proverb of Solomon, King of Israel)*

. . .a man sharpeneth the countenance of his friend.

LOVE ONE ANOTHER

John 13:34-35 *(Jesus Christ to his disciples)*

34.   A new commandment I give unto you, That ye love one another; as I have loved you, that ye also love one another.

35.   By this shall all men know that ye are my disciples if ye have love one to another.

CHRIST GAVE HIS LIFE FOR HIS FRIENDS

John 15:13 *(Jesus Christ to his disciples)*

Greater love hath no man than this, that a man lay down his life for his friends.

ABRAHAM WAS THE FRIEND OF GOD

James 2:23 *(Epistle of James to the twelve tribes)*

And the scripture was fulfilled which saith, Abraham believed God, and it was imputed unto him for righteousness: and he was called the Friend of God.

MAN MUST LOVE OTHERS IN ORDER TO LOVE GOD

1 John 4:20-21 *(Epistle of John the Beloved)*

20.   If a man say, I love God, and hateth his brother, he is a liar: for he that loveth not his brother whom he hath seen, how can he love God whom he hath not seen?

21.   And this commandment have we from him, That he who loveth God love his brother also.

LOVE YOUR BROTHER AS YOURSELF

D & C 38:24-25 *(Revelation given to Joseph Smith — January, 1831)*

24. And let every man esteem his brother as himself, and practise virtue and holiness before me.

25. And again I say unto you, let every man esteem his brother as himself.

CHRIST CALLED CHURCH LEADERS HIS FRIENDS

D & C 84:77 *(Revelation given to Joseph Smith — September, 1832)*

And again I say unto you, my friends, for from henceforth I shall call you friends, it is expedient that I give unto you this commandment, that ye become even as my friends in days when I was with them, traveling to preach the gospel in my power-

D & C 93:45 *(Revelation given to Joseph Smith — May, 1833)*

Verily, I say unto my servant Joseph Smith, Jun., or in other words, I will call you friends, for you are my friends, and ye shall have an inheritance with me —

GOOD FRIENDS SUPPORT YOU IN TIMES OF TRIALS

D & C 121:7-10 *(Writings of Joseph Smith from the jail at Liberty, Missouri — March, 1839)*

7. My son, peace be unto thy soul; thine adversity and thine afflictions shall be but a small moment;

8. And then, if thou endure it well, God shall exalt thee on high; thou shalt triumph over all thy foes.

9.   Thy friends do stand by thee, and they shall hail thee again with warm hearts and friendly hands.

10.   Thou art not yet as Job; thy friends do not contend against thee, neither charge thee with transgression, as they did Job.

FUNERAL MESSAGES

(See Death, Resurrection)

THE LORD IS MY SHEPHERD

Psalms 23:1-6 *(A psalm of David, King of Israel)*

1. The Lord is my shepherd; I shall not want.

2. He maketh me to lie down in green pastures: he leadeth me beside the still waters.

3. He restoreth my soul: he leadeth me in the paths of righteousness for his name's sake.

4. Yea, though I walk through the valley of the shadow of death, I will fear no evil: for thou art with me; thy rod and thy staff they comfort me.

5. Thou preparest a table before me in the presence of mine enemies: thou anointest my head with oil; my cup runneth over.

6. Surely goodness and mercy shall follow me all the days of my life: and I will dwell in the house of the Lord for ever.

DEAD SHALL LIVE BECAUSE OF CHRIST

John 11:25-26 *(Jesus Christ to Martha before he raised Lazarus from the dead)*

25. Jesus said unto her, I am the resurrection, and the life: he that believeth in me, though he were dead, yet shall he live:

26. And whosoever liveth and believeth in me shall never die. Believest thou this?

IN MY FATHER'S HOUSE ARE MANY MANSIONS

John 14:1-4 *(Jesus Christ to his disciples)*

1.   Let not your heart be troubled: ye believe in God, believe also in me.

2.   In my Father's house are many mansions: if it were not so, I would have told you. I go to prepare a place for you.

3.   And if I go and prepare a place for you, I will come again, and receive you unto myself; that where I am, there ye may be also.

4.   And whither I go ye know, and the way ye know.

DEATH HAS NO VICTORY

1 Corinthians 15:55,57 *(Paul to the Corinthians)*

55.   O death, where is thy sting? O grave, where is thy victory?

57.   But thanks be to God, which giveth us the victory through our Lord Jesus Christ.

REWARD FOR THE RIGHTEOUS

2 Timothy 4:7-8 *(Paul to Timothy)*

7.   I have fought a good fight, I have finished my course, I have kept the faith:

8.   Henceforth there is laid up for me a crown of righteousness, which the Lord, the righteous judge, shall give me at that day: and not to me only, but unto all them also that love his appearing.

GOD SHALL WIPE AWAY ALL TEARS AND THERE SHALL BE NO MORE DEATH

Revelations 21:4 *(Revelations to John the Beloved)*

And God shall wipe away all tears from their eyes; and there shall be no more death, neither sorrow, nor crying, neither shall there be any more pain: for the former things are passed away.

MEETING GOD WILL BE A PLEASURE

Enos Verse 27 *(Enos's testimony of the resurrection)*

For I soon go to the place of my rest, which is with my Redeemer; for I know that in him I shall rest. And I rejoice in the day when my mortal shall put on immortality, and shall stand before him; then shall I see his face with pleasure, and he will say unto me: Come unto me, ye blessed, there is a place prepared for you in the mansions of my father.

FOR SOMEONE WHO HAS ENJOYED SINGING

Mosiah 2:28 *(King Benjamin's discourse to the people of Zarahemla — 124 BC)*

. . .I am about to go down to my grave. . .and my immortal spirit may join the choirs above in singing the praises of a just God.

WHERE THE SPIRIT GOES AFTER DEATH

Alma 40:11-12 *(Alma explains death to his son, Corianton — 73 BC)*

11. Now, concerning the state of the soul between death and the resurrection — Behold, it has been made known unto me by an angel, that the spirits of all men, as soon as they are departed from this mortal

body, yea, the spirits of all men, whether they be good or evil, are taken home to that God who gave them life.

12.   And then shall it come to pass, that the spirits of those who are righteous are received into a state of happiness, which is called paradise, a state of rest, a state of peace, where they sahll rest from all their troubles and from all care, and sorrow.

DEATH SWEET TO THE RIGHTEOUS

D & C   42:44,46 *(Revelation to Joseph Smith — February, 1831)*

44.   And the elders of the church, two or more, shall be called, and shall pray for and lay their hands upon them in my name; and if they die they shall die unto me, and if they live they shall live unto me.

46.   And it shall come to pass that those that die in me shall not taste of death, for it shall be sweet unto them;

FOR CHILDREN WHO HAVE LOST A PARENT

D & C 61:36-39 *(Revelation to Joseph Smith — August, 1831)*

36.   And now, verily I say unto you, and what I say unto one I say unto all, be of good cheer, little children; for I am in your midst, and I have not forsaken you;

37.   And inasmuch as you have humbled yourselves before me, the blessings of the kingdom are yours.

38.   Gird up your loins and be watchful and be sober, looking forth for the coming of the Son of Man, for he cometh in an hour you think not.

39.   Pray always that you enter not into temptation, that you may abide the day of his coming, whether in life or in death. Even so. Amen.

GENEALOGY

(See Records, Judgment)

HEARTS OF CHILDREN SHALL TURN TO THEIR FATHERS

Malachi 4:5-6 *(also D & C 2:1-3) (Malachi tells the mission of Elijah)*

5. Behold, I will send you Elijah the prophet before the coming of the great and dreadful day of the Lord:

6. And he shall turn the heart of the fathers to the children, and the heart of the children to their fathers, lest I come and smite the earth with a curse.

SALVATION OF THE DEAD IS ESSENTIAL TO OUR SALVATION

Hebrews 11:40 *(Paul's letter to the Hebrews)*

God having provided some better thing for us, that they without us should not be made perfect.

D & C 128:15 *(Epistle of Joseph Smith to the saints in Nauvoo — September, 1842)*

And now, my dearly beloved brethren and sisters, let me assure you that these are principles in relation to the dead and the living that cannot be lightly passed over, as pertaining to our salvation. For their salvation is necessary and essential to our salvation, as Paul says concerning the fathers — that they without us cannot be made perfect — neither can we without our dead be made perfect.

ELIJAH RETURNS THE KEYS OF GENEALOGY

D & C 110:13-16 *(Visitation of Elijah to Joseph Smith and Oliver Cowdery in the Kirtland Temple — April, 1836)*

13. After this vision had closed, another great and glorious vision burst upon us; for Elijah the prophet, who was taken to heaven without tasting death, stood before us, and said:

14. Behold, the time has fully come, which was spoken of by the mouth of Malachi — testifying that he (Elijah) should be sent, before the great and dreadful day of the Lord come —

15. To turn the hearts of the fathers to the children, and the children to the fathers, lest the whole earth be smitten with a curse —

16. Therefore, the keys of this dispensation are committed into your hands; and by this ye may know that the great and dreadful day of the Lord is near, even at the doors.

EXPLANATION OF MALACHI'S PROPHECY

D & C 128:18 *(A letter from Joseph Smith to the saints in Nauvoo — September, 1842)*

. . .It is sufficient to know, in this case, that the earth will be smitten with a curse unless there is a welding link of some kind or other between the fathers and the children, upon some subject or other — and behold what is that subject? It is the baptism for the dead. For we without them cannot be made perfect; neither can they without us be made perfect. Neither can they nor we be made perfect without those who have died in the gospel also; for it is necessary in the ushering in of the dispensation of the fulness of times, which dispensation is now beginning to usher in, that a whole and complete and perfect union, and welding together of dispensations, and keys, and powers, and glories should take place, and be revealed from the days of Adam even to the present time. . .

BOOK OF REMEMBRANCE PATTERNED BY GOD

Moses 6:46 *(Enoch speaking to Mahijah)*

For a book of remembrance we have written among us, according to the pattern given by the finger of God; and it is given in our own language.

GIFTS

(See Charity, Friendship)

RECONCILE YOUR PROBLEMS BEFORE YOU BRING GIFTS TO GOD

Matthew 5:23-24 *(Compare to 3 Nephi 12:24) (Jesus Christ in the Sermon on the Mount)*

23. Therefore if thou bring thy gift to the altar, and there rememberest that thy brother hath ought against thee;

24. Leave there thy gift before the altar, and go thy way; first be reconciled to thy brother, and then come and offer thy gift.

SPIRITUAL GIFTS FOLLOW BELIEVERS

Mark 16:17-18 *(Jesus Christ to his apostles before his ascension into heaven)*

17. And these signs shall follow them that believe; In my name shall they cast out devils; they shall speak with new tongues;

18. They shall take up serpents; and if they drink any deadly thing, it shall not hurt them: they shall lay hands on the sick, and they shall recover.

GIVE AND IT SHALL BE GIVEN YOU

Luke 6:38 *(Jesus Christ to his disciples)*

Give, and it shall be given unto you; good measure, pressed down, and shaken together, and running over, shall men give into your bosom. For with the same measure that ye mete withal it shall be measured to you again.

HEAVENLY FATHER GIVES THE GIFT OF THE SPIRIT

Luke 11:13 *(Jesus Christ to his disciples)*

If ye then, being evil, know how to give good gifts unto your children: how much more shall your heavenly Father give the Holy Spirit to them that ask him?

SUCH AS JESUS HAD, HE GAVE

Acts 3:6 *(Peter heals the lame man at the temple gate)*

Then Peter said, Silver and gold have I none; but such as I have give I thee: In the name of Jesus Christ of Nazareth rise up and walk.

MORE BLESSED TO GIVE THAN RECEIVE

Acts 20:35 *(Paul talks to the elders at Ephesus)*

. . .remember the words of the Lord Jesus, how he said, It is more blessed to give than receive.

GOD LOVETH A CHEERFUL GIVER

2 Corinthians 9:7 *(Paul to the Corinthians)*

Every man according as he purposeth in his heart, so let him give; not grudingly, or of necessity: for God loveth a cheerful giver.

DO NOT OVERLOOK THE GIFTS THAT GOD HAS GIVEN

1 Timothy 4:14 *(Paul to Timothy)*

Neglect not the gift that is in thee. . .

EVERY GOOD GIFT COMETH FROM CHRIST

Moroni 10:18,30 *(Moroni's final testimony before he hid the gold plates in the hill Cumorah — 422 AD)*

18. And I would exhort you, my beloved brethren, that ye remember that every good gift cometh of Christ.

30. . . .come unto Christ, and lay hold upon every good gift, and touch not the evil gift, nor the unclean thing.

GIFT OF GOD IS SALVATION

D & C 6:13 *(Revelation to Joseph Smith and Oliver Cowdery — April, 1829)*

If you wilt do good, yea, and hold out faithful to the end, thou shalt be saved in the kingdom of God, which is the greatest of all the gifts of God; for there is no gift greater than the gift of salvation.

SEEK THE BEST GIFTS

D & C 46:8-9 *(Revelation to Joseph Smith — March, 1831)*

8. Wherefore, beware lest ye are deceived; and that ye may not be deceived seek ye earnestly the best gifts, always remembering for what they are given;

9. For verily I say unto you they are given for the benefit of those who love me and keep all my

commandments, and him that seeketh so to do; that all may be benefited that seek or that ask of me, that ask and not for a sign that they may consume it upon their lusts.

EVERY MAN IS GIVEN A GIFT BY THE SPIRIT OF GOD THAT ALL MAY PROFIT

D & C 46:11-12 *(Revelation to Joseph Smith — March, 1831)*

11.   . . .to every man is given a gift by the Spirit of God.

12.   To some is given one, and to some is given another, that all may be profited thereby.

WE BELIEVE IN SPIRITUAL GIFTS

Seventh Article of Faith

We believe in the gift of tongues, prophecy, revelation, visions, healing, interpretation of tongues, etc.

GOD

MAN CREATED IN GOD'S IMAGE

Genesis 1:27 *(Moses' account of the creation)*

So God created man in his own image, in the image of God created he him; male and female created he them.

WORSHIP AND SERVE ONLY GOD

Exodus 20:3-6 *(First and second commandments)*

3.   Thou shalt have no other gods before me.

4.   Thou shalt not make unto thee any graven image, or any likeness of any thing that is in heaven above, or that is in the earth beneath, or that is in the water under the earth:

5.   Thou shalt not bow down thyself to them, nor serve them: for I the Lord thy God am a jealous God, visiting the iniquity of the fathers upon the children unto the third and fourth generation of them that hate me;

6.   And shewing mercy unto thousands of them that love me, and keep my commandments.

Matthew 4:10 *(Jesus Christ's comment to Satan)*

. . .Thou shalt worship the Lord thy God, and him only shalt thou serve.

MOSES TALKED WITH THE LORD

Exodus 33:11 *(Moses talked to God in the tabernacle by Mt. Sinai)*

And the Lord spake unto Moses face to face, as a man speaketh unto his friend. . .

Moses 1:11 *(Revelation to Joseph Smith — June, 1830)*

And now mine own eyes have beheld God; but not my natural, but my spiritual eyes, for my natural eyes could not have beheld. . .

GOD'S THOUGHTS ARE DIFFERENT THAN MAN'S

Numbers 23:19 *(Balaam, the prophet, to Balak the prince of Moab)*

God is not a man, that he should lie; neither the son of man, that he should repent: hath he said, and shall he not do it? or hath he spoken, and shall he not make it good?

Isaiah 55:8-9 *(Prophecies of Isaiah)*

8. For my thoughts are not your thoughts, neither are your ways my ways, saith the Lord.

9. For as the heavens are higher than the earth, so are my ways higher than your ways, and my thoughts than your thoughts.

Luke 18:27 *(Jesus Christ to his disciples)*

. . .The things which are impossible with men are possible with God.

THE LORD LOVES THOSE WHOM HE CORRECTETH

Proverbs 3:11-12 *(Proverb of Solomon, King of Israel)*

11. My son, despise not the chastening of the Lord; neither be weary of his correction:

12. For whom the Lord loveth he correcteth; even as a father the son in whom he delighteth.

SIX THINGS DOTH THE LORD HATE

Proverbs 6:16-19 *(Proverb of Solomon, King of Israel)*

16. These six things doth the Lord hate: yea, seven are an abomination unto him:

17. A proud look, a lying tongue, and hands that shed innocent blood,

18. An heart that deviseth wicked imaginations, feet that be swift in running to mischief,

19. A false witness that speaketh lies, and he that soweth discord among brethren.

BE PERFECT

Matthew 5:48 *(Jesus Christ in the Sermon on the Mount)*

Be ye therefore perfect, even as your Father which is in heaven is perfect.

THE FATHER IS GREATER THAN THE SON

John 14:28 *(Jesus Christ talks of his death to his apostles)*

. . .If ye loved me, ye would rejoice, because I said, I go unto the Father: for my Father is greater than I.

STEPHEN SAW GOD AND THE SON

Acts 7:55-56 *(Stephen's testimony before he was stoned by a mob)*

55.   But he, being full of the Holy Ghost, looked up stedfastly into heaven, and saw the glory of God, and Jesus standing on the right hand of God.

56.   And said, Behold, I see the heavens opened, and the Son of man standing on the right hand of God.

GOD IS NO RESPECTER OF PERSONS

Acts 10:34-35 *(Peter to Cornelius)*

34.   . . .Of a truth I perceive that God is no respecter of persons:

35.   But in every nation he that feareth him, and worketh righteousness, is accepted with him.

2 Nephi 26:33 *(Nephi predictions of the last days — 545 BC)*

For none of these iniquities come of the Lord; for he doeth that which is good among the children of men; and he doeth nothing save it be plain unto the children of men; and he inviteth them all to come unto him and partake of his goodness; and he denieth none that come unto him, black and white, bond and free, male and female; and he remembereth the heathen; and all are alike unto God, both Jew and Gentile.

D & C 1:35 *(Revelation known as the preface to the Doctrine & Covenants given to Joseph Smith — November, 1831)*

For I am no respecter of persons, and will that all men shall know that the day speedily cometh; the hour is not yet, but is nigh at hand, when peace shall be taken from the earth, and the devil shall have power over his own dominion.

THE UNKNOWN GOD

Acts 17:23,27-29 *(Paul talks to the men of Athens on Mars Hill)*

23.   For as I passed by, and beheld your devotions, I found an altar with this inscription, TO THE UNKNOWN GOD. Whom therefore ye ignorantly worship, him declare I unto you.

27.   That they should seek the Lord, if haply they might feel after him, and find him, though he be not far from every one of us:

28.   For in him we live, and move, and have our being; as certain also of your own poets have said, For we are also his offspring.

29.   Forasmuch then as we are the offspring of God, we ought not to think that the Godhead is like unto gold, or silver, or stone, graven by art and man's device.

IMPORTANCE OF HAVING GOD'S HELP

Romans 8:31 *(Paul to the Romans)*

What shall we then say to these things? If God be for us, who can be against us?

GOD IS NOT THE AUTHOR OF CONFUSION

1 Corinthians 14:33 *(Paul to the Corinthians)*

For God is not the author of confusion, but of peace. . .

ONE DAY OF THE LORD'S TIME IS A THOUSAND YEARS TO MAN

2 Peter 3:8 *(Epistle of Peter)*

> But, beloved, be not ignorant of this one thing, that one day is with the Lord as a thousand years, and a thousand years as one day.

ALL GOOD COMES FROM GOD

Alma 5:40 *(Alma to the people of Nephi — 83 BC)*

> . . .whatsoever is good cometh from God, and whatsoever is evil cometh from the devil.

MEN SEEK THEIR OWN GOD

D & C 1:16 *(Revelation known as the preface to the Doctrine & Covenants given to Joseph Smith — November, 1831)*

> They seek not the Lord to establish his righteousness, but every man walketh in his own way, and after the image of his own God, whose image is in the likeness of the world, and whose substance is that of an idol, which waxeth old and shall perish in Babylon, even Babylon the great, which shall fall.

GOD KNOWS OUR THOUGHTS

D & C 6:16 *(Revelation to Joseph Smith and Oliver Cowdery — April, 1829)*

> Yea, I tell thee, that thou mayest know that there is none else save God that knowest thy thoughts and the intents of thy heart.

UNTO GOD ALL THINGS ARE SPIRITUAL

D & C 29:34 *(Revelation to Joseph Smith — September, 1830)*

...that all things unto me are spiritual, and not at any time have I given unto you a law which was temporal; neither any man, nor the children of men;...

DESCRIPTION OF THE GODHEAD

D & C 130:22 *(Instruction given by Joseph Smith — April, 1843)*

The Father has a body of flesh and bones as tangible as man's; the Son also; but the Holy Ghost has not a body of flesh and bones, but is a personage of Spirit. Were it not so, the Holy Ghost could not dwell in us.

GOD'S WORK

Moses 1:39 *(The Lord to Moses)*

For behold, this is my work and my glory — to bring to pass the immortality and eternal life of man.

JOSEPH SMITH'S VISION

Joseph Smith 2:17 *(Joseph Smith telling his own story)*

. . .When the light rested upon me I saw two Personages, whose brightness and glory defy all description, standing above me in the air. One of them spake unto me, calling me by name and said, pointing to the other — ***This is My Beloved Son. Hear Him!***

WE BELIEVE IN A DISTINCT TRINITY

First Article of Faith

We believe in God, the Eternal Father, and in His Son, Jesus Christ, and in the Holy Ghost.

GOSSIP

GOSSIP ABOUT CHURCH LEADERS IS GOSSIP AGAINST GOD

Exodus 16:8 *(Moses to the people of Israel)*

. . .what are we? your murmurings are not against us, but against the Lord.

NINTH COMMANDMENT

Exodus 20:16 *(also Mosiah 13:23 and Deuteronomy 5:20)*
(given to Moses by the Lord on Mt. Sinai)

Thou shalt not bear false witness against thy neighbor.

THE RIGHTEOUS FEED MANY

Proverbs 10:21 *(Proverb of Solomon, King of Israel)*

The lips of the righteous feed many: but fools die for want of wisdom.

LYING IS AN ABOMINATION UNTO THE LORD

Proverbs 12:22 *(Proverb of Solomon, King of Israel)*

Lying lips are abomination to the Lord: but they that deal truly are his delight.

A TIME TO SPEAK

Ecclesiastes 3:1,7 *(Teachings of Ecclesiastes, son of King David)*

1. To every thing there is a season, and a time to every purpose under the heaven:

7. . . .a time to keep silence, and a time to speak.

FOOLS TALK TOO MUCH

Ecclesiastes 5:2-3 *(Teachings of Ecclesiastes, son of King David)*

2. Be not rash with thy mouth, and let not thine heart be hasty to utter any thing before God: for God is in heaven, and thou upon the earth: therefore let thy words be few. . .

3. . . .a fool's voice is known by multitude of words.

REFUSE TO LISTEN TO DIRTY STORIES AND GOSSIP

1 Timothy 4:7 *(Paul to Timothy)*

But refuse profane and old wives' fables, and exercise thyself rather unto godliness.

2 Timothy 2:16 *(Paul to Timothy)*

But shun profane and vain babblings: for they will increase unto more ungodliness.

SPEAK NOT EVIL

James 4:11 *(Epistle of James the brother of Jesus)*

Speak not evil one of another. . .

IN THE ELECT THERE WAS FOUND NO GUILE

Revelation 14:5 *(John's prophecy about the elect of God)*

And in their mouth was found no guile: for they are without fault before the throne of God.

TRIFLE NOT WITH SACRED THINGS

D & C 6:12 *(Revelation to Joseph Smith and Oliver Cowdery — April, 1829)*

. . .Trifle not with sacred things.

STRENGTHEN YOUR BRETHREN IN CONVERSATION

D & C 108:7 *(Revelation to Joseph Smith — December 26, 1835)*

Therefore, strengthen your brethren in all your conversation, in all your prayers, in all your exhortations, and in all your doings.

ḤAPPINESS

(See Peace)

GOD'S CORRECTION BRINGS HAPPINESS

Job 5:17 *(Job's comments to his friends)*

Behold, happy is the man whom God correcteth: therefore despise not thou the chastening of the Almighty:

WISDOM BRINGS HAPPINESS

Proverbs 3:13-14 *(Proverb of Solomon, King of Israel)*

13. Happy is the man that findeth wisdom, and the man that getteth understanding.

14. For the merchandise of it is better than the merchandise of silver, and the gain thereof than fine gold.

HAPPINESS COMES BY OBEYING THE LAW

Proverbs 29:18 *(Proverb of Solomon)*

Where there is no vision, the people perish: but he that keepeth the law, happy is he.

BE OF GOOD CHEER

John 16:33 *(Jesus to his disciples)*

. . .In the world ye shall have tribulation: but be of good cheer; I have overcome the world.

MEN ARE THAT THEY MIGHT HAVE JOY

2 Nephi 2:25 *(Lehi to his son Jacob — 570 BC)*

Adam fell that men might be; and men are, that they might have joy.

KEEPING THE COMMANDMENTS BRINGS HAPPINESS

Mosiah 2:41 *(King Benjamin's address — 124 BC)*

And moreover, I would desire that ye should consider on the blessed and happy state of those that keep the commandments of God. For behold, they are blessed in all things, both temporal and spiritual; and if they hold out faithful to the end they are received into heaven, that thereby they may dwell with God in a state of never-ending happiness. O remember, remember that these things are true; for the Lord God hath spoken it.

RIGHTEOUSNESS BRINGS HAPPINESS

4 Nephi Vs. 15-16 *(Nephi explains how the people lived — 35-201 AD)*

15.   And it came to pass that there was no contention in the land, because of the love of God which did dwell in the hearts of the people.

16.   And there were no envyings, nor strifes, nor tumults, nor whoredomes, nor lyings, nor murders, nor any manner of lasciviousness; and surely there could not be a happier people among all the people who had been created by the hand of God.

SPIRIT AND BODY MUST BE UNITED TO RECEIVE JOY

D & C 93:33-34 *(Revelation to Joseph Smith — May, 1833)*

33. For man is spirit. The elements are eternal, and spirit and element, inseparably connected, receive a fulness of joy.

34. And when separated, man cannot receive a fulness of joy.

ᴅOLY GHOST

CHRIST HAD THE POWER TO BESTOW THE HOLY GHOST

Matthew 3:11 *(John the Baptist comments about the Savior)*

I indeed baptize you with water unto repentance: but he that cometh after me is mightier than I, whose shoes I am not worthy to bear: he shall baptize you with the Holy Ghost, and with fire:

BLASPHEMY AGAINST THE HOLY GHOST SHALL NOT BE FORGIVEN

Matthew 12:31-32 *(Jesus Christ to the Pharisees)*

31. . . . All manner of sin and blasphemy shall be forgiven unto men: but the blasphemy against the Holy Ghost shall not be forgiven unto men.

32. And whosoever speaketh a word against the Son of man, it shall be forgiven him: but whosoever speaketh against the Holy Ghost, it shall not be forgiven him, neither in this world, neither in the world to come.

THE COMFORTER AND THE SPIRIT OF TRUTH WILL BEAR TESTIMONY OF JESUS CHRIST AND GUIDE MAN INTO ALL TRUTH

John 14:16-17, 26 *(Jesus Christ to his disciples)*

16. And I will pray the Father, and he shall give you another Comforter, that he may abide with you for ever;

17.   Even the Spirit of truth; whom the world cannot receive, because it seeth him not, neither knoweth him: but ye know him; for he dwelleth with you, and shall be in you.

26.   But the Comforter, which is the Holy Ghost, whom the Father will send in my name, he shall teach you all things, and bring all things to your remembrance, whatsoever I have said unto you.

John 15:26 *(Jesus Christ promises the Holy Ghost to his disciples)*

But when the Comforter is come, whom I will send unto you from the Father, even the Spirit of truth, which proceedeth from the Father, he shall testify of me:

John 16:13 *(Jesus Christ to his disciples)*

Howbeit when he, the Spirit of truth, is come, he will guide you into all truth: for he shall not speak of himself; but whatsoever he shall hear, that shall he speak: and he will shew you things to come.

HOLY GHOST IS THE POWER OF GOD TO THOSE WHO DILIGENTLY SEEK HIM

1 Nephi 10:17 *(Nephi's predictions of the captivity of Israel — 592 BC)*

. . .the Holy Ghost which power he (Nephi) received by faith on the Son of God . . . is the gift of God unto all those who diligently seek him. . .

THE HOLY GHOST IS A GUIDE

2 Nephi 32:5 *(Nephi's teachings — approximately 550 BC)*

For behold, again I say unto you that if ye will enter in by the way, and receive the Holy Ghost, it will show unto you all things what ye should do.

THE HOLY GHOST CARRIES THE MESSAGE TO THE HEART

2 Nephi 33:1 *(Nephi's last testimony — 559 BC)*

. . .for when a man speaketh by the power of the Holy Ghost the power of the Holy Ghost carrieth it unto the hearts of the children of men.

D & C 8:2 *(Revelation for Oliver Cowdery — April, 1829)*

Yea, behold, I will tell you in your mind and in your heart, by the Holy Ghost, which shall come upon you and which shall dwell in your heart.

THE HOLY GHOST IS A REVELATOR

Moroni 10:5 *(Moroni's last testimony before he hid the gold plates in the Hill Cumorah — 421 AD)*

And by the power of the Holy Ghost ye may know the truth of all things.

THE COMFORTER TEACHES

D & C 75:10 *(Revelation to Joseph Smith for Luke Johnson — January, 1832)*

Calling on the name of the Lord for the Comforter, which shall teach them all things that are expedient for them —

THE HOLY GHOST SHOULD BE YOUR CONSTANT COMPANION

D & C 121:46 *(Prayer of Joseph Smith in Liberty jail — March 20, 1839)*

The Holy Ghost shall be thy constant companion, and thy scepter an unchanging scepter of righteousness and truth; and thy dominion shall be an everlasting dominion, and without compulsory means it shall flow unto thee forever and ever.

GIFT OF HOLY GHOST GIVEN BY LAYING ON OF HANDS

Fourth Article of Faith

We believe that the first principles and ordinances of the Gospel are: first, Faith in the Lord Jesus Christ; second, Repentance; third, Baptism by immersion for the remission of sins; fourth, Laying on of hands for the gift of the Holy Ghost.

Ʌonesty

THEFT

Exodus 20:15 *(also Mosiah 13:22 and Deuteronomy 5:19) (Eighth Commandment)*

Thou shalt not steal.

FALSE WITNESS

Exodus 20:16 *(also Mosiah 13:23 and Deuteronomy 5:20) (Ninth Commandment)*

Thou shalt not bear false witness against thy neighbor.

BETTER TO NOT MAKE A PROMISE THAN BREAK A PROMISE

Ecclesiastes 5:4-5 *(Teachings of Ecclesiastes, son of King David)*

4.   When thou vowest a vow unto God, defer not to pay it; for he hath no pleasure in fools: pay that which thou hast vowed.

5.   Better is it that thou shouldest not vow, than that thou shouldest vow and not pay.

TITHING

Malachi 3:8-10 *(also 3 Nephi 24:8-10) (Malachi's prophecy of the last days)*

8.   Will a man rob God? Yet ye have robbed me. But ye say, Wherein have we robbed thee? In tithes and offerings.

9.   Ye are cursed with a curse: for ye have robbed me, even this whole nation.

10.   Bring ye all the tithes into the storehouse, that there may be meat in mine house, and prove me now herewith, saith the Lord of hosts, if I will not open you the windows of heaven, and pour you out a blessing, that there shall not be room enough to receive it.

PAUL DESIRED A CLEAR CONSCIENCE

Acts 24:16 *(Paul to the Roman Governor)*

And herein do I exercise myself, to have always a conscience void of offence toward God, and toward men.

SEEK AFTER HONESTY

Philippians 4:8 *(also Thirteenth Article of Faith) (Paul to the Philippians)*

Finally, brethren, whatsoever things are true, whatsoever things are honest, whatsoever things are just, whatsoever things are pure, whatsoever things are lovely, whatsoever things are of good report; if there be any virtue, and if there be any praise, think on these things.

DO NOT JUSTIFY LIES BECAUSE OTHERS LIE

D & C 10:28 *(Revelation to Joseph Smith — Summer, 1828)*

. . .wo be unto him that lieth to deceive because he supposeth that another lieth to deceive, for such are not exempt from the justice of God.

THE LORD CANNOT LIE

D & C 62:6 *(Revelation to Joseph Smith — August, 1831)*

. . .I, the Lord, promise the faithful and cannot lie.

WE BELIEVE IN BEING HONEST

Thirteenth Article of Faith

We believe in being honest, true, chaste, benevolent, virtuous, and in doing good to all men; indeed, we may say that we follow the admonition of Paul — We believe all things, we hope all things, we have endured many things, and hope to be able to endure all things. If there is anything virtuous, lovely, or of good report or praiseworthy, we seek after these things.

ⱧUMILITY

THE HUMBLE SHALL BE EXALTED

Matthew 23:12 *(Jesus Christ to the multitude)*

And whosoever shall exalt himself shall be abased; and he that shall humble himself shall be exalted.

DO NOT BE OFFENDED IN JESUS CHRIST

Luke 7:23 *(Jesus Christ to his disciples)*

And blessed is he, whosoever shall not be offended in me.

MEN MUST HUMBLE THEMSELVES AS LITTLE CHILDREN

Mosiah 3:18-19 *(King Benjamin's farewell address to the Nephites — 124 BC)*

18. . . .men drink damnation to their own souls except they humble themselves and become as little children, and believe that salvation was, and is, and is to come, in and through the atoning blood of Christ, the Lord Omnipotent.

19. For the natural man is an enemy to God, and has been from the fall of Adam, and will be, forever and ever, unless he yields to the enticings of the Holy Spirit, and putteth off the natural man and becometh a saint through the atonement of Christ the Lord, and becometh as a child, submissive, meek, humble, patient, full of love, willing to submit to all things

which the Lord seeth fit to inflict upon him, even as a child doth submit to his father.

HUMILITY IS THE KEY TO LEARNING THE MYSTERIES OF GOD

Alma 12:9-11 *(Alma's teachings — 82 BC)*

9. . . .It is given unto many to know the mysteries of God; nevertheless they are laid under a strict command that they shall not impart only according to the portion of his word which he doth grant unto the children of men, according to the heed and diligence which they give unto him.

10. And therefore, he that will harden his heart, the same receiveth the lesser portion of the word; and he that will not harden his heart, to him is given the greater portion of the word, until it is given unto him to know the mysteries of God until he know them in full.

11. And they that will harden their hearts, to them is given the lesser portion of the word until they know nothing concerning his mysteries; and then they are taken captive by the devil, and led by his will down to destruction. Now this is what is meant by the chains of hell.

BLESSED ARE THOSE WHO HUMBLE THEMSELVES

Alma 32:16 *(Alma's discourse on faith — 74 BC)*

Therefore, blessed are they who humble themselves without being compelled to be humble; or rather in other words, blessed is he that believeth in the word of God, and is baptized without stubbornness of heart, yea, without being brought to know the word, or even compelled to know before they will believe.

THE HUMBLE SHALL BE MADE STRONG

D & C 1:28 *(Revelation to Joseph Smith — November, 1831)*

And inasmuch as they were humble they might be made strong, and blessed from on high, and receive knowledge from time to time.

ONLY THOSE WHO ARE HUMBLE AND FULL OF LOVE ARE CALLED TO SERVE

D & C 12:8 *(Revelation for Joseph Knight, Sen. — May, 1829)*

And no one can assist in this work except he shall be humble and full of love, having faith, hope, and charity, being temperate in all things, whatsoever shall be entrusted to his care.

BE HUMBLE AND THE LORD WILL LEAD YOU

D & C 112:10 *(Revelation for Thomas B. Marsh, President of the Quorum of Twelve — July, 1837)*

Be thou humble; and the Lord thy God shall lead thee by the hand, and give thee answer to thy prayers.

ꞲESUS CHRIST'S PRE-MORTAL ROLE

(See Creation, Pre-Mortal Life)

THE EARTH IS THE LORD'S

Psalms 24:1 *(A psalm of David, King of Israel)*

The earth is the Lord's, and the fulness thereof; the world, and they that dwell therein.

CHRIST TO BE BORN IN BETHLEHEM

Micah 5:2 *(Micah's vision of Christ's kingdom)*

But thou, Bethlehem Ephratah, though thou be little among the thousands of Judah, yet out of thee shall he come forth unto me that is to be ruler in Israel; whose goings forth have been from of old, from everlasting.

CHRIST CREATED THE WORLD

John 1:1-5 *(John's account of the creation)*

1. In the beginning was the Word, and the Word was with God, and the Word was God.

2. The same was in the beginning with God.

3. All things were made by him; and without him was not any thing made that was made.

4. In him was life; and the life was the light of men.

5. And the light shineth in darkness; and the darkness comprehended it not.

Ephesians 3:9 *(Paul to the people of Ephesus)*

And to make all men see what is the fellowship of the mystery, which from the beginning of the world hath been hid in God, who created all things by Jesus Christ.

Moses 1:33 *(The Lord speaking to Moses)*

And worlds without number have I created; and I also created them for mine own purpose; and by the Son I created them, which is mine Only Begotten.

CHRIST'S SPIRIT LOOKS LIKE HIS BODY

Ether 3:15-16 *(Jesus Christ appeared in His spirit body to the brother of Jared — 2200 BC)*

15. And never have I showed myself unto man whom I have created, for never has man believed in me as thou hast. Seest thou that ye are created after mine own image? Yea, even all men were created in the beginning after mine own image.

16. Behold, this body, which ye now behold, is the body of my spirit; and man have I created after the body of my spirit; and even as I appear unto thee to be in the spirit will I appear unto my people in the flesh.

ℐESUS CHRIST'S MORTAL MINISTRY

PROPHECIES OF CHRIST'S BIRTH

Isaiah 7:14 *(Isaiah prophesies Christ's birth)*

Therefore the Lord himself shall give you a sign; Behold, a virgin shall conceive, and bear a son, and shall call his name Immanuel.

Isaiah 9:6 *(Isaiah prophesies Christ's birth)*

For unto us a child is born, unto us a son is given: and the government shall be upon his shoulder: and his name shall be called Wonderful, Counsellor, The mighty God, The everlasting Father, The Prince of Peace.

1 Nephi 11:20-21 *(Nephi's vision of Christ's birth — 600 BC)*

20. And I looked and beheld the virgin again, bearing a child in her arms.

21. And the angel said unto me: Behold the Lamb of God, yea, even the Son of the Eternal Father!. . .

Mosiah 3:5-8 *(King Benjamin's address to the Nephites — 124 BC)*

5. For behold, the time cometh, and is not far distant, that with power, the Lord Omnipotent who reigneth, who was, and is from all eternity to all eternity, shall come down from heaven among the children of men, and shall dwell in a tabernacle of clay, and shall go forth amongst men, working mighty miracles, such as healing the sick, raising the

dead, causing the lame to walk, the blind to receive their sight, and the deaf to hear, and curing all manner of diseases.

6. And he shall cast out devils, or the evil spirits which dwell in the hearts of the children of men.

7. And lo, he shall suffer temptations, and pain of body, hunger, thirst, and fatigue, even more than man can suffer, except it be unto death; for behold blood cometh from every pore, so great shall be his anguish for the wickedness and the abominations of his people.

8. And he shall be called Jesus Christ, the Son of God, the Father of heaven and earth, the Creator of all things from the beginning; and his mother shall be called Mary.

3 Nephi 1:13 *(Jesus Christ to Nephi — 1 AD)*

Lift up your head and be of good cheer; for behold, the time is at hand, and on this night shall the sign be given, and on the morrow come I into the world. . .

JESUS WAS LAUGHED TO SCORN BY HIS PEERS

Matthew 9:24 *(The response of the crowds when Jesus said he could raise Jairus' daughter from the dead)*

He said unto them, Give place: for the maid is not dead, but sleepeth. And they laughed him to scorn.

COME UNTO JESUS

Matthew 11:28-30 *(Christ to his disciples)*

28. Come unto me, all ye that labour and are heavy laden, and I will give you rest.

29.   Take my yoke upon you, and learn of me; for I am meek and lowly in heart: and ye shall find rest unto your souls.

30.   For my yoke is easy, and my burden is light.

JESUS' FAMILY

Matthew 13:55-56 *(Jesus Christ's wisdom is questioned in his hometown of Nazareth)*

55.   Is not this the carpenter's son? is not his mother called Mary? And his brethren, James, and Joses, and Simon, and Judas?

56.   And his sisters, are they not all with us?

PETER'S TESTIMONY OF JESUS CHRIST

Matthew 16:13,16,17 *(Jesus talks to his disciples)*

13.   . . .he asked his disciples, saying, Whom do men say that I the Son of man am?

16.   And Simon Peter answered and said, Thou art the Christ, the Son of the living God.

17.   And Jesus answered and said unto him, Blessed art thou, Simon Bar-jona: for flesh and blood hath not revealed it unto thee, but my Father which is in heaven.

THE BIRTH OF JESUS CHRIST

Luke 2:4-14 *(Luke recounts the story of Christ's birth)*

4.   And Joseph also went up from Galilee, out of the city of Nazareth, into Judea, unto the city of David, which is called Bethlehem; (because he was of the house and lineage of David:)

5.   To be taxed with Mary his espoused wife, being great with child.

6.   And so it was, that, while they were there, the days were accomplished that she should be delivered.

7.   And she brought forth her firstborn son, and wrapped him in swaddling clothes, and laid him in a manger; because there was no room for them in the inn.

8.   And there were in the same country shepherds abiding in the field, keeping watch over their flock by night.

9.   And, lo, the angel of the Lord came upon them, and the glory of the Lord shone round about them: and they were sore afraid.

10.   And the angel said unto them, Fear not: for, behold, I bring you good tidings of great joy, which shall be to all people.

11.   For unto you is born this day in the city of David a Saviour, which is Christ the Lord.

12.   And this shall be a sign unto you; Ye shall find the babe wrapped in swaddling clothes, lying in a manger.

13.   And suddenly there was with the angel a multitude of the heavenly host praising God, and saying,

14.   Glory to God in the highest, and on earth peace, good will toward men.

CHRIST IS THE LIGHT OF THE WORLD

John 8:12 *(Jesus to the Pharisees)*

Then spake Jesus again unto them, saying, I am the light of the world: he that followeth me shall not walk in darkness, but shall have the light of life.

CHRIST GAVE UP HIS LIFE

John 10:17-18 *(Christ to the Jews)*

17. Therefore doth my Father love me, because I lay down my life, that I might take it again.

18. No man taketh it from me, but I lay it down of myself. I have power to lay it down, and I have power to take it again. This commandment have I received of my Father.

CHRIST THE TRUTH, THE WAY, AND THE LIFE

John 14:6 *(Jesus to Thomas)*

Jesus saith unto him, I am the way, the truth, and the life: no man cometh unto the Father, but by me.

I AM NOT ASHAMED OF THE GOSPEL OF JESUS CHRIST

Romans 1:16 *(Paul to the Romans)*

For I am not ashamed of the gospel of Christ: for it is the power of God unto salvation to every one that believeth. . .

JESUS CHRIST IS THE CORNERSTONE OF THE CHURCH

Ephesians 2:19-20 *(Paul to the Ephesians)*

19. Now therefore ye are no more strangers and foreigners, but fellow citizens with the saints, and of the household of God;

20. And are built upon the foundation of the apostles and prophets, Jesus Christ himself being the chief corner stone;

CHRIST CAME TO SAVE SINNERS

1 Timothy 1:15 *(Paul to Timothy)*

. . .Christ Jesus came into the world to save sinners; of whom I am chief.

ONLY ONE MEDIATOR BETWEEN GOD AND MAN

1 Timothy 2:5-6 *(Paul to Timothy)*

5. For there is one God, and one mediator between God and men, the man Christ Jesus;

6. Who gave himself a ransom for all, to be testified in due time.

DO NOT COUNSEL THE LORD

Jacob 4:10 *(Jacob to the Nephites — 421 BC)*

Wherefore, brethren, seek not to counsel the Lord, but to take counsel from his hand. For behold, ye yourselves know that he counseleth in wisdom, and in justice, and in great mercy, over all his works.

MAN SHOULD BE LIKE JESUS CHRIST

3 Nephi 27:21,27 *(Jesus Christ teaches the Nephites — 34 AD)*

21. ...this is my gospel; and ye know the things that ye must do in my church; for the works ye have seen me do that shall ye also do...

27. ...what manner of men ought ye to be? Verily I say unto you, even as I am.

CHRIST CAME TO BEAR THE SINS OF THE WORLD

D & C 76:41 *(Vision given to Joseph Smith and Sidney Rigdon — February, 1832)*

That he came into the world, even Jesus, to be crucified for the world, and to bear the sins of the world, and to sanctify the world, and to cleanse it from all unrighteousness;

JESUS CHRIST'S RESURRECTION AND SPIRITUAL MINISTRY

(See Resurrection)

WHEN GATHERED IN CHRIST'S NAME, HE WILL ALSO BE THERE

Matthew 18:20 *(Jesus Christ to his disciples)*

For where two or three are gathered together in my name, there am I in the midst of them.

THE RESURRECTED CHRIST

Luke 24:36,38-39 *(Christ to his disciples after the resurrection)*

36.   And as they thus spake, Jesus himself stood in the midst of them, and saith unto them, Peace be unto you.

38.   And he said unto them, Why are ye troubled? and why do thoughts arise in your hearts?

39.   Behold my hands and my feet, that it is I myself: handle me, and see; for a spirit hath not flesh and bones, as ye see me have.

LIFE ETERNAL IS TO KNOW CHRIST

John 17:3 *(Jesus Christ's prayer to God the Father)*

And this is life eternal, that they might know thee the only true God, and Jesus Christ, whom thou hast sent.

CHRIST RETURNED TO HIS FATHER

John 20:17 *(Christ to Mary Magdalene)*

Jesus saith unto her, Touch me not; for I am not yet ascended to my Father: but go to my brethren, and say unto them, I ascend unto my Father, and your Father; and to my God, and your God.

JESUS CHRIST IS THE ONLY NAME WHEREBY MAN CAN BE SAVED

Acts 4:12 *(Peter and John testify of Christ to Jewish leaders in the temple)*

Neither is there salvation in any other: for there is none other name under heaven given among men, whereby we must be saved;

D & C 18:23 *(Revelation to Joseph Smith, Oliver Cowdery, and David Whitmer — June 1829)*

Behold, Jesus Christ is the name which is given of the Father, and there is none other name given whereby man can be saved.

JESUS CHRIST TAUGHT THE SPIRITS IN PRISON

1 Peter 3:18-19 *(also D & C 138) (Epistle of Peter)*

18. For Christ also hath once suffered for sins, the just for the unjust, that he might bring us to God, being put to death in the flesh, but quickened by the Spirit:

19. By which also he went and preached unto the spirits in prison;

1 Peter 4:6 *(also D & C 76:73 and D & C 138) (Epistle of Peter)*

For for this cause was the gospel preached also to them that are dead, that they might be judged according to men in the flesh, but live according to God in the spirit.

JESUS CHRIST IS THE KEEPER OF THE GATES

2 Nephi 9:41 *(Jacob's teachings to the Nephites — 559 BC)*

. . .the keeper of the gate is the Holy One of Israel; and he employeth no servant there; and there is none other way save it be by the gate; for he cannot be deceived, for the Lord God is his name.

WE ARE SAVED BY GRACE AFTER ALL WE CAN DO

2 Nephi 25:23 *(Nephi's predictions of the last days — 545 BC)*

. . .for we know that it is by grace that we are saved, after all we can do.

APPEARANCE OF THE RESURRECTED JESUS CHRIST TO THE NEPHITES

3 Nephi 11:1,3,7-8,10-11 *(Nephi's account of Jesus Christ — 34 AD)*

1.　And now it came to pass that there were a great multitude gathered together, of the people of Nephi, round about the temple which was in the land Bountiful. . .

3.　And it came to pass that while they were thus conversing one with another, they heard a voice as if it came out of heaven; and they cast their eyes round about, for they understood not the voice which they heard; and it was not a harsh voice, neither was it a loud voice; nevertheless, and notwithstanding it being a small voice it did pierce them that did hear to the center, insomuch that there was no part of their frame that it did not cause to quake; yea, it did pierce them to the very soul, and did cause their hearts to burn.

7.   Behold my Beloved Son, in whom I am well pleased, in whom I have glorified my name — hear ye him.

8.   . . .they cast their eyes up again towards heaven; and behold, they saw a Man descending out of heaven; and he was clothed in a white robe; and he came down and stood in the midst of them. . .

10.   Behold, I am Jesus Christ, whom the prophets testified shall come into the world.

11.   And behold, I am the light and the life of the world; and I have drunk out of the bitter cup which the Father hath given me, and have glorified the Father in taking upon me the sins of the world, in the which I have suffered the will of the Father in all things from the beginning.

THE SPIRIT OF CHRIST IS GIVEN TO EVERY MAN

Moroni 7:16 *(Mormon's epistle to Moroni — 400 AD)*

For behold, the Spirit of Christ is given to every man, that he may know good from evil. . .

D & C 84:45-46 *(Revelation on priesthood — September, 1832)*

45.   For the word of the Lord is truth, and whatsoever is truth is light, and whatsoever is light is Spirit, even the Spirit of Jesus Christ.

46. And the Spirit giveth light to every man that cometh into the world; and the Spirit enlighteneth every man through the world, that hearkeneth to the voice of the Spirit.

JOSEPH SMITH'S AND SIDNEY RIGDON'S TESTIMONY

D & C 76:22-24 *(The Lord appeared in a vision to Joseph Smith and Sidney Rigdon — February, 1832)*

22. And now, after the many testimonies which have been given of him, this is the testimony, last of all, which we give of him: That he lives!

23. For we saw him, even on the right hand of God; and we heard the voice bearing record that he is the Only Begotten of the Father —

24. That by him, and through him, and of him, the worlds are and were created, and the inhabitants thereof are begotten sons and daughters unto God.

OUR ADVOCATE WITH THE FATHER

D & C 110:4 *(Jesus Christ appeared in vision to Joseph Smith and Oliver Cowdery in the Kirtland Temple — April, 1836)*

I am the first and the last; I am he who liveth, I am he who was slain; I am your advocate with the Father.

JESUS CHRIST'S SECOND COMING

(See Last Days)

THE KINGDOM OF GOD

Daniel 7:13-14,27 *(Daniel's vision of Christ's kingdom)*

13. I saw in the night visions, and, behold, one like the Son of man came with the clouds of heaven, and came to the Ancient of days, and they brought him near before him.

14. And there was given him dominion, and glory, and a kingdom, that all people, nations, and languages, should serve him: his dominion is an everlasting dominion, which shall not pass away, and his kingdom that which shall not be destroyed.

27. And the kingdom and dominion, and the greatness of the kingdom under the whole heaven, shall be given to the people of the saints of the most High, whose kingdom is an everlasting kingdom, and all dominions shall serve and obey him.

JEWS WILL ACCEPT CHRIST'S SECOND COMING

Zechariah 12:10 *(Zechariah explains Christ's second coming)*

And I will pour upon the house of David, and upon the inhabitants of Jerusalem, the spirit of grace and of supplications: and they shall look upon me whom they have pierced, and they shall mourn for him, as one mourneth for his only son, and shall be in bitterness for him, as one that is in bitterness for his firstborn.

Zechariah 13:6 *(Zechariah explains Christ's second coming)*

And one shall say unto him, What are these wounds in thine hands? Then he shall answer, Those with which I was wounded in the house of my friends.

THE SECOND COMING OF CHRIST SHALL BE A REFINER'S FIRE

Malachi 3:1-2 *(Malachi prophesies of the second coming)*

1. . . .the Lord, whom ye seek, shall suddenly come to his temple. . .

2. But who may abide the day of his coming? and who shall stand when he appeareth? for he is like a refiner's fire, and like fullers' soap:

THE SECOND COMING SHALL BE AS LIGHTNING FROM THE EAST

Matthew 24:27 *(Jesus Christ to his disciples)*

For as the lightning cometh out of the east, and shineth even unto the west; so shall also the coming of the Son of man be.

NO ONE KNOWETH WHEN CHRIST COMES, NOT EVEN THE ANGELS

Matthew 24:36 *(Jesus Christ to his disciples)*

But of that day and hour knoweth no man, no, not the angels of heaven, but my Father only.

D & C 49:7 *(Revelation to Joseph Smith — March, 1831)*

I, the Lord God, have spoken it; but the hour and the day no man knoweth, neither the angels in heaven, nor shall they know until he comes.

THE ANGEL TELLS THE APOSTLES OF CHRIST'S SECOND COMING

Acts 1:11 *(Angels talk to the apostles on the day of Christ's ascension into heaven)*

. . .Ye men of Galilee, why stand ye gazing up into heaven? this same Jesus, which is taken up from you into heaven, shall so come in like manner as ye have seen him go into heaven.

JESUS WILL COME IN GLORY

D & C 29:11 *(Revelation about the last days — September, 1830)*

For I will reveal myself from heaven with power and great glory, with all the hosts thereof, and dwell in righteousness with men on earth a thousand years, and the wicked shall not stand.

ᴊUDGMENT

(See Genealogy, Resurrection)

GOD SHALL BRING EVERY WORK INTO JUDGMENT

Ecclesiastes 12:13-14 *(Advice of Ecclesiastes, the preacher, son of David)*

13.   Let us hear the conclusion of the whole matter: Fear God, and keep his commandments: for this is the whole duty of man.

14.   For God shall bring every work into judgment, with every secret thing, whether it be good, or whether it be evil.

JUDGE NOT, THAT YE BE NOT JUDGED

Matthew 7:1-2 *(also 3 Nephi 14:1-2) (Jesus Christ in the Sermon on the Mount)*

1.   Judge not, that ye be not judged.

2.   For with what judgment ye judge, ye shall be judged: and with what measure ye mete, it shall be measured to you again.

Luke 6:37 *(Jesus to his disciples)*

Judge not, and ye shall not be judged: condemn not, and ye shall not be condemned: forgive, and ye shall be forgiven.

THE FIRST SHALL BE LAST

Matthew 19:30 *(Jesus to his disciples)*

But many that are first shall be last; and the last shall be first.

Matthew 20:16 *(Jesus to his disciples)*

So the last shall be first, and the first last: for many be called, but few chosen.

JUDGE NOT BY APPEARANCE

John 7:24 *(Jesus to the Jews of Galilee)*

Judge not according to the appearance, but judge righteous judgment.

IF THE RIGHTEOUS SCARCELY BE SAVED

1 Peter 4:18 *(Epistle of Peter)*

And if the righteous scarcely be saved, where shall the ungodly and the sinner appear?

THE DEAD ARE JUDGED FROM THE BOOKS

Revelation 20:12 *(Vision of John the Revelator)*

And I saw the dead, small and great, stand before God; and the books were opened: and another book was opened, which is the book of life: and the dead were judged out of those things which were written in the books, according to their works.

3 Nephi 27:25-26 *(The resurrected Jesus Christ to the Nephites — 34 AD)*

25. For behold, out of the books which have been written, and which shall be written, shall this people be judged, for by them shall their works be known unto men.

26. And behold, all things are written by the Father; therefore out of the books which shall be written shall the world be judged.

JESUS CHRIST IS THE KEEPER OF THE GATES

2 Nephi 9:41 *(Jacob's teachings to the Nephites — 500 BC)*

. . .the keeper of the gate is the Holy One of Israel; and he employeth no servant there; and there is none other way save it be by the gate; for he cannot be deceived, for the Lord God is his name.

MAN WILL JUDGE HIMSELF

Mosiah 2:38 *(King Benjamin's address — 124 BC)*

Therefore if that man repenteth not, and remaineth and dieth an enemy to God, the demands of divine justice do awaken his immortal soul to a lively sense of his own guilt, which doth cause him to shrink from the presence of the Lord, and doth fill his breast with guilt, and pain, and anguish, which is like an unquenchable fire, whose flame ascendeth up forever and ever.

A PERFECT REMEMBRANCE OF GUILT

Alma 5:16-19 *(Alma the Younger to the Nephites — 83 BC)*

16. I say unto you, can you imagine to yourselves that ye hear the voice of the Lord, saying unto you, in that day: Come unto me ye blessed, for behold, your works have been the works of righteousness upon the face of the earth?

17. Or do ye imagine to yourselves that ye can lie unto the Lord in that day, and say — Lord, our works have been righteous works upon the face of the earth — and that he will save you?

18.   Or otherwise, can ye imagine yourselves brought before the tribunal of God with your souls filled with guilt and remorse, having a remembrance of all your guilt, yea, a perfect remembrance of all your wickedness, yea, a remembrance that ye have set at defiance the commandments of God?

19.   I say unto you, can ye look up to God at that day with a pure heart and clean hands? I say unto you, can you look up, having the image of God engraven upon your countenances?

JUDGMENT WILL COME AFTER THE RESURRECTION

Alma 11:41-43 *(Amulek's debate with Zeezrom, the anti-Christ — 82 BC)*

41.   Therefore the wicked remain as though there had been no redemption made, except it be the loosing of the bands of death; for behold, the day cometh that all shall rise from the dead and stand before God, and be judged according to their works.

42.   Now, there is a death which is called a temporal death; and the death of Christ shall loose the bands of this temporal death, that all shall be raised from this temporal death.

43.   The spirit and the body shall be reunited again in its perfect form; both limb and joint shall be restored to its proper frame, even as we now are at this time; and we shall be brought to stand before God, knowing even as we know now, and have a bright recollection of all our guilt.

MERCY CANNOT ROB JUSTICE

Alma 42:25 *(Alma's great discourse on repentance to his son, Corianton — 73 BC)*

What, do ye suppose that mercy can rob justice? I say unto you, Nay; not one whit. If so, God would cease to be God.

NO UNCLEAN THING CAN ENTER INTO THE KINGDOM OF GOD

3 Nephi 27:19-20 *(The resurrected Jesus Christ teaches the Nephites — 34 AD)*

19. And no unclean thing can enter into his kingdom; therefore nothing entereth into his rest save it be those who have washed their garments in my blood, because of their faith, and the repentance of all their sins, and their faithfulness unto the end.

20. Now this is the commandment: Repent, all ye ends of the earth, and come unto me and be baptized in my name, that ye may be sanctified by the reception of the Holy Ghost, that ye may stand spotless before me at the last day.

EVERY STEWARD WILL HAVE TO ACCOUNT FOR HIS STEWARDSHIP

D & C 72:3-4 *(Revelation to Joseph Smith — December, 1831)*

3. And verily in this thing ye have done wisely, for it is required of the Lord, at the hand of every steward, to render an account of his stewardship, both in time and in eternity.

4. For he who is faithful and wise in time is accounted worthy to inherit the mansions prepared for him of my Father.

HE THAT CANNOT LIVE A CELESTIAL LAW CANNOT RECEIVE A CELESTIAL GLORY

D & C 88:22 *(Revelation to Joseph Smith — December, 1832)*

For he who is not able to abide the law of a celestial kingdom cannot abide a celestial glory.

Ⅼast Days

(See Millennium, Jesus Christ: Second Coming)

Note: There are many scriptures concerning the last days. However, the most popular are found in Doctrine and Covenants 45:16-59 and in Matthew 24:3-51.

GOSPEL SHALL BE TAKEN TO THE GENTILES

Matthew 24:14 *(also D & C 45:20) (Jesus to his disciples)*

And this gospel of the kingdom shall be preached in all the world for a witness unto all nations; and then shall the end come.

FALSE PROPHETS SHALL DECEIVE MANY

Matthew 24:24 *(Jesus to his disciples)*

For there shall arise false Christs, and false prophets, and shall shew great signs and wonders; insomuch that, if it were possible, they shall deceive the very elect.

CHARACTERISTICS OF MEN IN THE LAST DAYS

2 Timothy 3:1-7 *(Paul's epistle to Timothy)*

1. This know also, that in the last days perilous times shall come.

2. For men shall be lovers of their own selves, covetous, boasters, proud, blasphemers, disobedient to parents, unthankful, unholy,

3. Without natural affection, trucebreakers, false accusers, incontinent, fierce, despisers of those that are good,

4. Traitors, heady, highminded, lovers of pleasures more than lovers of God;

5. Having a form of godliness, but denying the power thereof: from such turn away.

6. For of this sort are they which creep into houses, and lead captive silly women laden with sins, led away with divers lusts.

7. Ever learning, and never able to come to the knowledge of the truth.

JEWS SHALL GATHER AT JERUSALEM

D & C 45:24-25 *(Revelation given to Joseph Smith — February, 1831)*

24. And this I have told you concerning Jerusalem; and when that day shall come, shall a remnant be scattered among all nations;

25. But they shall be gathered again; but they shall remain until the times of the Gentiles be fulfilled.

WARS AND RUMORS OF WARS

D & C 45:26 *(Revelation given to Joseph Smith — February, 1831)*

And in that day shall be heard of wars and rumors of wars, and the whole earth shall be in commotion, and men's hearts shall fail them, and they shall say that Christ delayeth his coming until the end of the earth.

A DESOLATING SICKNESS SHALL COVER THE LAND

D & C 45:31 *(also Matthew 24:21) (Revelation given to Joseph Smith — February, 1831)*

. . .for a desolating sickness shall cover the land.

EARTHQUAKES

D & C 45:33 *(also Matthew 24:7) (Revelation given to Joseph Smith — February, 1831)*

And there shall be earthquakes also in divers places, and many desolations; . . .

SUN DARKENED, MOON TURNED TO BLOOD

D & C 45:42 *(also Matthew 24:29) (Revelation given to Joseph Smith — February, 1831)*

And before the day of the Lord shall come, the sun shall be darkened, and the moon be turned into blood, and the stars fall from heaven.

SAINTS SHALL GATHER

D & C 45:46 *(also Matthew 24:16) (Revelation given to Joseph Smith — February, 1831)*

. . .and the saints shall come forth from the four quarters of the earth.

MOUNT OF OLIVES SHALL SPLIT

D & C 45:48 *(Revelation given to Joseph Smith — February, 1831)*

And then shall the Lord set his foot upon this mount, and it shall cleave in twain, and the earth shall tremble, and reel to and fro, and the heavens also shall shake.

JEWS SHALL ACCEPT CHRIST

D & C 45:51-53 *(Revelation given to Joseph Smith — February, 1831)*

51. And then shall the Jews look upon me and say: What are these wounds in thine hands and in thy feet?

52. Then shall they know that I am the Lord; for I will say unto them: These wounds are the wounds with which I was wounded in the house of my friends. I am he who was lifted up. I am Jesus that was crucified. I am the Son of God.

53. And then shall they weep because of their iniquities; then shall they lament because they persecuted their king.

SATAN SHALL BE BOUND

D & C 45:55 *(Revelation given to Joseph Smith — February, 1831)*

And Satan shall be bound, that he shall have no place in the hearts of the children of men.

CHRIST WILL BE THE KING

D & C 45:59 *(Revelation given to Joseph Smith — February 1831)*

For the Lord shall be in their midst, and his glory shall be upon them, and he will be their king and their lawgiver.

LAMANITES SHALL BLOSSOM AS A ROSE

D & C 49:24 *(Revelation to the missionaries to the Lamanites — March, 1831)*

But before the great day of the Lord shall come, Jacob shall flourish in the wilderness, and the Lamanites shall blossom as the rose.

ISTENING

A WISE MAN SHALL HEAR

Proverbs 1:5 *(Proverb of Solomon, King of Israel)*

A wise man will hear, and will increase learning; and a man of understanding shall attain unto wise counsels:

PEOPLE FEAR TO LISTEN AND BELIEVE

Matthew 13:15 *(Jesus speaks to the multitude from a ship)*

For this people's heart is waxed gross, and their ears are dull of hearing, and their eyes they have closed; lest at any time they should see with their eyes, and hear with their ears, and should understand with their heart, and should be converted, and I should heal them.

TAKE HEED; IF YE HAVE EARS TO HEAR, HEAR

Mark 4:23-24 *(Jesus Christ to the multitude from a ship)*

23.   If any man have ears to hear, let him hear.

24.   . . .Take heed what ye hear: with what measure ye mete, it shall be measured to you: and unto you that hear shall more be given.

CHRIST THANKS GOD FOR LISTENING TO HIS PRAYER

John 11:41 *(Jesus Christ to his father just before he raises from the dead)*

. . .And Jesus lifted up his eyes, and said, Father, I thank thee that thou hast heard me.

FAITH COMES THROUGH HEARING

Romans 10:17 *(Paul to the Romans)*

So then faith cometh by hearing, and hearing by the word of God.

BE DOERS OF THE WORD

James 1:22 *(Epistle to James, the brother of Christ)*

But be ye doers of the word, and not hearers only, deceiving your own selves.

CHRIST WILL JOIN THOSE WHO HEAR HIS VOICE

Revelations 3:20,22 *(John's vision of Christ)*

20.   Behold, I stand at the door, and knock: if any man hear my voice, and open the door, I will come in to him, and will sup with him, and he with me.

22.   He that hath an ear, let him hear what the Spirit saith unto the churches.

THOSE WHO WILL NOT LISTEN TO THE PROPHETS WILL BE CUT OFF

D & C 1:14 *(Revelation to Joseph Smith — November, 1831)*

. . .they who will not hear the voice of the Lord, neither the voice of his servants, neither give heed to the words of the prophets and apostles, shall be cut off from among the people;

LISTEN TO GOD'S WORDS AND HAVE PEACE

D & C 19:23 *(A commandment of God through Joseph Smith to Martin Harris — March, 1830)*

Learn of me, and listen to my words; walk in the meekness of my Spirit, and you shall have peace in me.

LISTEN AND FOLLOW THE SPIRIT

D & C 46:7 *(Revelation to Joseph Smith — March, 1831)*

. . .and that which the Spirit testifies unto you even so I would that ye should do in all holiness of heart, walking uprightly before me, considering the end of your salvation, doing all things with prayer and thanksgiving, that ye may not be seduced by evil spirits, or doctrines of devils, or the commandments of men; for some are of men, and others of devils.

Ḷove

(See Charity, Friendship)

LOVE THY NEIGHBOR

Leviticus 19:18 *(also Matthew 22:39, James 2:8, Mosiah 23:15, D & C 59:6) (Moses to the Israelites)*

Thou shalt not avenge, nor bear any grudge against the children of thy people, but thou shalt love thy neighbour as thyself. . .

Romans 13:9-10 *(Paul to the saints in Rome)*

9. . . .if there by any other commandment, it is briefly comprehended in this saying, namely, Thou shalt love thy neighbour as thyself.

10. Love worketh no ill to his neighbour: therefore love is the fulfilling of the law.

LOVE YOUR ENEMIES

Matthew 5:44,46 *(also Luke 6:27,35 and 3 Nephi 12:44) (Jesus Christ in the Sermon on the Mount)*

44. But I say unto you, Love your enemies, bless them that curse you, do good to them that hate you, and pray for them which despitefully use you, and persecute you;

46. For if ye love them which love you, what reward have ye? do not even the publicans the same?

LOVE IS A COMMANDMENT

Matthew 22:36-40 *(Christ's response to the Pharisee lawyer)*

36. Master, which is the great commandment in the law?

37. Jesus said unto him, Thou shalt love the Lord thy God with all thy heart, and with all thy soul, and with all thy mind.

38. This is the first and great commandment.

39. And the second is like unto it, Thou shalt love thy neighbor as thyself.

40. On these two commandments hang all the law and the prophets.

John 13:34-35 *(Jesus Christ to his disciples)*

34. A new commandment I give unto you, That ye love one another; as I have loved you, that ye also love one another.

35. By this shall all men know that ye are my disciples, if ye have love one for another.

Romans 13:8 *(Paul to the saints in Rome)*

Owe no man any thing, but to love one another; for he that loveth another hath fulfilled the law.

INIQUITY CAUSES LOVE TO WAX COLD

Matthew 24:12-13 *(Jesus Christ to his disciples)*

12. And because iniquity shall abound, the love of many shall wax cold.

13. But he that shall endure unto the end, the same shall be saved.

GOD'S LOVE FOR MAN

John 3:16 *(Jesus Christ to Nicodemus, a ruler of the Jews)*

For God so loved the world, that he gave his only begotten Son, that whosoever believeth in him should not perish, but have everlasting life.

1 John 4:16 *(Epistle of John the Beloved)*

And we have known and believed the love that God hath to us. God is love; and he that dwelleth in love dwelleth in God, and God in him.

GOD'S LOVE FOR JESUS

John 10:17 *(Jesus to his disciples)*

Therefore doth my Father love me, because I lay down my life, that I might take it again.

THOSE WHO LOVE GOD KEEP THE COMMANDMENTS

John 14:15 *(Jesus to Philip)*

If ye love me, keep my commandments.

D & C 42:29 *(Revelation to Joseph Smith — February, 1831)*

If thou lovest me thou shalt serve me and keep all my commandments.

GREATER LOVE HATH NO MAN

John 15:13 *(Jesus to his disciples)*

Greater love hath no man than this, that a man lay down his life for his friends.

REWARD OF THOSE WHO LOVE

1 Corinthians 2:9 *(Paul to the Corinthians)*

But as it is written, Eye hath not seen, nor ear heard, neither have entered into the heart of man, the things which God hath prepared for them that love him.

CHRIST'S LOVE IS TOO GREAT TO UNDERSTAND

Ephesians 3:17-19 *(Paul to the Church at Ephesus)*

17.   That Christ may dwell in your hearts by faith; that ye, being rooted and grounded in love,

18.   May be able to comprehend with all saints what is the breadth, and length, and depth, and height;

19.   And to know the love of Christ, which passeth knowledge, that ye might be filled with all the fulness of God.

MAN CANNOT LOVE GOD AND HATE HIS BROTHER

1 John 4:20-21 *(Epistle of John the Beloved)*

20.   If a man say, I love God, and hateth his brother, he is a liar: for he that loveth not his brother whom he hath seen, how can he love God whom he hath not seen?

21.   And this commandment have we from him, That he who loveth God love his brother also.

'HE FAITHFUL SHALL BE ENCIRCLED IN THE ARMS OF GOD'S LOVE

2 Nephi 1:15 *(Lehi's exhortation to his sons — 588 BC)*

> But behold the Lord hath redeemed my soul from hell; I have beheld his glory, and I am encircled about eternally in the arms of his love.

D & C 6:20 *(Jesus Christ to Oliver Cowdery — April, 1829)*

> . . .Be faithful and diligent in keeping the commandments of God, and I will encircle thee in the arms of my love.

CHARITY IS THE PURE LOVE OF CHRIST

Moroni 7:47 *(Mormon's teachings to his son Moroni — 400 AD)*

> But charity is the pure love of Christ, and it endureth forever; and whoso is found possessed of it at the last day, it shall be well with him.

ᴔARRIAGE

(See Covenants, Love)

GOD MADE A HELP MEET FOR MAN

Genesis 2:18,24 *(also Moses 3:18) (Moses' account of the creation)*

18.　And the Lord God said, It is not good that the man should be alone; I will make him an help meet for him.

24.　Therefore shall a man leave his father and his mother, and shall cleave unto his wife: and they shall be one flesh.

WHITHER THOU GOEST, I WILL GO

Ruth 1:16 *(Ruth speaking to Naomi)*

. . .Intreat me not to leave thee, or to return from following after thee: for whither thou goest, I will go; and where thou lodgest, I will lodge: thy people shall be my people, and thy God my God.

TWO ARE BETTER THAN ONE

Ecclesiastes 4:9-10 *(Advice of Ecclesiastes, the preacher, son of David)*

9.　Two are better than one; because they have a good reward for their labour.

10.　For if they fall, the one will lift up his fellow: but woe to him that is alone when he falleth; for he hath not another to help him up.

LOVE YOUR WIFE AND LIVE JOYFULLY

Ecclesiastes 9:9 *(Advice of Ecclesiastes, the preacher, Son of David)*

Live joyfully with the wife whom thou lovest. . .

MEN AND WOMEN ARE BOTH IMPORTANT TO THE LORD

1 Corinthians 11:11-12 *(Paul to the saints in Corinth)*

11. Nevertheless neither is the man without the woman, neither the woman without the man, in the Lord.

12. For as the woman is of the man, even so is the man also by the woman; but all things of God.

MAN AND WIFE SHALL BE AS ONE FLESH

Ephesians 5:31 *(also Moses 3:24)* *(Paul to the Ephesians)*

For this cause shall a man leave his father and mother, and shall be joined unto his wife, and they two shall be one flesh.

LOVE YOUR HUSBAND OR WIFE

Ephesians 5:33 *(Paul to the Ephesians)*

Nevertheless let every one of you in particular so love his wife even as himself; and the wife see that she reverence her husband.

MARRIAGE IS ORDAINED OF GOD

D & C 49:15 *(Revelation to Joseph Smith — March, 1831)*

And again, verily I say unto you, that whoso forbiddeth to marry is not ordained of God, for marriage is ordained of God unto man.

THE HIGHEST DEGREE OF CELESTIAL GLORY REQUIRES MARRIAGE

D & C 131:1-4 *(Instructions on temple marriage to the saints by Joseph Smith — May, 1843)*

1. In the celestial glory there are three heavens or degrees;

2. And in order to obtain the highest, a man must enter into this order of the priesthood (meaning the new and everlasting covenant of marriage):

3. And if he does not, he cannot obtain it.

4. He may enter into the other, but that is the end of his kingdom; he cannot have an increase.

PROMISE TO THOSE WHO REJECT TEMPLE MARRIAGE

D & C 132:15-17 *(Revelation on celestial marriage — July, 1843)*

15. Therefore, if a man marry him a wife in the world, and he marry her not by me nor by my word, and he covenant with her so long as he is in the world and she with him, their covenant and marriage are not of force when they are dead, and when they are out of the world; therefore, they are not bound by any law when they are out of the world.

16.   Therefore, when they are out of the world they neither marry nor are given in marriage; but are appointed angels in heaven; which angels are ministering servants, to minister for those who are worthy of a far more, and an exceeding, and an eternal weight of glory.

17.   For these angels did not abide my law; therefore, they cannot be enlarged, but remain separately and singly, without exaltation, in their saved condition, to all eternity; and from henceforth are not gods, but are angels of God forever and ever.

PROMISE TO THOSE WHO ACCEPT TEMPLE MARRIAGE

D & C 132:19-20 *(Revelation on celestial marriage — July, 1843)*

19.   And again, verily I say unto you, if a man marry a wife by my word, which is my law and by the new and everlasting covenant, and it is sealed unto them by the Holy Spirit of promise. . .Ye shall come forth in the first resurrection; and if it be after the first resurrection, in the next resurrection; and shall inherit thrones, kingdoms, principalities, and powers, dominions, all heights and depths. . .

20.   Then shall they be gods, because they have no end; therefore shall they be from everlasting to everlasting, because they continue; then shall they be above all, because all things are subject unto them. Then shall they be gods, because they have all power, and the angels are subject unto them.

MILLENNIUM

(See Jesus Christ: Second Coming, Last Days)

WILD BEASTS WILL BE TAME

Isaiah 11:5-9 *(also 2 Nephi 30:11-15) (Prophecies of Isaiah)*

5. And righteousness shall be the girdle of his loins, and faithfulness the girdle of his reins.

6. The wolf also shall dwell with the lamb, and the leopard shall lie down with the kid; and the calf and the young lion and the fatling together, and a little child shall lead them.

7. And the cow and the bear shall feed; their young ones shall lie down together: and the lion shall eat straw like the ox.

8. And the sucking child shall play on the hole of the asp, and the weaned child shall put his hand on the cockatrice' den.

9. They shall not hurt nor destroy in all my holy mountain: for the earth shall be full of the knowledge of the Lord, as the waters cover the sea.

THE DESERT SHALL BLOSSOM AS A ROSE

Isaiah 35:1-2 *(Prophecies of Isaiah)*

1. The wilderness and the solitary place shall be glad for them; and the desert shall rejoice, and blossom as the rose.

2. It shall blossom abundantly, and rejoice even with joy and singing: . . .

JERUSALEM WILL BE AT PEACE

Isaiah 65:19 *(Prophecies of Isaiah)*

And I will rejoice in Jerusalem, and joy in my people: and the voice of weeping shall be no more heard in her, nor the voice of crying.

Revelations 21:4 *(John the Revelator's vision of the last days)*

And God shall wipe away all tears from their eyes; and there shall be no more death, neither sorrow, nor crying, neither shall there be any more pain: for the former things are passed away.

THE EARTH WILL BE CLEANSED BY FIRE

Malachi 4:1 *(Prophecies of Malachi)*

For, behold, the day cometh, that shall burn as an oven; and all the proud, yea, and all that do wickedly, shall be stubble: and the day that cometh shall burn them up, saith the Lord of hosts, that it shall leave them neither root nor branch.

SATAN WILL BE BOUND

Revelations 20:1-3 *(John the Revelator's vision of the last days)*

1. And I saw an angel come down from heaven, having the key of the bottomless pit and a great chain in his hand.

2. And he laid hold on the dragon, that old serpent, which is the Devil, and Satan, and bound him a thousand years.

3. And cast him into the bottomless pit, and shut him up, and set a seal upon him, that he should

deceive the nations no more, till the thousand years should be fulfilled: and after that he must be loosed a little season.

1 Nephi 22:15 *(Nephi expounds the prophecies of Isaiah — 588 BC)*

For behold, saith the prophet, the time cometh speedily that Satan shall have no more power over the hearts of the children of men; for the day soon cometh that all the proud and they who do wickedly shall be as stubble; and the day cometh that they must be burned.

D & C 88:110 *(Revelation to Joseph Smith — December, 1832)*

. . .and Satan shall be bound, that old serpent, who is called the devil, and shall not be loosed for the space of a thousand years.

GREAT WAR AFTER THE MILLENNIUM

Revelations 20:7-8 *(John the Revelator's vision of the last days)*

7.   And when the thousand years are expired, Satan shall be loosed out of his prison,

8.   And shall go out to deceive the nations which are in the four quarters of the earth, Gog and Magog, to gather them together to battle: the number of whom is as the sand of the sea.

D & C 88:110-114 *(Revelation to Joseph Smith — December, 1832)*

110.   And so on, until the seventh angel shall sound his trump; and he shall stand forth upon the land and upon the sea, and swear in the name of him who

sitteth upon the throne, that there shall be time no longer; and Satan shall be bound, that old serpent, who is called the devil, and shall be loosed for the space of a thousand years.

111.   And then he shall be loosed for a little season, that he may gather together his armies.

112.   And Michael, the seventh angel, even the archangel, shall gather together his armies, even the hosts of heaven.

113.   And the devil shall gather together his armies; even the hosts of hell, and shall come up to battle against Michael and his armies.

114.   And then cometh the battle of the great God; and the devil and his armies shall be cast away into their own place, that they shall not have power over the saints any more at all.

THE CHILDREN OF ISRAEL SHALL BE GATHERED

1 Nephi 22:25-26 *(Nephi's prophecy — 588 BC)*

25.   And he gathereth his children from the four quarters of the earth; and he numbereth his sheep, and they know him; and there shall be one fold and one shepherd; and he shall feed his sheep, and in him they shall find pasture.

26.   And because of the righteousness of his people, Satan has no power; wherefore, he cannot be loosed for the space of many years; for he hath no power over the hearts of the people, for they dwell in righteousness, and the Holy One of Israel reigneth.

CHRIST WILL REIGN AND SATAN WILL BE BOUND

D & C 43:29-33 *(Revelation to Joseph Smith — February, 1831)*

29. For in mine own due time will I come upon the earth in judgment, and my people shall be redeemed and shall reign with me on earth.

30. For the great Millennium, of which I have spoken by the mouth of my servants, shall come.

31. For Satan shall be bound, and when he is loosed again he shall only reign for a little season, and then cometh the end of the earth.

32. And he that liveth in righteousness shall be changed in the twinkling of an eye, and the earth shall pass away so as by fire.

33. And the wicked shall go away into unquenchable fire, and their end no man knoweth on earth, nor ever shall know, until they come before me in judgment.

MORTALS WILL CHANGE TO IMMORTALS IN THE TWINKLING OF AN EYE

D & C 63:50-51 *(Revelation to Joseph Smith — August, 1831)*

50. And he that liveth when the Lord shall come, and hath kept the faith, blessed is he; nevertheless, it is appointed to him to die at the age of man.

51. Wherefore, children shall grow up until they become old; old men shall die; but they shall not sleep in the dust, but they shall be changed in the twinkling of an eye.

D & C 101:28-31 *(Revelation to Joseph Smith — December, 1833)*

28.   And in that day Satan shall not have power to tempt any man.

29.   And there shall be no sorrow because there is no death.

30.   In that day an infant shall not die until he is old; and his life shall be as the age of a tree;

31.   And when he dies he shall not sleep, that is to say in the earth, but shall be changed in the twinkling of an eye, and shall be caught up, and his rest shall be glorious.

MILLENNIUM WILL LAST 1000 YEARS

Moses 7:64-65 *(The writings of Moses are revealed to Joseph Smith — December, 1830)*

64.   And there shall be mine abode, and it shall be Zion, which shall come forth out of all the creations which I have made; and for the space of a thousand years the earth shall rest.

65.   And it came to pass that Enoch saw the day of the coming of the Son of Man, in the last days, to dwell on the earth in righteousness for the space of a thousand years;

(D)IRACLES

AN EVIL AND ADULTEROUS GENERATION ASKS FOR SIGNS

Matthew 12:39 *(Jesus to the Pharisees)*

. . .An evil and adulterous generation seeketh after a sign. . .

Matthew 16:4 *(Jesus to the Pharisees and Sadducees)*

A wicked and adulterous generation seeketh after a sign; and there shall no sign be given unto it. . .

PEOPLE FOLLOWED JESUS BECAUSE OF MIRACLES

John 6:26-27 *(Jesus to the people of Capernaum)*

26.   Jesus answered them and said, Verily, verily, I say unto you, Ye seek me, not because ye saw the miracles, but because ye did eat of the loaves, and were filled.

27.   Labour not for the meat which perisheth, but for that meat which endureth unto everlasting life, which the Son of man shall give unto you: for him hath God the Father sealed.

MIRACLES ARE TO BENEFIT MANKIND

Mosiah 8:18 *(Ammon talks to King Lemhi about prophets and the power of the priesthood — 121 BC)*

Thus God has provided a means that man, through faith, might work mighty miracles; therefore he becometh a great benefit to his fellow beings.

FAITH IS ESSENTIAL BEFORE MIRACLES CAN BE PERFORMED

Ether 12:12 *(Moroni explains the fall of the Jaredites — 420 AD)*

For if there be no faith among the children of men God can do no miracle among them; wherefore, he showed not himself until after their faith.

⑪ISSIONARY WORK

WHY WE HAVE COMPANIONS

Ecclesiastes 4:9-10 *(Teachings of Ecclesiastes, son of David)*

9. Two are better than one; because they have a good reward for their labour.

10. For if they fall, the one will lift up his fellow: but woe to him that is alone when he falleth; for he hath not another to help him up.

Matthew 18:20 *(also D & C 6:32) (Christ to his disciples)*

For where two or three are gathered together in my name, there am I in the midst of them.

Luke 10:1 *(Christ to his disciples)*

After these things the Lord appointed other seventy also, and sent them two and two before his face into every city and place, whither he himself would come.

D & C 42:6 *(Revelation to Joseph Smith — February, 1831)*

And ye shall go forth in the power of my Spirit, preaching my gospel, two by two, in my name, lifting up your voices as with the sound of a trump, declaring my word like unto angels of God.

PARENTS AND MISSIONARIES SHOULD WRITE OFTEN

Proverbs 25:25 *(Proverb of Solomon, King of Israel)*

As cold waters to a thirsty soul, so is good news from a far country.

PARABLE OF THE LOST SHEEP

Matthew 18:12-13 *(Jesus Christ to his disciples)*

12.   How think ye? If a man have an hundred sheep, and one of them be gone astray, doth he not leave the ninety and nine, and goeth into the mountains, and seeketh that which is gone astray?

13.   And if so be that he find it, verily I say unto you, he rejoiceth more of that sheep, than of the ninety and nine which went not astray.

THE GOSPEL SHALL BE PREACHED IN ALL THE WORLD

Matthew 24:14 *(Jesus Christ to his disciples)*

And this gospel of the kingdom shall be preached in all the world for a witness unto all nations; and then shall the end come.

CHRIST'S ADMONITION TO TEACH ALL NATIONS

Matthew 28:19-20 *(Christ to his apostles prior to his ascension)*

19.   Go ye therefore, and teach all nations, baptizing them in the name of the Father, and of the Son, and of the Holy Ghost:

20. Teaching them to observe all things whatsoever I have commanded you: and, lo, I am with you always, even unto the end of the world. Amen.

Mark 16:15-16 *(Christ to his apostles prior to his ascension)*

15. And he said unto them, Go ye into all the world, and preach the gospel to every creature.

16. He that believeth and is baptized shall be saved; but he that believeth not shall be damned.

BELIEVERS SHALL HAVE THE POWER TO CAST OUT DEVILS, SPEAK IN NEW TONGUES, AND HEAL THE SICK

Mark 16:17-18 *(Jesus to his disciples)*

17. And these signs shall follow them that believe; In my name shall they cast out devils; they shall speak with new tongues;

18. They shall take up serpents; and if they drink any deadly thing, it shall not hurt them: they shall lay hands on the sick, and they shall recover.

WOE UNTO ME IF I PREACH NOT THE GOSPEL

1 Corinthians 9:16 *(Paul to the Corinthians)*

. . .woe is unto me, if I preach not the gospel!

WHY WE TEACH MISSIONARIES A LANGUAGE

1 Corinthians 14:19,33 *(Paul to the Corinthians)*

19. Yet in the church I had rather speak five words with my understanding, that by my voice I might teach others also, than ten thousand words in an unknown tongue.

33.　For God is not the author of confusion, but of peace, as in all churches of the saints.

THE GOSPEL SHALL BE PREACHED TO EVERY NATION, KINDRED, TONGUE, AND PEOPLE

Revelation 14:6-7 *(John's prophecy of the last days)*

6.　And I saw another angel fly in the midst of heaven, having the everlasting gospel to preach unto them that dwell on the earth, and to every nation, kindred, and tongue, and people.

7.　Saying with a loud voice, Fear God, and give glory to him; for the hour of his judgment is come: and worship him that made heaven, and earth, and the sea, and the fountains of waters.

D & C 133:37 *(Revelation to Joseph Smith — November, 1831)*

And this gospel shall be preached unto every nation, and kindred, and tongue, and people.

GOD IS MINDFUL OF ALL HIS CHILDREN

Alma 26:37 *(Ammon tells of his missionary experiences — 77 BC)*

Now my brethren, we see that God is mindful of every people, whatsoever land they may be in; yea, he numbereth his people, and his bowels of mercy are over all the earth. . .

O THAT I WERE AN ANGEL

Alma 29:1-3,6-7,9 *(Alma desires to preach to all — 76 BC)*

1.　O that I were an angel, and could have the wish of mine heart, that I might go forth and speak with the trump of God, with a voice to shake the earth, and cry repentance unto every people!

2. Yea, I would declare unto every soul, as with the voice of thunder, repentance and the plan of redemption, that they should repent and come unto our God, that there might not be more sorrow upon all the face of the earth.

3. But behold, I am a man, and do sin in my wish; for I ought to be content with the things which the Lord hath allotted unto me.

6. Now, seeing that I know these things, why should I desire more than to perform the work to which I have been called?

7. Why should I desire that I were an angel, that I could speak unto all the ends of the earth?

9. I know that which the Lord hath commanded me, and I glory in it. I do not glory of myself, but I glory in that which the Lord hath commanded me; yea, and this is my glory, that perhaps I may be an instrument in the hands of God to bring some soul to repentance; and this is my joy.

PREACHING THE WORD HAS A MORE POWERFUL EFFECT THAN THE SWORD

Alma 31:5 *(Alma speaking to the Zoramites — 74 BC)*

And now, as the preaching of the word had a great tendency to lead the people to do that which was just — yea, it had had more powerful effect upon the minds of the people than the sword, or anything else, which had happened unto them. . .

WHAT TO PREACH TO PEOPLE

Alma 37:33-35 *(Alma's exhortation to his son, Helaman)*

33.   Preach unto them repentance, and faith on the Lord Jesus Christ; teach them to humble themselves and to be meek and lowly in heart; teach them to withstand every temptation of the devil, with their faith on the Lord Jesus Christ.

34.   Teach them to never be weary of good works, but to be meek and lowly in heart; for such shall find rest to their souls.

35.   O, remember, my son, and learn wisdom in thy youth; yea, learn in thy youth to keep the commandments of God.

THE SIMPLE AND WEAK SHALL PROCLAIM THE FULLNESS OF THE GOSPEL

D & C 1:23 *(Revelation to Joseph Smith — November, 1831)*

That the fulness of my gospel might be proclaimed by the weak and the simple unto the ends of the world, and before kings and rulers.

WHETHER BY THE VOICE OF GOD OR HIS SERVANTS IT IS THE SAME

D & C 1:38 *(Revelation to Joseph Smith — November, 1831)*

What I the Lord have spoken, I have spoken, and I excuse not myself; and though the heavens and the earth pass away, my word shall not pass away, but shall all be fulfilled, whether by mine own voice or by the voice of my servants, it is the same.

QUALIFICATIONS OF A MISSIONARY

D & C 4:1-7 *(Revelation to Joseph Smith — February, 1829)*

1. Now behold, a marvelous work is about to come forth among the children of men.

2. Therefore, O ye that embark in the service of God, see that ye serve him with all your heart, might, mind and strength, that ye may stand blameless before God at the last day.

3. Therefore, if ye have desires to serve God ye are called to the work;

4. For behold the field is white already to harvest; and lo, he that thrusteth in his sickle with his might, the same layeth up in store that he perisheth not, but bringeth salvation to his soul;

5. And faith, hope, charity and love, with an eye single to the glory of God, qualify him for the work.

6. Remember faith, virtue, knowledge, temperance, patience, brotherly kindness, godliness, charity, humility, diligence.

7. Ask, and ye shall receive; knock, and it shall be opened unto you. Amen.

SERVE WITH ALL YOUR HEART, MIGHT, MIND AND STRENGTH

D & C 4:2 *(Revelation to Joseph smith — February, 1829)*

Therefore, O ye that embark in the service of God, see that ye serve him with all your heart, might, mind and strength, that ye may stand blameless before God at the last day.

MISSIONARY BLESSED EVEN IF THE MESSAGE IS REJECTED

D & C 6:29-30 *(Revelation to Joseph Smith and Oliver Cowdery — April, 1829)*

29.　Verily, verily, I say unto you, if they reject my words, and this part of my gospel and ministry, blessed are ye, for they can do no more unto you than unto me.

30.　And even if they do unto you even as they have done unto me, blessed are ye, for you shall dwell with me in glory.

THE WORTH OF SOULS IS GREAT

D & C 18:10,13,15-16 *(Revelation to Joseph Smith, Oliver Cowdery, and David Whitmer — June, 1829)*

10.　Remember the worth of souls is great in the sight of God;

13.　And how great is his joy in the soul that repenteth!

15.　And if it so be that you should labor all your days in crying repentance unto this people, and bring, save it be one soul unto me, how great shall be your joy with him in the kingdom of my Father!

16.　And now, if your joy will be great with one soul that you have brought unto me into the kingdom of my Father, how great will be your joy if you should bring many souls unto me!

MISSIONARIES MUST BE ORDAINED

D & C 42:11 *(Revelation to Joseph Smith — February, 1831)*

. . .it shall not be given to any one to go forth to preach my gospel, or to build up my church, except he be ordained by some one who has authority. . .

Fifth Article of Faith

We believe that a man must be called of God, by prophecy, and by the laying on of hands, by those who are in authority to preach the Gosepl and administer in the ordinances thereof.

DUTIES OF A MISSIONARY

D & C 58:47 *(The Lord to the Elders of the Church — August, 1831)*

Let them preach by the way, and bear testimony of the truth in all places, and call upon the rich, the high and the low, and the poor to repent.

THE GOSPEL MUST BE PREACHED TO THE UTTERMOST PARTS OF THE EARTH

D & C 58:64 *(The Lord to the Elders of the Church — August, 1831)*

For, verily, the sound must go forth from this place into all the world, and unto the uttermost parts of the earth — the gospel must be preached unto every creature, with signs following them that believe.

THE LORD IS NOT PLEASED WITH THOSE WHO DO NOT USE THEIR TALENTS

D & C 60:2-3 *(Joseph Smith for missionaries — August, 1831)*

2. But with some I am not well pleased, for they will not open their mouths, but they hide the talent which I have given unto them, because of the fear of man. Wo unto such, for mine anger is kindled against them.

3. And it shall come to pass, if they are not more faithful unto me, it shall be taken away, even that which they have.

THE GOSPEL IS THE STONE CUT WITHOUT HANDS

D & C 65:2 *(also Daniel 2:44-45) (Revelation to Joseph Smith — October, 1831)*

The keys of the kingdom of God are committed unto man on the earth, and from thence shall the gospel roll forth unto the ends of the earth, as the stone which is cut out of the mountain without hands shall roll forth, until it has filled the whole earth.

PREPARE YE THE WAY OF THE LORD

D & C 65:3-4 *(Revelation to Joseph Smith — October, 1831)*

3. . . .Prepare ye the way of the Lord. . .

4. Pray unto the Lord, call upon his holy name, make known his wonderful works among the people.

EVERY MAN SHOULD WARN HIS NEIGHBOR

D & C 88:81-82 *(Revelation to Joseph Smith — December, 1832)*

81. . . .it becometh every man who hath been warned to warn his neighbor.

82. Therefore, they are left without excuse, and their sins are upon their own heads.

EVERY MAN SHALL HEAR THE FULLNESS OF THE GOSPEL IN HIS OWN TONGUE

D & C 90:11 *(Revelation to Joseph Smith — March, 1833)*

For it shall come to pass in that day, that every man shall hear the fulness of the gospel in his own tongue, and in his own language, through those who are ordained unto this power, by the administration of the Comforter, shed forth upon them for the revelation of Jesus Christ.

A MAN MUST BE CALLED OF GOD TO PREACH THE GOSPEL

Fifth Article of Faith

We believe that a man must be called of God, by prophecy, and by the laying on of hands, by those who are in authority, to preach the Gospel and administer in the ordinances thereof.

⑩OTHERS

(See Fathers, Family, and Marriage)

EVE, THE MOTHER OF ALL

Genesis 3:20 *(Moses' record of the beginning of the world)*

And Adam called his wife's name Eve; because she was the mother of all living.

FIFTH COMMANDMENT

Exodus 20:12 *(also Mosiah 13:20; Deuteronomy 5:16) (Given to Moses on Mt. Sinai)*

Honour thy father and thy mother: that thy days may be long upon the land which the Lord thy God giveth thee.

OBEY THY MOTHER

Proverbs 1:8 *(Proverb of Solomon, King of Israel)*

My son, hear the instruction of thy father, and forsake not the law of thy mother.

Proverbs 10:1 *(Proverb of Solomon, King of Israel)*

A wise son maketh a glad father: but a foolish son is the heaviness of his mother.

Proverbs 23:22 *(Proverb of Solomon, King of Israel)*

Hearken unto thy father that begat thee, and despise not thy mother when she is old.

CHARACTERISTICS OF A MOTHER

Proverbs 31:10-31 *(Proverb of Solomon, King of Israel)*

10. Who can find a virtuous woman? for her price is far above rubies.

11. The heart of her husband doth safely trust in her, so that he shall have no need of spoil.

12. She will do him good and not evil all the days of her life.

13. She seeketh wool, and flax, and worketh willingly with her hands.

14. She is like the merchants' ships; she bringeth her food from afar.

15. She riseth also while it is yet night, and giveth meat to her household. . .

16. . . .with the fruit of her hands she planteth a vineyard.

17. She girdeth her loins with strength, and strengtheneth her arms.

18. She perceiveth that her merchandise is good: her candle goeth not out by night.

19. She layeth her hands to the spindle. . .

20. She stretcheth out her hand to the poor; yea, she reacheth forth her hands to the needy.

21. She is not afraid of the snow for her household: for all her household are clothed. . .

22. She maketh herself coverings of tapestry. . .

23. Her husband is known in the gates, when he sitteth among the elders of the land.

24.   She maketh fine linen, and selleth it. . .

25.   Strength and honour are her clothing; and she shall rejoice in time to come.

26.   She openeth her mouth with wisdom; and in her tongue is the law of kindness.

27.   She looketh well to the ways of her household, and eateth not the bread of idleness.

28.   Her children arise up, and call her blessed; her husband also, and he praiseth her. . .

29.   Many daughters have done virtuously, but thou excellest them all.

30.   Favour is deceitful, and beauty is vain: but a woman that feareth the Lord, she shall be praised.

31.   . . .and let her own works praise her in the gates.

MARY'S CALLING TO BE THE MOTHER OF CHRIST

Luke 1:27-30, 37-38 *(Luke records the events prior to Jesus' birth)*

27.   . . .and the virgin's name was Mary.

28.   And the angel came in unto her, and said, Hail, thou that art highly favoured, the Lord is with thee: blessed art thou among women.

29.   And when she saw him, she was troubled at his saying, and cast in her mind what manner of salutation this should be.

30.   And the angel said unto her, Fear not, Mary: for thou hast found favour with God.

37.   For with God nothing shall be impossible.

38.   And Mary said, Behold the handmaid of the Lord; be it unto me according to thy word. And the angel departed from her.

CHRIST'S CONCERN FOR HIS MOTHER

John 19:26-27 *(John records the events of the crucifixion of Jesus Christ)*

26.   When Jesus therefore saw his mother, and the disciple standing by, whom he loved, he saith unto his mother, Woman, behold thy son!

27.   Then saith he to the disciple, Behold thy mother! And from that hour that disciple took her unto his own home.

MOTHERS TEACH FAITH

Alma 56:47-48 *(Epistle of Helaman to General Moroni — 64 BC)*

47.   . . .yea, they had been taught by their mothers, that if they did not doubt, God would deliver them.

48.   And they rehearsed unto me the words of their mothers, saying: We do not doubt our mothers knew it.

USIC

(See Praise)

JESUS SANG WITH HIS APOSTLES

Matthew 26:30 *(Before they went to Gethsemane to pray they sang)*

. . .And when they had sung an hymn, they went out into the Mount of Olives.

SING WITH THE SPIRIT

1 Corinthians 14:15 *(Paul's epistle to the Corinthians)*

. . .I will sing with the spirit, and I will sing with the understanding also.

TEACH ONE ANOTHER WITH HYMNS

Colossians 3:16 *(Paul to Colossians)*

Let the word of Christ dwell in you richly in all wisdom; teaching and admonishing one another in psalms and hymns and spiritual songs, singing with grace in your hearts to the Lord.

SING UNTO THE LORD

2 Nephi 22:2,5 *(Nephi quotes Isaiah 12 — 545 BC)*

2.   . . .the Lord JEHOVAH is my strength and my song; he also has become my salvation.

5.   Sing unto the Lord; for he hath done excellent things; thus is known in all the earth.

THE CHOIRS ABOVE

Mosiah 2:28 *(King Benjamin's discourse to the people of Zarahemla — 124 BC)*

. . .I am about to go down to my grave. . .and my immortal spirit may join the choirs above in singing the praises of a just God.

THE LORD WILL BLESS THOSE WHO SING UNTO HIM

D & C 25:12 *(Revelation given to Joseph Smith — July, 1830)*

For my soul delighteth in the song of the heart; yea, the song of the righteous is a prayer unto me, and it shall be answered with a blessing upon their heads.

ZION SHALL SING SONGS OF JOY

D & C 45:71 *(Revelation to Joseph Smith — March, 1831)*

And it shall come to pass that the righteous shall be gathered out from among all nations, and shall come to Zion, singing with songs of everlasting joy.

OBEDIENCE

(See Diligence)

WHO IS ON THE LORD'S SIDE

Exodus 32:26 *(Moses' question to the drunken Israelites as they worshipped the golden calf upon his return from Mt. Sinai with the Ten Commandments)*

. . .Who is on the Lord's side? let him come unto me. . .

THE LORD BLESSES THE OBEDIENT

Deuteronomy 11:26-28 *(Moses exhorts the children of Israel to be obedient)*

26. Behold, I set before you this day a blessing and a curse;

27. A blessing, if ye obey the commandments of the Lord your God, which I command you this day:

28. And a curse, if ye will not obey the commandments of the Lord your God, but turn aside out of the way which I command you this day, to go after other gods, which ye have not known.

TO OBEY IS BETTER THAN SACRIFICE

1 Samuel 15:22 *(The prophet Samuel to King Saul)*

And Samuel said, Hath the Lord as great delight in burnt offerings and sacrifices, as in obeying the voice of the Lord? Behold, to obey is better than sacrifice, and to hearken than the fat of rams.

WHO SHALL ASCEND THE HILL OF THE LORD; HE THAT HATH CLEAN HANDS AND A PURE HEART

Psalms 24:3-4 *(A Psalm of David, King of Israel)*

3. Who shall ascend into the hill of the Lord? or who shall stand in his holy place?

4. He that hath clean hands, and a pure heart; who hath not lifted up his soul unto vanity, nor sworn deceitfully.

IF SINNERS ENTICE THEE, CONSENT NOT

Proverbs 1:10 *(Proverb of Solomon, King of Israel)*

My son, if sinners entice thee, consent thou not.

TRUST THE LORD

Proverbs 3:5-7 *(Proverb of Solomon, King of Israel)*

5. Trust in the Lord with all thine heart; and lean not unto thine own understanding.

6. In all thy ways acknowledge him, and he shall direct thy paths.

7. Be not wise in thine own eyes: fear the Lord, and depart from evil.

OBEYING THE LAW BRINGS HAPPINESS

Proverbs 29:18 *(Proverb of Solomon, King of Israel)*

Where there is no vision, the people perish: but he that keepeth the law, happy is he.

DUTY OF MAN IS TO KEEP THE COMMANDMENTS

Ecclesiastes 12:13-14 *(Teachings of Ecclesiastes, son of King David)*

13.   Let us hear the conclusion of the whole matter: Fear God, and keep his commandments: for this is the whole duty of man.

14.   For God shall bring every work into judgment, with every secret thing, whether it be good, or whether it be evil.

DO NOT EXCHANGE GLORY FOR THINGS OF NO VALUE

Jeremiah 2:11 *(The Lord speaking to Jeremiah)*

Hath a nation changed their gods, which are yet no gods? but my people have changed their glory for that which doth not profit.

THE BEATITUDES

Matthew 5:3-12 *(also 3 Nephi 12:3-12) (Jesus Christ in the Sermon on the Mount)*

3.   Blessed are the poor in spirit: for theirs is the kingdom of heaven.

4.   Blessed are they that mourn: for they shall be comforted.

5.   Blessed are the meek: for they shall inherit the earth.

6.   Blessed are they which do hunger and thirst after righteousness: for they shall be filled.

7.   Blessed are the merciful: for they shall obtain mercy.

8. Blessed are the pure in heart: for they shall see God.

9. Blessed are the peacemakers: for they shall be called the children of God.

10. Blessed are they which are persecuted for righteousness' sake: for theirs is the kingdom of heaven.

11. Blessed are ye, when men shall revile you, and persecute you, and shall say all manner of evil against you falsely, for my sake.

12. Rejoice, and be exceeding glad: for great is your reward in heaven: for so persecuted they the prophets which were before you.

THE PUNISHMENT FOR THOSE WHO TEACH OTHERS TO BREAK THE COMMANDMENTS

Matthew 5:19 *(Jesus Christ in the Sermon on the Mount)*

Whosoever therefore shall break one of these least commandments, and shall teach men so, he shall be called the least in the kingdom of heaven: but whosoever shall do and teach them, the same shall be called great in the kingdom of heaven.

WE MUST PROVE OURSELVES BY BEING OBEDIENT

Matthew 7:21 *(Jesus Christ in the Sermon on the Mount)*

Not every one that saith unto me, Lord, Lord, shall enter into the kingdom of heaven; but he that doeth the will of my Father which is in heaven.

HE THAT ENDURES TO THE END SHALL BE SAVED

Matthew 24:13 *(Jesus Christ to his disciples)*

But he that shall endure unto the end, the same shall be saved.

GOD'S WILL BE DONE

Matthew 26:39 *(also Luke 22:42) (Jesus Christ prays to his Father in Heaven in Gethsemane)*

. . .O my Father, if it be possible, let this cup pass from me: nevertheless not as I will, but as thou wilt.

JESUS DID HIS FATHER'S WORK

Luke 2:49 *(Jesus Christ to his mother, Mary, and his father, Joseph, when they found him in the temple with the doctors)*

And he said unto them, How is it that ye sought me? wist ye not that I must be about my Father's business?

THOSE WHO BELIEVE SHOULD OBEY

Luke 6:46 *(Jesus Christ to his disciples)*

And why call ye me, Lord, Lord, and do not the things which I say?

THE OBEDIENT WILL KNOW IF THE DOCTRINE IS TRUE

John 7:16-17 *(Jesus Christ teaching in the temple)*

16. . . .My doctrine is not mine, but his that sent me.

17. If any man will do his will, he shall know of the doctrine, whether it be of God, or whether I speak of myself.

OVERCOME EVIL BY GOOD

Romans 12:21 *(Paul to the Romans)*

Be not overcome of evil, but overcome evil with good.

WE SHOULD OBEY GOD AS WE OBEY OUR PARENTS

Hebrews 12:9 *(Paul's epistle to the Hebrews)*

Furthermore we have had fathers of our flesh which corrected us, and we gave them reverence: shall we not much rather be in subjection unto the Father of spirits, and live?

THOSE WHO ARE NOT FOR GOD ARE AGAINST HIM

2 Nephi 10:16 *(Jacob's teachings to the Nephites — 560 BC)*

. . .for they who are not for me are against me, saith our God.

IF WE KEEP THE COMMANDMENTS, WE SHALL PROSPER

Jarom vs. 9 *(Jarom quoting the word of the Lord — 399 BC)*

. . .Inasmuch as ye will keep my commandments, ye shall prosper in the land.

Omni vs. 6 *(Writings of Amaron — 279 BC)*

. . .Inasmuch as ye will not keep my commandments ye shall not prosper in the land.

THE LORD CANNOT ALLOW EVEN A LITTLE SIN

D & C 1:31 *(Revelation to Joseph Smith — November, 1831)*

For I the Lord cannot look upon sin with the least degree of allowance.

THE FAITHFUL WILL BE ENCIRCLED IN THE ARMS OF CHRIST'S LOVE

D & C 6:20 *(Lord's promise to Oliver Cowdery — April, 1829)*

. . .Be faithful and diligent in keeping the commandments of God, and I will encircle thee in the arms of my love.

ENDURE TO THE END, AND YE SHALL HAVE ETERNAL LIFE

D & C 14:7 *(Revelation through Joseph Smith to David Whitmer — June, 1829)*

And, if you keep my commandments and endure to the end you shall have eternal life, which gift is the greatest of all the gifts of God.

HE THAT RECEIVETH MY LAW AND LIVES IT IS MY DISCIPLE

D & C 41:5 *(Revelation to Joseph Smith — February, 1831)*

He that receiveth my law and doeth it, the same is my disciple; and he that saith he receiveth it and doeth it not, the same is not my disciple, and shall be cast out from among you.

THE PURPOSE OF LIFE IS TO LEARN OBEDIENCE

D & C 58:6 *(Revelation to Joseph Smith — August, 1831)*

. . .for this cause I have sent you — that you might be obedient, and that your hearts might be prepared to bear testimony of the things which are to come.

THE LORD IS BOUND WHEN MEN OBEY

D & C 82:10 *(Revelation to Joseph Smith — January, 1832)*

I, the Lord, am bound when ye do what I say; but when ye do not what I say, ye have no promise.

BLESSINGS ARE BASED ON OBEDIENCE TO A LAW DECREED IN HEAVEN

D & C 130:20-21 *(Instructions to Joseph Smith — April, 1843)*

20. There is a law, irrevocably decreed in heaven before the foundations of this world, upon which all blessings are predicated —

21. And when we obtain any blessing from God, it is by obedience to that law upon which it is predicated.

QATIENCE

(See Peace)

CHRIST HAS OVERCOME

John 16:33 *(Jesus to his disciples)*

These things I have spoken unto you, that in me ye might have peace. In the world ye shall have tribulation: but be of good cheer; I have overcome the world.

TRIBULATION WORKETH PATIENCE

Romans 5:3-5 *(Paul to the Romans)*

3. And not only so, but we glory in tribulations also: knowing that tribulation worketh patience;

4. And patience, experience; and experience, hope:

5. And hope maketh not ashamed; because the love of God is shed abroad in our hearts by the Holy Ghost which is given unto us.

James 1:2-4 *(Epistle of James, the brother of Jesus)*

2. My brethren, count it all joy when ye fall into divers temptations;

3. Knowing this, that the trying of your faith worketh patience.

4. But let patience have her perfect work, that ye may be perfect and entire, wanting nothing.

PROCEED WITH PATIENCE

Hebrews 12:1 *(Paul's epistle to the Hebrews)*

. . .let us lay aside every. . .sin which doth so easily beset us, and let us run with patience the race that is set before us.

THE QUALITIES OF A MISSIONARY

D & C 4:6 *(Revelation to Joseph Smith — February, 1829)*

Remember faith, virtue, knowledge, temperance, patience, brotherly kindness, godliness, charity, humility, diligence.

PATIENCE EARNS REWARDS

D & C 127:4 *(Epistle of Joseph Smith — September, 1842)*

. . .let your diligence, and your perseverance, and patience, and your works be redoubled, and you shall in nowise lose your reward. . .

PATRIOTISM

(See America)

WHERE THE SPIRIT OF THE LORD IS, THERE IS LIBERTY

2 Corinthians 3:17 *(Paul to the Corinthians)*

. . .where the spirit of the Lord is, there is liberty.

THIS LAND SHALL BE A LAND OF LIBERTY

2 Nephi 1:7 *(Lehi's exortation to his sons — 570 BC)*

Wherefore, this land is consecrated unto him whom he shall bring. And if it so be that they shall serve him according to the commandments which he hath given, it shall be a land of liberty unto them; wherefore, they shall never be brought down into captivity; if so, it shall be because of iniquity; for if iniquity shall abound cursed shall be the land for their sakes, but unto the righteous it shall be blessed forever.

THE MAJORITY WILL NORMALLY CHOOSE THE RIGHT

Mosiah 29:26-27 *(Mosiah recommends a representative government rather than a king — 92 BC)*

26. Now it is not common that the voice of the people desireth anything contrary to that which is right; but it is common for the lesser part of the people to desire that which is not right; therefore this shall ye observe and make it your law — to do your business by the voice of the people.

27. And if the time comes that the voice of the people doth choose iniquity, then is the time that the judgments of God will come upon you; yea, then is the time he will visit you with great destruction even as he has hitherto visited this land.

THE CURSE AND BLESSING OF THE AMERICAN CONTINENT

Alma 45:16 *(Alma to his son, Helaman — 73 BC)*

. . .Thus saith the Lord God — Cursed shall be the land, yea, this land, unto every nation, kindred, tongue, and people, unto destruction, which do wickedly, when they are fully ripe; and as I have said so shall it be; for this is the cursing and the blessing of God upon the land, for the Lord cannot look upon sin with the least degree of allowance.

THE LORD'S WARNING TO THE NEPHITES

Helaman 7:28 *(Nephi's prophecy of the destruction of the Nephites — 23 BC)*

And except ye repent ye shall perish; yea, even your lands shall be taken from you, and ye shall be destroyed from off the face of the earth.

THE AMERICAN CONTINENT IS A CHOICE LAND, A LAND OF PROMISE, AND THE PEOPLE SHALL BE FREE IF THEY SERVE JESUS CHRIST

Ether 2:9-10,12 *(The Lord to the brother of Jared — 2200 BC)*

9. And now, we can behold the decrees of God concerning this land, that it is a land of promise; and whatsoever nation shall possess it shall serve God, or they shall be swept off when the fulness of his wrath

shall come upon them. And the fulness of his wrath cometh upon them when they are ripened in iniquity.

10.   For behold, this is a land which is choice above all other lands; wherefore he that doth possess it shall serve God or shall be swept off; for it is the everlasting decree of God. And it is not until the fulness of iniquity among the children of the land, that they are swept off.

12.   Behold, this is a choice land, and whatsoever nation shall possess it shall be free from bondage, and from captivity, and from all other nations under heaven, if they will but serve the God of the land, who is Jesus Christ, who hath been manifested by the things which we have written.

OBEY THE LAW OF THE LAND

D & C 58:21-22 *(Revelation to Joseph Smith — August, 1831)*

21.   Let no man break the laws of the land, for he that keepeth the laws of God hath no need to break the laws of the land.

22.   Wherefore, be subject to the powers that be, until he reigns whose right it is to reign, and subdues all enemies under his feet.

GOD ESTABLISHED THE CONSTITUTION

D & C 101:80 *(Revelation to Joseph Smith — December, 1833)*

. . .I established the Constitution of this land, by the hands of wise men whom I raised up unto this very purpose, and redeemed the land by the shedding of blood.

GOVERNMENTS WERE INSTITUTED OF GOD FOR THE BENEFIT OF MAN

D & C 134:1-2 *(A declaration of belief regarding governments and laws, adopted by unanimous vote of the Saints at Kirtland, Ohio — August, 1835)*

1. We believe the governments were instituted of God for the benefit of man; and that he holds men accountable for their acts in relation to them, both in making laws and administering them, for the good and safety of society.

2. We believe that no government can exist in peace, except such laws are framed and held inviolate as will secure to each individual the free exercise of conscience, the right and control of property, and the protection of life.

WE BELIEVE IN OBEYING THE LAW

Twelfth Article of Faith

We believe in being subject to kings, presidents, rulers, and magistrates, in obeying, honoring, and sustaining the law.

PEACE

(See Happiness, Contentment)

PEACE IN CHRIST

Isaiah 52:7 *(Isaiah's prophecies of Christ)*

How beautiful upon the mountains are the feet of him that bringeth good tidings, that publisheth peace; . . .

John 14:27 *(Jesus Christ to his disciples)*

Peace I leave with you, my peace I give unto you: not as the world giveth, give I unto you. Let not your heart be troubled, neither let it be afraid.

John 16:33 *(Jesus Christ to his disciples)*

These things I have spoken unto you, that in me ye might have peace. In the world ye shall have tribulations: but be of good cheer; I have overcome the world.

John 20:21 *(Jesus Christ to his disciples)*

. . .Peace be unto you: as my Father hath sent me, even so send I you.

SEARCH FOR PEACE

Jeremiah 6:14 *(Jeremiah's prophecies)*

. . .Peace, peace; when there is no peace.

BLESS THE PEACEMAKERS

Matthew 5:9 *(also 3 Nephi 12:9) (Jesus Christ in the Sermon on the Mount)*

Blessed are the peacemakers: for they shall be called the children of God.

THE ANGELS PROCLAIMED PEACE AT CHRIST'S BIRTH

Luke 2:14 *(Multitude of angels announce the birth of Jesus Christ)*

Glory to God in the highest, and on earth peace, good will toward men.

GOD IS THE AUTHOR OF PEACE

1 Corinthians 14:33 *(Paul to the saints at Corinth)*

For God is not the author of confusion, but of peace, as in all churches of the saints.

PEACE AND ETERNAL LIFE PROMISED TO THE OBEDIENT

D & C 59:23 *(Revelation to Joseph Smith — August, 1831)*

But learn that he who doeth the works of righteousness shall receive his reward, even peace in this world, and eternal life in the world to come.

PRAISE

(See Music)

PRAISE THE LORD WITH SINGING

Isaiah 12:4-5 *(Isaiah's prophecy of the last days)*

4.   And in that day shall ye say, Praise the Lord, call upon his name, declare his doings among the people, make mention that his name is exalted.

5.   Sing unto the Lord; for he hath done excellent things: this is known in all the earth.

D & C 136:28 *(Revelation to Brigham Young — January, 1847)*

If thou art merry, praise the Lord with singing, with music, with dancing, and with a prayer of praise and thanksgiving.

IN THE BEGINNING THE SONS OF GOD SANG AND SHOUTED FOR JOY

Job 38:4,7 *(The Lord speaks to Job)*

4.   Where wast thou when I laid the foundations of the earth? declare, if thou hast understanding.

7.   When the morning stars sang together, and all the sons of God shouted for joy?

ANGELS SANG AT CHRIST'S BIRTH

Luke 2:13-14 *(Angels sang to the shepherds)*

13. And suddenly there was with the angel a multitude of the heavenly host praising God, and saying,

14. Glory to God in the highest, and on earth peace, good will toward men.

THE SONG OF THE RIGHTEOUS IS A PRAYER UNTO ME

D & C 25:12 *(Revelation through Joseph Smith to his wife Emma Smith — July, 1830)*

For my soul delighteth in the song of the heart; yea, the song of the righteous is a prayer unto me, and it shall be answered with a blessing upon their heads.

PRAYER

USE NOT VAIN REPETITIONS

Matthew 6:7 *(Jesus Christ in the Sermon on the Mount)*

But when we pray, use not vain repetitions. . .

THE LORD'S PRAYER

Matthew 6:9-13 *(Jesus Christ in the Sermon on the Mount)*

9.   After this manner therefore pray ye: Our Father which art in heaven, Hallowed be thy name.

10.   Thy kingdom come. Thy will be done in earth, as it is in heaven.

11.   Give us this day our daily bread.

12.   And forgive us our debts, as we forgive our debtors.

13.   And lead us not into temptation, but deliver us from evil: For thine is the kingdom, and the power, and the glory, for ever. Amen.

ASK AND IT SHALL BE GIVEN YOU

Matthew 7:7-8 *(Jesus Christ in the Sermon on the Mount)*

7.   Ask, and it shall be given you; seek, and ye shall find; knock, and it shall be opened unto you;

8.   For every one that asketh receiveth; and he that seeketh findeth; and to him that knocketh it shall be opened.

ASK IN FAITH

Matthew 21:22 *(Jesus to his disciples)*

And all things, whatsoever ye shall ask in prayer, believing, ye shall receive.

Moroni 7:26 *(Mormon quotes Christ's teachings to the Nephites — 400 AD)*

. . .And as sure as Christ liveth he spake these words unto our fathers, saying: Whatsoever thing ye shall ask the Father in my name, which is good, in faith believing that ye shall receive, behold, it shall be done unto you.

WHY WE CLOSE PRAYERS IN THE NAME OF JESUS CHRIST

John 15:16 *(Jesus Christ's instructions to his disciples)*

. . .whatsoever ye shall ask of the Father in my name, he may give it to you.

IF ANY LACK WISDOM LET THEM ASK OF GOD

James 1:5-6 *(Epistle of James, the brother of Christ)*

5. If any of you lack wisdom, let him ask of God, that giveth to all men liberally, and upbraideth not; and it shall be given him.

6. But let him ask in faith, nothing wavering. For he that wavereth is like a wave of the sea driven with the wind and tossed.

POWER OF THE PRAYERS OF THE RIGHTEOUS

James 5:16 *(Writings of James, the brother of Jesus)*

Confess your faults one to another, and pray one for another, that ye may be healed. The effectual fervent prayer of a righteous man availeth much.

Alma 62:40 *(Writing of Helaman, son of Alma, about the Nephite-Lamanite wars — 60 BC)*

. . .because of the prayers of the righteous, they were spared.

THE EVIL SPIRIT TEACHES A MAN NOT TO PRAY

2 Nephi 32:8 *(Nephi's testimony — 545 BC)*

. . .if ye would hearken unto the Spirit which teacheth a man to pray ye would know that ye must pray; for the evil spirit teacheth not a man to pray, but teacheth him that he must not pray.

PRAYER ALONE IS NOT ENOUGH. WE MUST IMPART OF OUR SUBSTANCE AND VISIT THOSE IN NEED.

Alma 34:27-29 *(Amulek's testimony — 74 BC)*

27.   . . .let your hearts be full, drawn out in prayer unto him continually for your welfare, and also for the welfare of those who are around you.

28.   And now behold, my beloved brethren, I say unto you, do not suppose that this is all; for after ye have done all these things, if ye turn away the needy, and the naked, and visit not the sick and afflicted, and impart of your substance, if ye have, to those who stand in need — I say unto you, if ye do not any of these things, behold, your prayer is vain, and

availeth you nothing, and ye are as hypocrites who do deny the faith.

COUNSEL WITH THE LORD MORNING AND NIGHT

Alma 37:37 *(Alma's counsel to his son, Helaman — 73 BC)*

Counsel with the Lord in all thy doings, and he will direct thee for good; yea, when thou liest down at night lie down unto the Lord, that he may watch over you in your sleep; and when thou risest in the morning let thy heart be full of thanks unto God; and if ye do these things, ye shall be lifted up at the last day.

CHRIST TEACHES FAMILY PRAYER

3 Nephi 18:21 *(The resurrected Christ teaches the Nephites — 34 AD)*

Pray in your families unto the Father, always in my name, that your wives and your children may be blessed.

PRAY ALWAYS

D & C 31:12 *(Revelation for Thomas B. Marsh — September, 1830)*

Pray always, lest you enter into temptation and lose your reward.

D & C 93:49 *(Revelation to Joseph Smith — May, 1833)*

. . .pray always lest that wicked one have power in you, and remove you out of your place.

THOSE WHO ASK SHALL RECEIVE REVELATION AND KNOWLEDGE

D & C 42:61 *(Revelation to Joseph Smith — February, 1831)*

If thou shalt ask, thou shalt receive revelation upon revelation, knowledge upon knowledge, that thou mayest know the mysteries and peaceable things — that which bringeth joy, that which bringeth life eternal.

PREPARATION

PREPARE YE THE WAY OF THE LORD

Isaiah 40:3 *(Isaiah prophecies of John the Baptist)*

The voice of him that crieth in the wilderness, Prepare ye the way of the Lord, make straight in the desert a highway for our God.

CHRIST WILL PREPARE THE WAY FOR US

John 14:1-4 *(Christ to his disciples)*

1. Let not your heart be troubled: ye believe in God, believe also in me.

2. In my Father's house are many mansions: if it were not so, I would have told you. I go to prepare a place for you.

3. And if I go and prepare a place for you, I will come again, and receive you unto myself; and where I am, there ye may be also.

4. And whither I go ye know, and the way ye know.

NOW IS THE TIME TO PREPARE TO MEET GOD

Alma 34:32 *(Alma preaching upon the hill Onidah — 74 BC)*

For behold, this life is the time for men to prepare to meet God; yea, behold the day of this life is the day for men to perform their labors.

PREPARE FOR THE COMING OF THE LORD

D & C 1:12 *(Revelation to Joseph Smith — November, 1831)*

Prepare ye, prepare ye for that which is to come, for the Lord is nigh;

PREPARED SHALL NOT FEAR

D & C 38:30 *(Revelation given to Joseph Smith — January, 1831)*

. . .if ye are prepared ye shall not fear.

PREPARE YOURSELF FOR CELESTIAL THINGS

D & C 78:7 *(Revelation to Joseph Smith — March, 1832)*

For if you will that I give unto you a place in the celestial world, you must prepare yourselves by doing the things which I have commanded you and required of you.

THE CHURCH MUST PREPARE TO STAND INDEPENDENTLY

D & C 78:13-15 *(Revelation to Joseph Smith — March, 1832)*

13. Behold, this is the preparation wherewith I prepare you, and the foundation, and the ensample which I give unto you, whereby you may accomplish the commandments which are given you;

14. That through my providence, notwithstanding the tribulation which shall descend upon you, that the church may stand independent above all other creatures beneath the celestial world;

15.   That you may come up unto the crown prepared for you, and be made rulers over many kingdoms, saith the Lord God, the Holy One of Zion, who hath established the foundations of Adam-ondi-Ahman;

PRIESTHOOD

NOT EVERYONE WHO SAYS LORD, LORD, OR PERFORMS MIRACLES IS OF GOD

Matthew 7:21-23 *(Jesus Christ in the Sermon on the Mount)*

21. Not every one that saith unto me Lord, Lord, shall enter into the kingdom of heaven; but he that doeth the will of my Father which is in heaven.

22. Many will say to me in that day, Lord, Lord, have we not prophesied in thy name? and in thy name have cast out devils? and in thy name done many wonderful works?

23. And then will I profess unto them, I never knew you: depart from me, ye that work iniquity.

KEYS TO THE KINGDOM OF HEAVEN

Matthew 16:19 *(Jesus Christ to Peter)*

And I will give unto thee the keys of the kingdom of heaven: and whatsoever thou shalt bind on earth shall be bound in heaven: and whatsoever thou shalt loose on earth shall be loosed in heaven.

MANY CALLED BUT FEW CHOSEN BECAUSE OF WORLDLY ASPIRATIONS

Matthew 22:14 *(also Matthew 20:16) (Jesus Christ to his disciples)*

For many are called, but few are chosen.

D & C 121:34-37 *(Prayers and prophecies of Joseph Smith while a prisoner in Liberty jail, Missouri — March, 1839)*

34. Behold, there are many called, but few are chosen. And why are they not chosen?

35. Because their hearts are set so much upon the things of this world, and aspire to the honors of men, that they do not learn this one lesson —

36. That the rights of the priesthood are inseparably connected with the powers of heaven, and that the powers of heaven cannot be controlled nor handled only upon the principles of righteousness.

37. That they may be conferred upon us, it is true; but when we undertake to cover our sins, or to gratify our pride, our vain ambition, or to exercise control or dominion or compulsion upon the souls of the children of men, in any degree of unrighteousness, behold the heavens withdraw themselves; the Spirit of the Lord is grieved; and when it is withdrawn, Amen to the priesthood or the authority of that man.

GOD SELECTS THOSE WHO RECEIVE THE PRIESTHOOD

John 15:16 *(Jesus Christ's instructions to his disciples)*

Ye have not chosen me, but I have chosen you, and ordained you, that ye should go and bring forth fruit. . .

ADMINISTRATION OF THE SICK

James 5:14-15 *(Epistle of James, the brother of Christ)*

14. Is any sick among you? let him call for the elders of the church; and let them pray over him, anointing him with oil in the name of the Lord:

15. And the prayer of faith shall save the sick, and the Lord shall raise him up; and if he have committed sins, they shall be forgiven him.

A ROYAL PRIESTHOOD

1 Peter 2:9 *(Epistle of Peter to the saints)*

But ye are a chosen generation, a royal priesthood, an holy nation, a peculiar people; that ye should shew forth the praises of him who hath called you out of darkness into his marvellous light.

DEFINITION OF PRIESTCRAFTS

2 Nephi 26:29 *(Nephi's prediction of the last days — 545 BC)*

He commandeth that there shall be no priestcrafts, for; behold, priestcrafts are that men preach and set themselves up for a light unto the world, that they may get gain and praise of the world; but they seek not the welfare of Zion.

WHY THE FIRST PRIESTHOOD IS CALLED THE MELCHIZEDEK PRIESTHOOD

Alma 13:18-19

18. But Melchizedek having exercised mighty faith, and received the office of the high priesthood according to the holy order of God, did preach

repentance unto his people. And behold, they did repent; and Melchizedek did establish peace in the land in his days; therefore he was called the prince of peace, for he was the king of Salem; and he did reign under his father.

19. Now, there were many before him, and also there were many afterwards, but none were greater; therefore, of him they have more particularly made mention.

D & C 107:2-4 *(A revelation on priesthood to Joseph Smith — March, 1835)*

2. Why the first is called the Melchizedek Priesthood is because Melchizedek was such a great high priest.

3. Before his day it was called the Holy Priesthood, after the Order of the Son of God.

4. But out of respect or reverence to the name of the Supreme Being, to avoid the too frequent repetition of his name, they, the church, in ancient days, called that priesthood after Melchizedek, or the Melchizedek Priesthood.

NAME OF THE CHURCH

3 Nephi 27:3,5,8 *(The resurrected Jesus Christ talks to his Nephite disciples — 34 AD)*

3. . . .tell us the name whereby we shall call this church; for there are disputations among the people concerning this matter.

5. Have they not read the scriptures, which say ye must take upon you the name of Christ, which is my name? For by this name shall ye be called at the last day;

8.   And how be it my church save it be called in my name? For if a church be called in Moses' name then it be Moses' church; or if it be called in the name of a man then it be the church of a man; but if it be called in my name then it is my church, if it so be that they are built upon my gospel.

D & C 115:4 *(Revelation to Joseph Smith — April, 1838)*
For thus shall my church be called in the last days, even the Church of Jesus Christ of Latter-day Saints.

RIGHTS OF THE AARONIC PRIESTHOOD

D & C 13 *(Ordination of Joseph Smith and Oliver Cowdery to the Aaronic Priesthood — May 15, 1829)*

Upon you my fellow servants, in the name of Messiah I confer the Priesthood of Aaron, which holds the keys of the ministering of angels, and of the gospel of repentance, and of baptism by immersion for the remission of sins; and this shall never be taken again from the earth, until the sons of Levi do offer again an offering unto the Lord in righteousness.

D & C 84:26-27 *(A revelation on priesthood to Joseph Smith — September, 1832)*

26.   And the lesser . . . priesthood holdeth the key of the ministering of angels and the preparatory gospel;

27.   Which gospel is the gospel of repentance and of baptism, and the remission of sins, and the law of carnal commandments. . .

PRIESTHOOD HOLDERS ARE AGENTS ON THE LORD'S ERRAND

D & C 64:29 *(Revelation to the elders of the Church — September, 1831)*

Wherefore, as ye are agents, ye are on the Lord's errand; and whatever ye do according to the will of the Lord is the Lord's business.

OATH AND COVENANT OF THE PRIESTHOOD

D & C 84:33-40 *(A revelation on the priesthood to Joseph Smith — September, 1832)*

33.   For whoso is faithful unto the obtaining these two priesthoods of which I have spoken, and the magnifying their calling, are sanctified by the Spirit unto the renewing of their bodies.

34.   They become the sons of Moses and of Aaron and the seed of Abraham, and the church and kingdom, and the elect of God.

35.   And also all they who receive this priesthood receive me, saith the Lord.

36.   For he that receiveth my servants receiveth me;

37.   And he that receiveth me receiveth my Father;

38.   And he that receiveth my Father receiveth my Father's kingdom; therefore all that my Father hath shall be given unto him.

39.   And this is according to the oath and covenant which belongeth to the priesthood.

40.   Therefore, all those who receive the priesthood, receive this oath and covenant of my Father, which he cannot break, neither can it be moved.

RIGHTS OF THE MELCHIZEDEK PRIESTHOOD

D & C 107:5,8 *(A revelation on priesthood to Joseph Smith — March, 1835)*

5. All other authorities or offices in the church are appendages to this priesthood.

8. The Melchizedek Priesthood holds the right of presidency, and has power and authority over all the offices in the church in all ages of the world, to administer in spiritual things.

WHY THE SECOND PRIESTHOOD IS CALLED AARONIC PRIESTHOOD

D & C 107:13-14 *(A revelation on priesthood to Joseph Smith — March, 1835)*

13. The second priesthood is called the Priesthood of Aaron, because it was conferred upon Aaron and his seed, throughout all their generations.

14. Why it is called the lesser priesthood is because it is an appendage to the greater, or the Melchizedek Priesthood, and has power in administering outward ordinances.

A BISHOP IS TO ADMINISTER IN ALL TEMPORAL THINGS

D & C 107:68 *(A revelation on priesthood to Joseph Smith — March, 1835)*

Wherefore, the office of a bishop is not equal unto it; for the office of a bishop is in administering all temporal things. . .

EVERY MAN SHOULD ACT DILIGENTLY IN ANY OFFICE HE IS GIVEN

D & C 107:99-100 *(A revelation on priesthood to Joseph Smith — March, 1835)*

99. Wherefore, now let every man learn his duty, and to act in the office in which he is appointed, in all diligence.

100. He that is slothful shall not be counted worthy to stand, and he that learns not his duty and shows himself not approved shall not be counted worthy to stand. Even so. Amen.

PRIESTHOOD SHOULD NOT BE USED UNRIGHTEOUS-LY

D & C 121:39-40 *(Prayers and prophecies of Joseph Smith while a prisoner at Liberty jail, Missouri — March, 1839)*

39. We have learned by said experience that it is the nature and disposition of almost all men, as soon as they get a little authority, as they suppose, they will immediately begin to exercise unrighteous dominion.

40. Hence many are called, but few are chosen.

D & C 121:41-43

41. No power or influence can or ought to be maintained by virtue of the priesthood, only by persuasion, by long-suffering, by gentleness and meekness, and by love unfeigned;

42. By kindness, and pure knowledge, which shall greatly enlarge the soul without hypocrisy, and without guile —

WE BELIEVE IN THE SAME ORGANIZATION AS THE CHURCH OF GOD

Sixth Article of Faith

We believe in the same organization that existed in the Primitive Church, viz., apostles, prophets, pastors, teachers, evangelists, etc.

PRE-MORTAL LIFE

(See Jesus Christ's Pre-mortal Role)

WHEN THE HEAVENS WERE PREPARED

Proverbs 8:27-30 *(Proverb of Solomon, King of Israel)*

27. When he prepared the heavens, I was there: when he set a compass upon the face of the depth:

28. When he established the clouds above: when he strengthened the fountains of the deep:

29. When he gave to the sea his decree, that the waters should not pass his commandment: when he appointed the foundations of the earth:

30. Then I was by him, as one brought up with him: and I was daily his delight, rejoicing always before him;

ORDAINED A PROPHET BEFORE BIRTH

Jeremiah 1:5 *(The Lord speaking to Jeremiah)*

Before I formed thee in the belly I knew thee; and before thou camest forth out of the womb I sanctified thee, and I ordained thee a prophet unto the nations.

CHOSEN BEFORE THE WORLD

Ephesians 1:4 *(Paul to the people of Ephesus)*

According as he hath chosen us in him before the foundation of the world, that we should be holy and without blame before him in love:

43.   Reproving betimes with sharpness, when moved upon by the Holy Ghost; and then showing forth afterwards an increase of love toward him whom thou has reproved, lest he esteem thee to be his enemy;

WAR IN HEAVEN

Revelation 12:7-9 *(Vision of John the Revelator)*

7.   And there was war in heaven: Michael and his angels fought against the dragon; and the dragon fought and his angels,

8.   And prevailed not; neither was their place found any more in heaven.

9.   And the great dragon was cast out, that old serpent, called the Devil, and Satan, which deceiveth the whole world: he was cast out into the earth, and his angels were cast out with him.

ABRAHAM WAS IN THE COUNCIL OF GOD

Abraham 3:22-23 *(Joseph Smith's translation of the ancient scriptures of Abraham)*

22.   Now the Lord has shown unto me, Abraham, the intelligences that were organized before the world was; and among all these there were many of the noble and great ones;

23.   And God saw these souls that they were good, and he stood in the midst of them, and he said: These I will make my rulers; for he stood among those that were spirits, and he saw that they were good; and he said unto me: Abraham, thou art one of them; thou wast chosen before thou wast born.

PRIDE

TENTH COMMANDMENT

Exodus 20:17 *(also Mosiah 13:24 and Deuteronomy 5:21)*
(The Lord to Moses on Mt. Sinai)

Thou shalt not covet thy neighbour's house, thou shalt not covet thy neighbour's wife . . . nor any thing that is thy neighbour's.

THE LORD HATES A PROUD LOOK

Proverbs 6:16-19 *(Proverb of Solomon, King of Israel)*

16.   These six things doth the Lord hate: yea, seven are an abomination unto him:

17.   A proud look, a lying tongue, and hands that shed innocent blood,

18.   An heart that deviseth wicked imaginations, feet that be swift in running to mischief,

19.   A false witness that speaketh lies, and he that soweth discord among brethren.

BEAUTY IS VAIN

Proverbs 31:30 *(Proverb of Solomon, King of Israel)*

Favour is deceitful, and beauty is vain: but a woman that fearth the Lord, she shall be praised.

HONOR GOD WITH YOUR HEART

Isaiah 29:13 *(Isaiah prophesies of the last days)*

Wherefore the Lord said, Forasmuch as this people draw near me with their mouth, and with their lips do honour me, but have removed their heart far from me, and their fear toward me is taught by the precept of men:

Joseph Smith 2:19 *(Jesus Christ speaking to Joseph Smith)*

. . ."they draw near to me with their lips, but their hearts are far from me, they teach for doctrines the commandments of men, having a form of godliness, but they deny the power thereof."

PRIDE IN WORLDLY THINGS

Jeremiah 2:32 *(Teachings of Jeremiah)*

Can a maid forget her ornaments, or a bride her attire? yet my people have forgotten me days without number.

D & C 38:39 *(Revelation to Joseph Smith — January, 1831)*

. . .the riches of the earth are mine to give; but beware of pride, lest ye become as the Nephites of old.

RESULTS OF ATTITUDES

Matthew 6:21 *(Jesus in the Sermon on the Mount)*

For where your treasure is, there will your heart be also.

THE REWARD OF PRIDE AND FOOLISHNESS IS DESTRUCTION

2 Nephi 26:10 *(Nephi's prediction of the last days — 545 BC)*

. . .they sell themselves for naught; for, for the reward of their pride and their foolishness they shall reap destruction. . .

PRIDE OF THE HEART CAN DESTROY THE SOUL

Jacob 2:16 *(Jacob teaches the Nephites — 421 BC)*

. . .O that ye would listen unto the word of his commands, and let not this pride of your hearts destroy your souls!

MEN SHOULD BE EQUAL

Mosiah 27:3-4 *(King Mosiah's proclamation to the Nephites — 120 BC)*

3. . . .that there should be an equality among all men;

4. That they should let no pride nor haughtiness disturb their peace; that every man should esteem his neighbor as himself, laboring with their own hands for their support.

STRIPPED OF PRIDE

Alma 5:28 *(Alma preaches the gospel to the Nephites — 83 BC)*

Behold, are ye stripped of pride? I say unto you, if ye are not ye are not prepared to meet God. Behold ye must prepare quickly; for the kingdom of heaven is soon at hand, and such an one hath not eternal life.

PROCRASTINATION

SEEK THE LORD TODAY

Isaiah 55:6 *(Isaiah exhorts the people to repentance)*

Seek ye the Lord while he may be found, call ye upon him while he is near.

BE READY FOR THE COMING OF THE SAVIOR

Matthew 24:44 *(Jesus Christ to his disciples)*

Therefore be ye also ready: for in such an hour as ye think not the Son of man cometh.

QUICK TO SIN BUT SLOW TO OBEY

1 Nephi 17:45 *(Nephi chastises his brethren — 59 BC)*

Ye are swift to do iniquity but slow to remember the Lord your God. . .

DON'T PROCRASTINATE THE DAY OF REPENTANCE

Alma 34:32-33 *(Amulek's testimony — 74 BC)*

32. For behold, this life is the time for men to prepare to meet God; yea, behold the day of this life is the day for men to perform their labors.

33. . . .do not procrastinate the day of your repentance until the end; for after this day of life, which is given us to prepare for eternity, behold, if we do not improve our time while in this life, then cometh the night of darkness wherein there can be no labor performed.

NO DEATH BED REPENTANCE

Alma 34:34-35 *(Amulek's testimony — 74 BC)*

34. Ye cannot say, when ye are brought to that awful crisis, that I will repent, that I will return to my God. Nay, ye cannot say this; for that same spirit which doth possess your bodies at the time that ye go out of this life, that same spirit will have power to possess your body in that eternal world.

35. For behold, if ye have procrastinated the day of your repentance even until death, behold, ye have become subjected to the spirit of the devil, and he doth seal you his; therefore, the Spirit of the Lord hath withdrawn from you, and hath no place in you, and the devil hath all power over you; and this is the final state of the wicked.

MEN SHOULD DO THINGS WITHOUT BEING TOLD

D & C 58:27 *(Revelation to Joseph Smith — August, 1831)*

Verily I say, men should be anxiously engaged in a good cause, and do many things of their own free will, and bring to pass much righteousness;

PREPARE YOURSELVES

D & C 133:10 *(Revelation to Joseph Smith — November, 1831)*

. . .Prepare yourselves for the great day of the Lord.

PROFANITY

(See Gossip)

NEVER TAKE THE LORD'S NAME IN VAIN

Exodus 20:7 *(also Deuteronomy 5:11 and Mosiah 13:15)*
(Third Commandment)

Thou shalt not take the name of the Lord thy God in
vain; for the Lord will not hold him guiltless that
taketh his name in vain.

D & C 63:61-62 *(Jesus Christ to Joseph Smith — August,
1831)*

61. Wherefore, let all men beware how they take my
name in their lips —

62. For behold, verily I say, that many there be who
are under this condemnation, who use the name of
the Lord, and use it in vain, having not authority.

SWEAR NOT AT ALL

Matthew 5:34-35 *(Jesus Christ in the Sermon on the
Mount)*

34. But I say unto you, Swear not at all; neither by
heaven; for it is God's throne:

35. Nor by the earth; for it is his footstool: . . .

MEN SHALL BE JUDGED BY THEIR SPEECH

Matthew 12:36-37 *(Jesus Christ to the Pharisees)*

36. But I say unto you, That every idle word that
men shall speak, they shall give account thereof in the
day of judgment.

37.   For by the words thou shalt be justified, and by thy words thou shalt be condemned.

SPOKEN WORDS DEFILETH A MAN

Matthew 15:11 *(Jesus Christ to the Pharisees and Scribes)*

Not that which goeth into the mouth defileth a man; but that which cometh out of the mouth, this defileth a man.

THE RELIGIOUS MAN WILL NOT USE PROFANITY

James 1:26 *(Epistle of James, the brother of Christ)*

If any man among you seem to be religious, and bridleth not his tongue, but deceiveth his own heart, this man's religion is vain.

KEEP YOUR THOUGHTS VIRTUOUS

D & C 121:45 *(Prayer and prophecies of Joseph Smith while a prisoner in the Liberty jail, Missouri — March, 1839)*

. . .let virtue garnish thy thoughts unceasingly; then shall thy confidence wax strong in the presence of God; and the doctrine of the priesthood shall distil upon thy soul as the dews from heaven.

PROPHETS

(See Revelation)

GOD WISHES THAT ALL MEN WERE WORTHY TO BE PROPHETS

Numbers 11:29 *(Moses to the people of Israel)*

> . . .would God that all the Lord's people were prophets, and that the Lord would put his spirit upon them!

VOICE OF THE PROPHET IS THE SAME AS THE VOICE OF THE LORD

1 Samuel 8:7 *(The Lord to Samuel)*

> . . .they have not rejected thee, but they have rejected me, that I should not reign over them.

D & C 1:38 *(Revelation given to Joseph Smith — November, 1831, known as the preface to the Doctrine and Covenants)*

> . . .whether by mine own voice or by the voice of my servants, it is the same.

D & C 21:5 *(Revelation to Joseph Smith regarding organization of the Church — April, 1830)*

> For his word ye shall receive, as if from mine own mouth, in all patience and faith.

WHERE THERE IS NO VISION, THE PEOPLE FAIL

Proverbs 29:18 *(Proverb of Solomon, King of Israel)*

> Where there is no vision, the people perish: but he that keepeth the law, happy is he.

WOMEN AND CHILDREN CAN RECEIVE THE WORD OF GOD FROM ANGELS

Joel 2:28-29 *(Joel prophecies about the last days)*

28. And it shall come to pass afterward, that I will pour out my spirit upon all flesh; and your sons and your daughters shall prophesy, your old men shall dream dreams, your young men shall see visions:

29. And also upon the servants and upon the handmaids in those days will I pour out my spirit.

Alma 32:23 *(Alma preaches to the Zoromites — 74 BC)*

And now, he imparteth his word by angels unto men, yea, not only men but women also. Now this is not all; little children do have words given unto them many times which confound the wise and the learned.

GOD REVEALETH SECRETS THROUGH THE PROPHETS

Amos 3:7 *(Teachings of Amos the Prophet)*

Surely the Lord God will do nothing, but he revealeth his secret unto his servants the prophets.

BEWARE OF FALSE PROPHETS

Matthew 7:15 *(also 3 Nephi 14:15) (Jesus Christ in the Sermon on the Mount)*

Beware of false prophets, which come to you in sheep's clothing, but inwardly they are ravening wolves.

A PROPHET IS WITHOUT HONOR IN HIS OWN COUNTRY

Matthew 13:57 *(also Mark 6:4) (Jesus Christ's response when he was rejected in his home town of Nazareth)*

> . . .A prophet is not without honour, save in his own country, and in his own house.

FALSE PROPHETS SHALL TRY TO DECEIVE THE VERY ELECT

Matthew 24:24 *(Jesus Christ to his disciples)*

> For there shall arise false Christs, and false prophets, and shall shew great signs and wonders; insomuch that, if it were possible, they shall deceive the very elect.

PROPHECY COMES FROM HOLY MEN

2 Peter 1:21 *(Epistle of Peter)*

> For the prophecy came not in old time by the will of man: but holy men of God spake as they were moved by the Holy Ghost.

JOSEPH'S PROPHECY ABOUT JOSEPH SMITH

2 Nephi 3:15 *(Lehi explains to his son Joseph the prophecies of old — 570 BC)*

> And his name shall be called after me; and it shall be after the name of his father. And he shall be like unto me; for the thing, which the Lord shall bring forth by his hand, by the power of the Lord shall bring my people unto salvation.

THE PROPHETS HAVE WRITTEN AND TESTIFIED OF CHRIST

Jacob 7:11 *(Jacob confounds Sherem, the Anti-Christ — 421 BC)*

. . .Behold, I say unto you that none of the prophets have written, nor prophesied, save they have spoken concerning this Christ.

DEFINITION OF A SEER

Mosiah 8:16-17 *(Ammon describes a seer to King Limhi — 121 BC)*

16. . . .A seer is a revelator and a prophet also; and a gift which is greater can no man have, except he should posses the power of God, which no man can; yet a man may have great power given him from God.

17. But a seer can know of things which are past, and also of things which are to come, and by them shall all things be revealed, or, rather, shall secret things be made manifest, and hidden things shall come to light, and things which are not known shall be made known by them, and also things shall be made known by them which otherwise could not be known.

VOICE OF THE LORD IS UNTO ALL MEN

D & C 1:2 *(Revelation given to Joseph Smith — November, 1831, known as the preface to the Doctrine and Covenants)*

For verily the voice of the Lord is unto all men, and there is none to escape; and there is no eye that shall not see, neither ear that shall not hear, neither heart that shall not be penetrated.

THE LORD'S CALL TO JOSEPH SMITH

D & C 1:17 *(Revelation given to Joseph Smith — November, 1831, known as the preface to the Doctrine and Covenants)*

Wherefore, I the Lord, knowing the calamity which should come upon the inhabitants of the earth, called upon my servant Joseph Smith, Jun., and spake unto him from heaven, and gave him commandments.

HOW IMPORTANT WAS THE WORK OF JOSEPH SMITH

D & C 135:3 *(See History of the Church, vol. 6, p. 612)*

Joseph Smith, the Prophet and Seer of the Lord, has done more, save Jesus only, for the salvation of men in this world, than any other man that ever lived in it. In the short space of twenty years, he has brought forth the Book of Mormon, which he translated by the gift and power of God, and has been the means of publishing it on two continents; has sent the fulness of the everlasting gospel, which it contained, to the four quarters of the earth; has brought forth the revelations and commandments which compose this book of Doctrine and Covenants, and many other wise documents and instructions for the benefit of the children of men; gathered many thousands of the Latter-day Saints, founded a great city, and left a fame and name that cannot be slain. He lived great, and he died great in the eyes of God and his people; and like most of the Lord's anointed in ancient times, has sealed his mission and his works with his own blood; and so has his brother Hyrum. In life they were not divided, and in death they were not separated!

QURPOSE OF LIFE

(See Preparation)

LIFE IS A PROBATIONARY TIME

Alma 12:24 *(Alma speaking to the people — 82 BC)*

And we see that death comes upon mankind, yea, the death which has been spoken of by Amulek, which is the temporal death; nevertheless there was a space granted unto man in which he might repent; therefore this life became a probationary state; a time to prepare to meet God; a time to prepare for that endless state which has been spoken of by us, which is after the resurrection of the dead.

LIFE IS A TIME TO PREPARE

Alma 34:32 *(Amulek's testimony — 74 BC)*

For behold, this life is the time for men to prepare to meet God; yea, behold the day of this life is the day for men to perform their labors.

LIFE IS A TIME OF TESTING

Abraham 3:25-26 *(The Lord to Abraham)*

25. And we will prove them herewith, to see if they will do all things whatsoever the Lord their God shall command them;

26. And they who keep their first estate shall be added upon; and they who keep not their first estate shall not have glory in the same kingdom with those who keep their first estate; and they who keep their second estate shall have glory added upon their heads for ever and ever.

℞ECORDS

(See Genealogy, Judgment)

NAMES OF THE RIGHTEOUS IN THE BOOK OF LIFE

Alma 5:57-58 *(Alma calls the people to repentance — 83 BC)*

57. . . .The names of the wicked shall not be mingled with the names of my people;

58. For the names of the righteous shall be written in the book of life, and unto them will I grant an inheritance at my right hand.

CHRIST CHASTISES NEPHI FOR NOT KEEPING ACCURATE RECORDS

3 Nephi 23:7-13 *(The resurrected Jesus Christ talks to the Nephites — 34 AD)*

7. . . .Bring forth the record which ye have kept.

8. And when Nephi had brought forth the records and laid them before him, he cast his eyes upon them and said:

9. Verily I say unto you, I commanded my servant Samuel, the Lamanite, that he should testify unto this people, . . . Was it not so?

10. And his disciples answered him and said: Yea, Lord, Samuel did prophesy according to thy words, and they were all fulfilled.

11. And Jesus said unto them: How be it that ye have not written this thing? . . .

12. . . . .Nephi remembered that this thing had not been written.

13. And it came to pass that Jesus commanded that it should be written; therefore it was written according as he commanded.

PEOPLE WILL BE JUDGED FROM THE RECORDS

3 Nephi 27:25-26 *(Jesus Christ admonishes the saints to keep records — 34 AD)*

25. For behold, out of the books which have been written, and which shall be written, shall this people be judged, for by them shall their works be known unto men.

26. And behold, all things are written by the Father; therefore out of the books which shall be written shall the world be judged.

THE LORD COMMANDS JOSEPH SMITH TO KEEP RECORDS

D & C 21:1 *(Revelation given at the organization of the Church — April 6, 1830)*

Behold, there shall be a record kept among you; . . .

IF RECORDS ARE NOT KEPT PROPERLY ON EARTH, THEY WILL NOT BE COMPLETE IN HEAVEN

D & C 128:8 *(Epistle from Joseph Smith to the saints in Nauvoo — September, 1842)*

. . .whatsoever you record on earth shall be recorded in heaven, and whatsoever you do not record on earth shall not be recorded in heaven; for out of the books shall your dead be judged, according to their own works.

REPENTANCE

(See Forgiveness, Obedience, and Sin)

CHRIST CAME TO CALL SINNERS TO REPENTANCE

Matthew 9:12-13 *(Jesus Christ's response to the Pharisees)*

12. . . .They that be whole need not a physician, but they that are sick.

13. . . .for I am not come to call the righteous, but sinners to repentance.

REPENT THAT SINS MAY BE BLOTTED OUT

Acts 3:19 *(Peter preaches to the people)*

Repent ye therefore, and be converted, that your sins may be blotted out, when the times of refreshing shall come from the presence of the Lord.

GODLY SORROW WORKETH REPENTANCE

2 Corinthians 7:10 *(Paul's second epistle to the saints at Corinth)*

For godly sorrow worketh repentance to salvation not to be repented of: but the sorrow of the world worketh death.

REPENT OF SINS AND FORSAKE THEM

Mosiah 4:10 *(King Benjamin's address — 124 BC)*

And again, believe that ye must repent of your sins and forsake them, and humble yourselves before

God; and ask in sincerity of heart that he would
forgive you; and now, if you believe all these things
see that ye do them.

NO DEATH BED REPENTANCE

Alma 34:34-35 *(Amulek's testimony — 74 BC)*

34.   Ye cannot say, when ye are brought to that
awful crisis, that I will repent, that I will return to my
God. Nay, ye cannot say this; for that same spirit
which doth possess your bodies at the time that ye go
out of this life, that same spirit will have power to
possess your body in that eternal world.

35.   For behold, if ye have procrastinated the day of
your repentance even until death, behold, ye have
become subjected to the spirit of the devil, and he
doth seal you his; therefore, the Spirit of the Lord
hath withdrawn from you, and hath no place in you,
and the devil hath all power over you; and this is the
final state of the wicked.

MERCY CANNOT ROB JUSTICE

Alma 42:25 *(Alma's discourse on repentance given to his son, Corianton — 73 BC)*

What, do ye suppose that mercy can rob justice? I say
unto you, Nay; not one whit. If so, God would cease
to be God.

THE INWARD VESSEL SHALL BE CLEANSED FIRST, THEN THE OUTER VESSEL

Alma 60:23 *(Moroni, the great Nephite general, writes to Pahoran, the chief judge — 62 BC)*

. . .God has said that the inward vessel shall be cleansed first, and then shall the outer vessel be cleansed also.

THE NEPHITE DISSENTERS SHOWED TRUE REPENTANCE

Helaman 5:17 *(Nephi and Lehi convert Lamanites and dissenters from the Nephites — 30 BC)*

. . .they came forth and did confess their sins and were baptized unto repentance, and immediately returned to the Nephites to endeavor to repair unto them the wrongs which they had done.

REPENT FOR THE KINGDOM OF HEAVEN IS AT HAND

Helaman 5:32 *(A voice from heaven to the Lamanites who held Nephi and Lehi, the sons of Helaman, captive — 30 BC)*

And behold the voice came again, saying: Repent ye, repent ye, for the kingdom of heaven is at hand. . .

AS OFTEN AS PEOPLE REPENT AND SEEK FORGIVENESS, THEY ARE FORGIVEN

Moroni 6:8 *(Moroni regarding Church membership — 421 AD)*

But as oft as they repented and sought forgiveness, with real intent, they were forgiven.

THE UNREPENTANT SHALL LOSE THE LIGHT OF THE GOSPEL

D & C 1:32-33 *(Revelation to Joseph Smith — November, 1831)*

32.   Nevertheless, he that repents and does the commandments of the Lord shall be forgiven;

33.   And he that repents not, from him shall be taken even the light which he has received; for my Spirit shall not always strive with man, saith the Lord of Hosts.

THE WORTH OF A SOUL IS GREAT

D & C 18:10,13,15-16 *(Revelation to Joseph Smith, Oliver Cowdery, and David Whitmer — June, 1829)*

10.   Remember the worth of souls is great in the sight of God;

13.   And how great is his joy in the soul that repenteth!

15.   And if it so be that you should labor all your days in crying repentance unto this people, and bring, save it be one soul unto me, how great shall be your joy with him in the kingdom of my Father!

16.   And now, if your joy will be great with one soul that you have brought unto me into the kingdom of my Father, how great will be your joy if you should bring many souls unto me!

MAN MUST REPENT OR SUFFER

D & C 19:4,16-18 *(Revelation to Joseph Smith — March, 1830)*

4. And surely every man must repent or suffer. . .

16. For behold, I, God, have suffered these things for all, that they might not suffer if they would repent;

17. But if they would not repent they must suffer even as I;

18. Which suffering caused myself, even God, the greatest of all, to tremble because of pain, and to bleed at every pore, and to suffer both body and spirit — and would that I might not drink the bitter cup, and shrink. . .

THE LORD WILL NOT REMEMBER THE SINS OF THE REPENTANT

D & C 58:42 *(Revelation to Joseph Smith — August, 1831)*

Behold, he who has repented of his sins, the same is forgiven, and I, the Lord, remember them no more.

TRUE REPENTANCE REQUIRES CONFESSING AND FORSAKING SIN

D & C 58:43 *(Revelation to Joseph Smith — August, 1831)*

By this ye may know if a man repenteth of his sins — behold, he will confess them and forsake them.

HE WHO FORSAKES HIS SINS AND OBEYS THE COMMANDMENTS SHALL SEE JESUS CHRIST FACE TO FACE

D & C 93:1 *(Revelation to Joseph Smith — May, 1833)*

. . .It shall come to pass that every soul who forsaketh his sins and cometh unto me, and calleth on my name, and obeyeth my voice, and keepeth my commandments, shall see my face and know that I am.

THE LORD CHASTENS THOSE WHOM HE LOVES SO THEY MIGHT REPENT AND BE FORGIVEN

D & C 95:1 *(Revelation to Joseph Smith — June, 1833)*

. . .whom I love I also chasten that their sins may be forgiven, for with the chastisement I prepare a way for their deliverance in all things out of temptation, and I have loved you.

BE CLEAN

D & C 133:5 *(Revelation to Joseph Smith — November, 1831)*

. . .Be ye clean that bear the vessels of the Lord.

REPENTANCE IS ONE OF THE FIRST PRINCIPLES OF THE GOSPEL

Fourth Article of Faith

We believe that the first principles and ordinances of the Gospel are: first, Faith in the Lord Jesus Christ; second, Repentance; third, Baptism by immersion for the remission of sins; fourth, Laying on of hands for the gift of the Holy Ghost.

ℜESURRECTION

(See Atonement, Death, Funeral Messages,
Jesus Christ's Resurrection)

TESTIMONIES THAT JESUS LIVES

Job 19:25-27 *(Teachings of Job)*

25. For I know that my redeemer liveth, and that he shall stand at the latter day upon the earth:

26. And though after my skin worms destroy this body, yet in my flesh shall I see God:

27. Whom I shall see for myself, and mine eyes shall behold, and not another; though my reins be consumed within me.

D & C 76:22-23 *(Vision of Jesus Christ to Joseph Smith and Sidney Rigdon — February, 1832)*

22. And now, after the many testimonies which have been given of him, this is the testimony, last of all, which we give of him: That he lives!

23. For we saw him, even on the right hand of God; and we heard the voice bearing record that he is the Only Begotten of the Father.

BODY RETURNS TO DUST, BUT THE SPIRIT TO GOD

Ecclesiastes 12:7 *(Words of Ecclesiastes, son of David)*

Then shall the dust return to the earth as it was: and the spirit shall return unto God who gave it.

UPON CHRIST'S RESURRECTION THE GRAVES WERE OPENED

Matthew 27:52-53 *(Matthew's account of the resurrection)*

52. And the graves were opened; and many bodies of the saints which slept arose,

53. And came out of the graves after his resurrection, and went into the holy city, and appeared unto many.

RESURRECTION MORNING

Luke 24:1-7 *(Experiences of Mary Magdalene and the other women when they went to the sepulchre)*

1. Now upon the first day of the week, very early in the morning, they came unto the sepulchre, bringing the spices which they had prepared, and certain others with them.

2. And they found the stone rolled away from the sepulchre.

3. And they entered in, and found not the body of the Lord Jesus.

4. And it came to pass, as they were much perplexed thereabout, behold, two men stood by them in shining garments:

5. And as they were afraid, and bowed down their faces to the earth, they said unto them, Why seek ye the living among the dead?

6. He is not here, but is risen: remember how he spake unto you when he was yet in Galilee,

7.   Saying, The Son of man must be delivered into the hands of sinful men, and be crucified, and the third day rise again.

A RESURRECTED BODY HAS FLESH AND BONES

Luke 24:36-39 *(Christ to his disciples after the resurrection)*

36.   And as they thus spake, Jesus himself stood in the midst of them, and saith unto them, Peace be unto you.

37.   But they were terrified and affrighted, and supposed that they had seen a spirit.

38.   And he said unto them, Why are ye troubled? and why do thoughts arise in your hearts?

39.   Behold my hands and my feet, that it is I myself: handle me, and see; for a spirit hath not flesh and bones, as ye see me have.

RESURRECTION OF LIFE AND RESURRECTION OF DAMNATION

John 5:28-29 *(Jesus to his disciples)*

28.   Marvel not at this: for the hour is coming, in the which all that are in the graves shall hear his voice,

29.   And shall come forth; they that have done good, unto the resurrection of life; and they that have done evil, unto the resurrection of damnation.

CHRIST IS THE RESURRECTION AND THE LIFE

John 11:25-26 *(Jesus' comments to Martha just before he raised Lazarus from the dead)*

25. Jesus said unto her, I am the resurrection, and the life: he that believeth in me, though he were dead, yet shall he live:

26. And whosoever liveth and believeth in me shall never die. . .

WE SHALL BE LIKE GOD

1 John 3:2 *(Epistle of John the Revelator)*

Beloved, now are we the sons of God, and it doth not yet appear what we shall be: but we know that, when he shall appear, we shall be like him; for we shall see him as he is.

Moroni 7:48 *(Mormon's teachings to his son Moroni — 400 AD)*

. . .pray unto the Father with all the energy of heart . . . that ye may become the sons of God; that when he shall appear we shall be like him, for we shall see him as he is . . .

ATTITUDES AREN'T CHANGED BY THE RESURRECTION

2 Nephi 9:16 *(Jacob's teachings on atonement — 559 BC)*

. . .the Lord God hath spoken it, and it is his eternal word, which cannot pass away, that they who are righteous shall be righteous still, and they who are filthy shall be filthy still; wherefore,they who are filthy are the devil and his angels; and they shall go away into everlasting fire; prepared for them; . . .

THE BODY SHALL BE RESTORED TO ITS PERFECT FRAME

Alma 40:23 *(Alma to his son Corianton — 73 BC)*

The soul shall be restored to the body, and the body to the soul; yea, and every limb and joint shall be restored to its body; yea, even a hair of the head shall not be lost; but all things shall be restored to their proper and perfect frame.

RESURRECTION IS REDEMPTION OF THE SOUL

D & C 88:15-16 *(Revelation to Joseph Smith — December, 1832)*

15. And the spirit and the body are the soul of man.

16. And the resurrection from the dead is the redemption of the soul.

SPIRIT AND BODY MUST BE RESURRECTED TO RECEIVE FULNESS OF JOY

D & C 93:33-34 *(Revelation to Joseph Smith — May, 1833)*

33. For man is spirit. The elements are eternal, and spirit and element, inseparably connected, receive a fulness of joy;

34. And when separated, man cannot receive a fulness of joy.

JOSEPH SMITH'S DESCRIPTION OF MORONI

Joseph Smith 2:32 *(Joseph Smith tells his own story)*

Not only was his robe exceedingly white, but his whole person was glorious beyond description. . .

℞EVELATION

(See Holy Ghost, Prophets)

GOD REVEALS SECRETS THROUGH THE PROPHETS

Amos 3:7 *(Teachings of Amos the Prophet)*

Surely the Lord God will do nothing, but he revealeth his secret unto his servants the prophets.

PETER KNEW OF CHRIST'S DIVINITY THROUGH REVELATION

Matthew 16:13,16,17 *(Jesus speaks to his disciples)*

13. When Jesus came into the coasts of Caesarea Philippi, he asked his disciples, saying, Whom do men say that I the Son of man am?

16. And Simon Peter answered and said, Thou art the Christ, the Son of the living God.

17. And Jesus answered and said unto him, Blessed art thou, Simon Bar-jona: for flesh and blood hath not revealed it unto thee, but my Father which is in heaven.

THERE IS NOTHING HID WHICH SHALL NOT BE MANIFEST

Mark 4:22-24 *(Jesus Christ talks to a multitude from a ship)*

22. For there is nothing hid, which shall not be manifested; neither was any thing kept secret, but that it should come abroad.

23. If any man have ears to hear, let him hear.

24. . . .Take heed what ye hear: with what measure ye mete, it shall be measured to you: and unto you that hear shall more be given.

MAN WILL RECEIVE WISDOM ONLY AS HE IS PREPARED

D & C 111:11 *(Revelation to Joseph Smith — August, 1836)*

Therefore, be ye as wise as serpents and yet without sin; and I will order all things for your good, as fast as ye are able to receive them.

WE BELIEVE IN REVELATION

Ninth Article of Faith

We believe all that God has revealed, all that He does now reveal, and we believe that He will yet reveal many great and important things pertaining to the Kingdom of God.

$\mathcal{S}$ABBATH DAY

KEEP THE SABBATH DAY HOLY

Exodus 20:8-10 *(also Deuteronomy 5:12-14 and Mosiah 13:16-19) (fourth Commandment given to Moses on Mt. Sinai)*

8. Remember the sabbath day, to keep it holy.

9. Six days shalt thou labour, and do all thy work:

10. But the seventh day is the sabbath of the Lord thy God: in it thou shalt not do any work, thou, nor thy son, nor thy daughter, thy manservant, nor thy maidservant, nor thy cattle, nor thy stranger that is within thy gates.

CHRIST IS LORD OF THE SABBATH; THEREFORE GOOD ACTS ARE ACCEPTABLE

Matthew 12:8,12 *(Jesus Christ to the Pharisees)*

8. For the Son of man is Lord even of the sabbath day.

12. . . .Wherefore it is lawful to do well on the sabbath days.

SABBATH IS FOR MAN

Mark 2:27-29 *(Christ to the Pharisees)*

27. And he said unto them, The sabbath was made for man, and not man for the sabbath:

28. Therefore the Son of man is Lord also of the sabbath.

WE SHOULD ATTEND CHURCH ON SUNDAY, BUT WORSHIP GOD EVERY DAY

D & C 59:9-13 *(Revelation to Joseph Smith — August, 1831)*

9. And that thou mayest more fully keep thyself unspotted from the world, thou shalt go to the house of prayer and offer up thy sacraments upon my holy day;

10. For verily this is a day appointed unto you to rest from your labors, and to pay thy devotions unto the Most High;

11. Nevertheless thy vows shall be offered up in righteousness on all days and at all times;

12. But remember that on this, the Lord's day, thou shalt offer thine oblations and thy sacraments unto the Most High, confessing thy sins unto thy brethren, and before the Lord.

13. And on this day thou shalt do none other thing, only let thy food be prepared with singleness of heart that thy fasting may be perfect, or, in other words, that thy joy may be full.

GOD BLESSED THE SEVENTH DAY AS A DAY OF REST

Moses 3:3 *(The Lord to Moses)*

And I, God, blessed the seventh day, and sanctified it; because that in it I had rested from all my work which I, God, had created and made.

$\mathcal{S}$ACRAMENT

SYMBOLISM OF THE SACRAMENT

Luke 22:19-20 *(also Matthew 26:26-28) (Christ at the last supper)*

19. And he took bread, and gave thanks, and brake it, and gave unto them, saying, This is my body which is given for you: this do in remembrance of me.

20. Likewise also the cup after supper, saying, This cup is the new testament in my blood, which is shed for you.

DO NOT TAKE THE SACRAMENT UNWORTHILY

3 Nephi 18:29 *(also 1 Corinthians 11:23-30) (The resurrected Jesus Christ to the Nephites — 34 AD)*

For whoso eateth and drinketh my flesh and blood unworthily eateth and drinketh damnation to his soul; therefore if ye know that a man is unworthy to eat and drink of my flesh and blood ye shall forbid him.

PRAYER ON THE BREAD

D & C 20:77 *(also Moroni 4:3) (Revelation of Church Organization and Government given to Joseph Smith — April, 1830)*

O God, the Eternal Father, we ask thee in the name of thy Son, Jesus Christ, to bless and sanctify this bread to the souls of all those who partake of it, that they may eat in remembrance of the body of thy Son, and witness unto thee, O God, the Eternal Father, that they are willing to take upon them the name of thy Son, and always remember him and keep his commandments which he has given them; that they may always have his Spirit to be with them. Amen.

PRAYER ON THE WATER

D & C 20:79 *(also Moroni 5:2) (Revelation of Church Organization and Government given to Joseph Smith — April, 1830)*

O God, the Eternal Father, we ask thee in the name of thy Son, Jesus Christ, to bless and sanctify this wine (water) to the souls of all those who drink of it, that they may do it in remembrance of the blood of thy Son, which was shed for them; that they may witness unto thee, O God, the Eternal Father, that they do always remember him, that they may have his Spirit to be with them. Amen.

WHY WE USE WATER, NOT WINE

D & C 27:2-3 *(Revelation to Joseph Smith — August, 1830)*

2. For, behold, I say unto you, that it mattereth not what ye shall eat or what ye shall drink when ye partake of the sacrament, if it so be that ye do it with an eye single to my glory — remembering unto the Father my body which was laid down for you, and my blood which was shed for the remission of your sins.

3. Wherefore, a commandment I give unto you, that you shall not purchase wine neither strong drink of your enemies.

$\mathcal{S}$ACRIFICE

TO OBEY IS BETTER THAN SACRIFICE

1 Samuel 15:22 *(Samuel to King Saul)*

And Samuel said, Hath the Lord as great delight in burnt offerings and sacrifices, as in obeying the voice of the Lord? Behold, to obey is better than sacrifice, and to hearken than the fat of rams.

BLOOD SACRIFICE ENDED WITH CHRIST

3 Nephi 9:19-20 *(Jesus to the Nephites — 34 AD)*

19. And ye shall offer up unto me no more the shedding of blood; yea, your sacrifices and your burnt offerings shall be done away, for I will accept none of your sacrifices and your burnt offerings.

20. And ye shall offer for a sacrifice unto me a broken heart and a contrite spirit. And whoso cometh unto me with a broken heart and a contrite spirit, him will I baptize with fire and with the Holy Ghost, even as the Lamanites, because of their faith in me at the time of their conversion, were baptized with fire and with the Holy Ghost, and they knew it not.

BLESSINGS THROUGH FAITHFULNESS IN TRIBULATION

D & C 58:2-7 *(Revelation to Joseph Smith — August, 1831)*

2. For verily I say unto you, blessed is he that keepeth my commandments, whether in life or in

death; and he that is faithful in tribulation, the reward of the same is greater in the kingdom of heaven.

3.   Ye cannot behold with your natural eyes, for the present time, the design of your God concerning those things which shall come hereafter, and the glory which shall follow after much tribulation.

4.   For after much tribulation come the blessings. Wherefore the day cometh that ye shall be crowned with much glory; the hour is not yet, but is nigh at hand.

5.   Remember this, which I tell you before, that you may lay it to heart, and receive that which is to follow.

6.   Behold, verily I say unto you, for this cause I have sent you — that you might be obedient, and that your hearts might be prepared to bear testimony of the things which are to come;

7.   And also that you might be honored in laying the foundation, and in bearing record of the land upon which the Zion of God shall stand;

ALL THINGS GIVE US EXPERIENCE

D & C 122:7-8 *(The Lord to Joseph Smith while a prisoner in jail at Liberty, Missouri — March, 1839)*

7.   And if thou shouldst be cast into the pit, or into the hands of murderers, and the sentence of death passed upon thee; if thou be cast into the deep; if the billowing surge conspire against thee; if fierce winds become thine enemy; if the heavens gather blackness, and all the elements combine to hedge up the way; and above all, if the very jaws of hell shall gape open

the mouth wide after thee, know thou, my son, that all these things shall give thee experience, and shall be for thy good.

8.   The Son of Man hath descended below them all. Art thou greater than he?

ADAM'S SACRIFICE

Moses 5:5-9 *(The Lord explains Adam's faithfulness to Moses)*

5.   And he gave unto them commandments, that they should worship the Lord their God, and should offer the firstlings of their flocks, for an offering unto the Lord. And Adam was obedient unto the commandments of the Lord.

6.   And after many days an angel of the Lord appeared unto Adam, saying: Why dost thou offer sacrifices unto the Lord? And Adam said unto him: I know not, save the Lord commanded me.

7.   And then the angel spake, saying: This thing is a similitude of the sacrifice of the Only Begotten of the Father, which is full of grace and truth.

8.   Wherefore, thou shalt do all that thou doest in the name of the Son, and thou shalt repent and call upon God in the name of the Son forevermore.

9.   And in that day the Holy Ghost fell upon Adam, which beareth record of the Father and the Son, saying: I am the Only Begotten of the Father from the beginning, henceforth and forever, that as thou hast fallen thou mayest be redeemed, and all mankind, even as many as will.

𝔖ATAN

WHY SATAN FELL FROM HEAVEN

Isaiah 14:12-15 *(also D & C 76:25-31) (Isaiah's vision of pre-mortal life)*

12. How art thou fallen from heaven, O Lucifer, son of the morning! how art thou cut down to the ground, which didst weaken the nations!

13. For thou hast said in thine heart, I will ascend into heaven, I will exalt my throne above the stars of God: I will sit also upon the mount of the congregation, in the sides of the north:

14. I will ascend above the heights of the clouds; I will be like the most High.

15. Yet thou shalt be brought down to hell, to the sides of the pit.

Moses 4:1-4 *(The Lord explains pre-mortal life to Moses)*

1. And I, the Lord God, spake unto Moses, saying: That Satan, whom thou hast commanded in the name of mine Only Begotten, is the same which was from the beginning, and he came before me, saying — Behold, here am I, send me, I will be thy son, and I will redeem all mankind, that one soul shall not be lost, and surely I will do it; wherefore give me thine honor.

2. But, behold, my Beloved Son, which was my Beloved and Chosen from the beginning, said unto

me — Father, thy will be done, and the glory be thine forever.

3. Wherefore, because that Satan rebelled against me, and sought to destroy the agency of man, which I, the Lord God, had given him, and also, that I should give unto him mine own power; by the power of mine Only Begotten, I caused that he should be cast down;

4. And he became Satan, yea, even the devil, the father of all lies, to deceive and blind men, and to lead them captive at his will, even as many as would not hearken unto my voice.

THE DEVIL WANTS MEN TO BE AS MISERABLE AS HIMSELF

2 Nephi 2:27 *(Lehi's teachings to his son, Jacob — 570 BC)*

Wherefore, men are free according to the flesh; and all things are given them which are expedient unto man. And they are free to choose liberty and eternal life, through the great mediation of all men, or to choose captivity and death, according to the captivity and power of the devil; for he seeketh that all men might be miserable like unto himself.

THE DEVIL CHEATETH THEIR SOULS AND CAREFULLY LEADS THEM TO HELL

2 Nephi 28:21 *(Nephi's testimony — 545 BC)*

. . .thus the devil cheateth their souls, and leadeth them away carefully down to hell.

SATAN GAINS CONTROL OF THE HEARTS OF THE WICKED

Alma 10:25 *(Amulek chastises the lawyer, Zeezrom — 82 BC)*

. . .O ye wicked and perverse generation, why hath Satan got such great hold upon your hearts? Why will ye yield yourselves unto him that he may have power over you, to blind your eyes, that ye will not understand the words which are spoken, according to their truth?

THE DEVIL CAN APPEAR AS AN ANGEL

Alma 30:53 *(Korihor, the anti-Christ, explains how he was deceived by the devil — 74 BC)*

But behold, the devil hath deceived me; for he appeared unto me in the form of an angel. . .

THE DEVIL SPEEDILY DRAGS HIS CHILDREN DOWN TO HELL

Alma 30:60 *(Alma explains how Korihor, the anti-Christ, was deceived by the deveil — 74 BC)*

. . .the devil will not support his children at the last day, but doth speedily drag them down to hell.

SATAN IS THE AUTHOR OF SIN

Helaman 6:30 *(Writing of Nephi, son of Helaman — 24 BC)*

And behold, it is he (Satan) who is the author of all sin. . .

THE DEVIL IS AN ENEMY OF GOD

Moroni 7:12,17 *(Mormon's writings — 400 AD)*

12.   Wherefore, all things which are good cometh of God; and that which is evil cometh of the devil; for the devil is an enemy unto God, and fighteth against him continually, and inviteth and enticeth to sin, and to do that which is evil continually.

17.   But whatsoever thing persuadeth men to do evil, and believe not in Christ, and deny him, and serve not God, then ye may know with a perfect knowledge it is of the devil; for after this manner doth the devil work, for he persuadeth no man to do good, no, not one; neither do his angels; neither do they who subject themselves unto him.

SATAN CAN BE CONQUERED THROUGH PRAYER

D & C 10:5 *(Revelation to Joseph Smith — Summer, 1828)*

Pray always, that you may come off conqueror; yea, that you may conquer Satan, and that you may escape the hands of the servants of Satan that do uphold his work.

ADAM'S CHILDREN LOVE SATAN MORE THAN GOD

Moses 5:13 *(Moses records the early history of the earth)*

And Satan came among them, saying: I am also a son of God; and he commanded them, saying: Believe it not; and they believed it not, and they loved Satan more than God. And men began from that time forth to be carnal, sensual, and devilish.

SCRIPTURES

(See Bible and Book of Mormon)

MAN SHALL NOT LIVE BY BREAD ALONE

Matthew 4:4 *(also Deuteronomy 8:3) (Jesus Christ to Satan during Jesus' four-day fast)*

. . .Man shall not live by bread alone, but by every word that proceedeth out of the mouth of God.

IF PEOPLE WON'T ACCEPT THE SCRIPTURES, THEY WOULDN'T ACCEPT AN ANGEL

Luke 16:31 *(Parable of the rich man who wanted to return to his family and tell them to listen to the Gospel message)*

And he said unto him, If they hear not Moses and the prophets, neither will they be persuaded, though one rose from the dead.

SEARCH THE SCRIPTURES

John 5:39 *(Jesus Christ to the multitudes)*

Search the scriptures; for in them ye think ye have eternal life: and they are they which testify of me.

PURPOSE OF THE SCRIPTURES

2 Timothy 3:16-17 *(Paul to Timothy)*

16. All scripture is given by inspiration of God, and is profitable for doctrine, for reproof, for correction, for instruction in righteousness:

17. That the man of God may be perfect, thoroughly furnished unto all good works.

1 Nephi 19:23 *(Nephi to his brethren — 570 BC)*

. . .for I did liken all scriptures unto us, that it might be for our profit and learning.

2 Nephi 4:15 *(Nephi's prayer — 570 BC)*

. . .For my soul delighteth in the scriptures, and my heart pondereth them, and writeth them for the learning and the profit of my children.

Mormon 9:31 *(Moroni's testimony of the scriptures — 421 AD)*

. . .that ye may learn to be more wise than we have been.

NO SCRIPTURE IS OF PRIVATE INTERPRETATION

2 Peter 1:20-21 *(Epistle of Peter)*

20. . . .no prophecy of the scripture is of any private interpretation.

21. For the prophecy came not in old time by the will of man: but holy men of God spake as they were moved by the Holy Ghost.

THE SCRIPTURES TESTIFY OF JESUS

Alma 33:14 *(Alma's discourse — 74 BC)*

Now behold, my brethren, I would ask if ye have read the scriptures? If ye have, how can ye disbelieve on the Son of God?

THE BOOK OF MORMON IS NOT A COMPLETE HISTORY

3 Nephi 26:6 *(Mormon's comment regarding which of Christ's teachings should be included — 400 AD)*

And now there cannot be written in this book even a hundredth part of the things which Jesus did truly teach unto the people.

WHAT THE GENERAL AUTHORITIES SPEAK BY THE POWER OF THE HOLY GHOST IS SCRIPTURE

D & C 68:4 *(Revelation to Joseph Smith — November, 1831)*

And whatsoever they shall speak when moved upon by the Holy Ghost shall be scripture, shall be the will of the Lord, shall be the mind of the Lord, shall be the word of the Lord, shall be the voice of the Lord, and the power of God unto salvation.

IMPACT OF SCRIPTURE ON JOSEPH SMITH

Joseph Smith 2:12 *(Joseph Smith tells his own story)*

Never did any passage of scripture come with more power to the heart of man than this did at this time to mine. It seemed to enter with great force into every feeling of my heart. I reflected on it again and again, knowing that if any person needed wisdom from God, I did; for how to act I did not know, and unless I could get more wisdom than I then had, I would never know; for the teachers of religion of the different sects understood the same passages of scripture so differently as to destroy all confidence in settling the question by an appeal to the Bible.

ERVICE

CHOOSE WHOM YOU WILL SERVE

Joshua 24:15 *(Joshua speaking to the tribes of Israel)*

. . .choose you this day whom ye will serve; . . . but as for me and my house, we will serve the Lord.

LET YOUR LIGHT SO SHINE

Matthew 5:16 *(Jesus Christ in the Sermon on the Mount)*

Let your light so shine before men, that they may see your good works, and glorify your Father which is in heaven.

JESUS ASKED US TO GO THE SECOND MILE

Matthew 5:41 *(Jesus Christ in the Sermon on the Mount)*

And whosoever shall compel thee to go a mile, go with him twain.

THE GOLDEN RULE

Matthew 7:12 *(also Luke 6:31) (Jesus Christ in the Sermon on the Mount)*

. . .whatsoever ye would that men should do to you, do ye even so to them. . .

HE THAT LOSES HIS LIFE SHALL FIND IT

Matthew 16:25-26 *(also Matthew 10:39) (Jesus Christ unto his disciples)*

25. For whosoever will save his life shall lose it: and whosoever will lose his life for my sake shall find it.

26. For what is a man profited, if he shall gain the whole world, and lose his own soul? or what shall a man give in exchange for his soul?

THE GREATEST SHALL BE THE SERVANT

Matthew 23:11 *(also Matthew 20:27) (Jesus Christ to his disciples)*

But he that is greatest among you shall be your servant.

PARABLE OF SERVICE

Matthew 25:34-40 *(A parable of Jesus Christ)*

34. Then shall the King say unto them on his right hand, Come be blessed of my Father, inherit the kingdom prepared for you from the foundation of the world:

35. For I was an hungred, and ye gave me meat: I was thirsty, and ye gave me drink: I was a stranger, and ye took me in:

36. Naked, and ye clothed me: I was sick, and ye visited me: I was in prison, and ye came unto me.

37. Then shall the righteous answer him, saying, Lord, when saw we thee an hungred, and fed thee? or thirsty, and gave thee drink?

38. When saw we thee a stranger, and took thee in? or naked and clothed thee?

39. Or when saw we thee sick, or in prison, and came unto thee?

40. And the King shall answer and say unto them, Verily I say unto you, Inasmuch as ye have done it unto one of the least of these my brethren, ye have done it unto me.

WHAT IS GIVEN IS RETURNED

Luke 6:38 *(Jesus Christ to his disciples)*

Give, and it shall be given unto you. . .

WHEN CONVERTED, STRENGTHEN OTHERS

Luke 22:32 *(Jesus Christ to Peter at the last supper)*

. . .I have prayed for thee, that thy faith fail not: and when thou art converted, strengthen thy brethren.

WHEN SERVING OTHERS, WE SERVE GOD

Mosiah 2:17 *(King Benjamin's address to the Nephites — 125 BC)*

And behold, I tell you these things that ye may learn wisdom; that ye may learn that when ye are in the service of your fellow beings ye are only in the service of your God.

D & C 42:38 *(Revelation to Joseph Smith — February, 1831)*

For inasmuch as ye do it unto the least of these, ye do it unto me.

THOSE WHO LOVE GOD SERVE HIM

D & C 42:29 *(Revelation to Joseph Smith — February, 1831)*

If thou lovest me thou shalt serve me and keep all my commandments.

$\mathfrak{S}$IN

(See Forgiveness and Repentance)

TO BE ACCEPTED, DO GOOD

Genesis 4:7 *(The Lord's comment to Cain after he offered a sacrifice according to Satan's instructions rather than the Lord's)*

If thou doest well, shalt thou not be accepted? and if thou doest not well, sin lieth at the door. . .

CONSENT NOT WHEN SINNERS ENTICE

Proverbs 1:10 *(Proverb of Solomon, King of Israel)*

My son, if sinners entice thee, consent thou not.

THOUGHTS OF FOOLISHNESS ARE SIN

Proverbs 24:9 *(Proverb of Solomon, King of Israel)*

The thought of foolishness is sin. . .

SINNERS HAVE DEFILED THE EARTH

Isaiah 24:5 *(Isaiah prophecies of the last days)*

The earth also is defiled under the inhabitants thereof; because they have transgressed the laws, changed the ordinance, broken the everlasting covenant.

SIN WITHHOLDS THE GOOD THINGS FROM YOU

Jeremiah 5:25 *(Teachings of Jeremiah, the Prophet)*

. . .your sins have withholden good things from you.

FEAR NOT THOSE WHO KILL THE BODY

Matthew 10:28 *(Jesus Christ to his disciples)*

And fear not them which kill the body, but are not able to kill the soul: but rather fear him which is able to destroy both soul and body in hell.

MEN LOVE DARKNESS RATHER THAN LIGHT

John 3:19 *(Jesus to Nicodemus)*

And this is the condemnation, that light is come into the world, and men loved darkness rather than light, because their deeds were evil.

HE WHO IS WITHOUT SIN

John 8:7 *(Jesus to the mob who was about to stone the adultress)*

. . .He that is without sin among you, let him first cast a stone at her.

A SINNER IS THE SERVANT OF SIN

John 8:34 *(Jesus Christ to the Jews who believed in him)*

. . .Whosoever committeth sin is the servant of sin.

SIN BRINGS SPIRITUAL DEATH

Romans 6:23 *(Paul to the Romans)*

For the wages of sin is death; but the gift of God is eternal life through Jesus Christ our Lord.

James 1:15 *(Epistle of James, the brother of Christ)*

. . .sin, when it is finished, bringeth forth death.

SIN IS THE STING OF DEATH

1 Corinthians 15:56 *(Paul to the Corinthians)*

The sting of death is sin; and the strength of sin is the law.

THE SIN OF OMISSION

James 4:17 *(Epistle of James, the brother of Christ)*

Therefore, to him that knoweth to do good, and doeth it not, to him it is sin.

Alma 32:19 *(Alma's discourse on faith — 74 BC)*

And now, how much more cursed is he that knoweth the will of God and doeth it not, than he that only believeth, or only hath cause to believe and falleth into transgression?

IF WE SAY WE HAVE NO SINS, WE ARE LIARS

1 John 1:8-10 *(Epistle of John the Beloved)*

8. If we say that we have no sin, we deceive ourselves, and the truth is not in us.

9. If we confess our sins, he is faithful and just to forgive us our sins, and to cleanse us from all unrighteousnes.

10. If we say that we have not sinned, we make him a liar, and his word is not in us.

ALL UNRIGHTEOUSNESS IS SIN

1 John 5:17 *(Epistle of John the Beloved)*

All unrighteousness is sin: and there is a sin not unto death.

QUICK TO SIN BUT SLOW TO OBEY

1 Nephi 17:45 *(Nephi chastises his brethren — 591 BC)*

Ye are swift to do iniquity but slow to remember the Lord your God. . . .

THE BLESSING OF ADAM'S FALL

2 Nephi 2:22-25 *(Lehi explains Adam and Eve's role to his son, Jacob — 588 BC)*

22. And now, behold, if Adam had not transgressed he would not have fallen, but he would have remained in the garden of Eden. And all things which were created must have remained in the same state in which they were after they were created; and they must have remained forever, and had no end.

23. And they would have had no children; wherefore they would have remained in a state of innocence, having no joy, for they knew no misery; doing no good, for they knew no sin.

24. But behold, all things have been done in the wisdom of him who knoweth all things.

25. Adam fell that men might be; and men are that they might have joy.

Moses 5:10-11 *(Adam and Eve praise the Lord for their transgression)*

10. . . .Blessed be the name of God, for because of my transgression my eyes are opened, and in this life I shall have joy, and again in the flesh I shall see God.

11. And Eve, his wife, heard all these things and was glad, saying: Were it not for our transgression we never should have had seed, and never should have

known good and evil, and the joy of our redemption, and the eternal life which God giveth unto all the obedient.

DO NOT DROOP IN SIN

2 Nephi 4:28 *(Nephi's prayer — 570 BC)*

Awake, my soul! No longer droop in sin. Rejoice, O my heart, and give place no more for the enemy of my soul.

SHAKE AT THE APPEARANCE OF SIN

2 Nephi 4:31 *(Nephi's prayer — 570 BC)*

. . .Wilt thou make me that I may shake at the appearance of sin?

MAN CANNOT BE SAVED IN SIN

Alma 11:37 *(Amulek's debate with Zeezrom, the anti-Christ — 82 BC)*

And I say unto you again that he cannot save them in their sins; for I cannot deny his word, and he hath said that no unclean thing can inherit the kingdom of heaven; therefore, how can ye be saved, except ye inherit the kingdom of heaven? Therefore, ye cannot be saved in your sins.

SIN WILL STAND AS A TESTIMONY AGAINST US

Alma 39:8 *(Alma to his son, Corianton — 73 BC)*

But behold, ye cannot hide your crimes from God; and except ye repent they will stand as a testimony against you at the last day.

WICKEDNESS NEVER WAS HAPPINESS

Alma 41:10 *(Alma to his son, Corianton — 73 BC)*

. . .Behold, I say unto you, wickedness never was happiness.

GOD CANNOT LOOK UPON SIN WITH THE LEAST DEGREE OF ALLOWANCE

Alma 45:16 *(Alma to his son, Helaman — 73 BC)*

. . .Thus saith the Lord God — Cursed shall be the land, yea, this land, unto every nation, kindred, tongue, and people, unto destruction, which do wickedly, when they are fully ripe; and as I have said so shall it be; for this is the cursing and the blessing of God upon the land, for the Lord cannot look upon sin with the least degree of allowance.

D & C 1:31 *(Revelation to Joseph Smith — November, 1831)*

For I the Lord cannot look upon sin with the least degree of allowance.

QUICK TO DO INIQUITY

Helaman 12:4 *(Nephi, the son of Helaman, describes the Nephites — 7 BC)*

. . .how quick to do iniquity, and how slow to do good, are the children of men; yea, how quick to hearken unto the words of the evil one, and to set their hearts upon the vain things of the world!

WHEN MUCH IS GIVEN, MUCH IS REQUIRED

D & C 82:3 *(Revelation to Joseph Smith — January, 1832)*

For of him unto whom much is given much is required; and he who sins against the greater light shall receive the greater condemnation.

SINS RETURN

D & C 82:7 *(Revelation to Joseph Smith — January, 1832)*

. . .go your ways and sin no more; but unto that soul who sinneth shall the former sins return, saith the Lord your God.

IT BECOMETH EVERY MAN WHO HAS BEEN WARNED TO WARN HIS NEIGHBOR

D & C 88:81-82 *(Revelation to Joseph Smith — December, 1832)*

81. . . .it becometh every man who hath been warned to warn his neighbor.

82. Therefore, they are left without excuse, and their sins are upon their own heads.

MEN WILL BE PUNISHED FOR THEIR OWN SINS

Second Article of Faith

We believe that men will be punished for their own sins, and not for Adam's transgression.

$\mathfrak{S}$PEAKING

MOSES COMPLAINS ABOUT HIS INABILITY TO SPEAK

Exodus 4:10-12 *(The Lord's answer to Moses)*

10. And Moses said unto the Lord, O my Lord, I am not eloquent, neither heretofore, nor since thou hast spoken unto thy servant: but I am slow of speech, and of a slow tongue.

11. And the Lord said unto him, Who hath made man's mouth? or who maketh the dumb, or deaf, or the seeing, or the blind? have not I the Lord?

12. Now therefore go, and I will be with thy mouth, and teach thee what thou shalt say.

PAUL, "THE WORLD'S GREATEST SALESMAN," WAS A POOR SPEAKER

1 Corinthians 2:1-4 *(Paul to the Corinthians)*

1. And I, brethren, when I came to you, came not with excellency of speech or of wisdom, declaring unto the testimony of God.

2. For I determined not to know any thing among you, save Jesus Christ, and him crucified.

3. And I was with you in weakness, and in fear, and in much trembling.

4. And my speech and my preaching was not with enticing words of man's wisdom, but in demonstration of the Spirit and of power:

THE HOLY GHOST CARRIES THE MESSAGE TO THE HEART

2 Nephi 33:1 *(Nephi's last testimony — 559 BC)*

> . . .for when a man speaketh by the power of the Holy Ghost the power of the Holy Ghost carrieth it unto the hearts of the children of men.

DESCRIPTION OF CHRIST'S VOICE

3 Nephi 11:3 *(Nephi describes Christ's voice — 34 AD)*

> . . .and it was not a harsh voice, neither was it a loud voice; nevertheless, and notwithstanding it being a small voice it did pierce them that did hear to the center, insomuch that there was no part of their frame that it did not cause to quake; yea, it did pierce them to the very soul, and did cause their hearts to burn.

⑤TEWARDSHIP

(See Diligence)

BELSHAZZAR'S STEWARDSHIP FOUND WANTING

Daniel 5:27 *(Daniel interprets the handwriting of the Lord on the temple wall of Belshazzar, the King of Babylon)*

. . .Thou art weighed in the balances, and art found wanting.

JESUS CHRIST CALLED HIS APOSTLES "FOLLOW ME AND I WILL MAKE YOU FISHERS OF MEN"

Matthew 4:18-20 *(Jesus calls Peter and Andrew)*

18. And Jesus, walking by the sea of Galilee, saw two brethren, Simon called Peter, and Andrew his brother, casting a net into the sea: or they were fishers.

19. And he saith unto them, Follow me, and I will make you fishers of men.

20. And they straightway left their nets, and followed him.

MAN SHOULD BE DILIGENT

Mosiah 4:27 *King Benjamin's address — 124 BC)*

. . .And again, it is expedient that he should be diligent, that thereby he might win the prize; therefore, all things must be done in order.

EVERY PERSON MUST ACCOUNT FOR HIS STEWARD-SHIP

D & C 70:3-4 *(Revelation to Joseph Smith — November, 1831)*

3. I, the Lord, have appointed them, and ordained them to be stewards over the revelations and commandments which I have given unto them, and which I shall hereafter given unto them;

4. And an account of this stewardship will I require of them in the day of judgment.

D & C 104:11-13 *(Revelation to Joseph Smith — April, 1834)*

11. It is wisdom in me; therefore, a commandment I give unto you, that ye shall organize yourselves and appoint every man his stewardship;

12. That every man may give an account unto me of the stewardship which is appointed unto him.

13. For it is expedient that I, the Lord, should make every man accountable, as a steward over earthly blessings, which I have made and prepared for my creatures.

UNTO WHOM MUCH IS GIVEN, MUCH IS EXPECTED

D & C 82:3 *(Revelation to Joseph Smith — April, 1832)*

For of him unto whom much is given much is required; and he who sins against the greater light shall receive the greater condemnation.

EVERY PERSON MUST LEARN TO FULFILL HIS DUTY

D & C 84:107-108 *(Revelation on priesthood — September, 1832)*

107. Therefore, take with you those who are ordained unto the lesser priesthood, and send them before you to make appointments, and to prepare the way and to fill appointments that you yourselves are not able to fill.

108. Behold, this is the way that mine apostles, in ancient days, built up my church unto me.

EVERYONE IS GIVEN A RESPONSIBILITY

D & C 84:109-110 *(also 1 Corinthians 12:14-29) (Revelation on the priesthood — September, 1832)*

109. Therefore, let every man stand in his own office, and labor in his own calling; and let not the head say unto the feet it hath no need of the feet; for without the feet how shall the body be able to stand?

110. Also the body hath need of every member, that all may be edified together, that the system may be kept perfect.

ᴛEACHING

TEACH LINE UPON LINE, PRECEPT UPON PRECEPT

Isaiah 28:9-10 *(Isaiah's prophecy of the last days)*

9.   Whom shall he teach knowledge? and whom shall he make to understand doctrine? . . .

10.   For precept must be upon precept, precept upon precept; line upon line, line upon line; here a little, and there a little:

JESUS CHRIST EXPLAINS THE REWARD FOR TEACHERS, BOTH GOOD AND BAD

Matthew 5:19 *(Jesus Christ in the Sermon on the Mount)*

Whosoever therefore shall break one of these least commandments, and shall teach men so, he shall be called the least in the kingdom of heaven: but whosoever shall do and teach them, the same shall be called great in the kingdom of heaven.

STRENGTHEN THY BRETHREN

Luke 22:32 *(Jesus Christ to Peter)*

But I have prayed for thee, that thy faith fail not: and when thou are converted, strengthen thy brethren.

PARABLE OF THE GOOD SHEPHERD

John 10:4-5 *(Jesus teaches through parables)*

4.   . . .he goeth before them, and the sheep follow him: for they know his voice.

5.   And a stranger will they not follow, but will flee from him: for they know not the voice of strangers.

IF YOU LOVE ME, FEED MY SHEEP

John 21:15-17 *(Jesus to Peter)*

15.   So when they had dined, Jesus saith to Simon Peter, Simon, son of Jonas, lovest thou me more than these? He saith unto him, Yea, Lord; thou knowest that I love thee. He saith unto him, Feed my lambs.

16.   He saith to him again the second time, Simon, son of Jonas, lovest thou me? He saith unto him, Yea, Lord; thou knowest that I love thee. He saith unto him, Feed my sheep.

17.   He saith unto him the third time, Simon, son of Jonas, lovest thou me? Peter was grieved because he said unto him the third time, Lovest thou me? And he said unto him, Lord, thou knowest all things; thou knowest that I love thee. Jesus saith unto him, Feed my sheep.

THOSE WHO PREACH THE GOSPEL MUST LIVE IT

1 Corinthians 9:14 *(Paul to the Corinthians)*

Even so hath the Lord ordained that they which preach the gospel should live of the gospel.

TEACH TO BE UNDERSTOOD

1 Corinthians 14:8-9 *(Paul's epistle to the Corinthians)*

8.   For if the trumpet give an uncertain sound, who shall prepare himself to the battle?

9.   So likewise ye, except ye utter by the tongue words easy to be understood, how shall it be known what is spoken? for ye shall speak into the air.

1 Corinthians 14:19 *(Paul to the Corinthians)*

Yet in the church I had rather speak five words with my understanding, that by my voice I might teach others also, than ten thousand words in an unknown tongue.

SEEK TO OBTAIN GOD'S WORD

D & C 11:21 *(Revelation through Joseph to Hyrum Smith — May, 1829)*

Seek not to declare my word, but first seek to obtain my word, and then shall your tongue be loosed; then, if you desire, you shall have my spirit and my word, yea, the power of God unto the convincing of men.

TEACH ONE ANOTHER

D & C 38:23-24 *(Revelation to Joseph Smith — January, 1831)*

23. But, verily I say unto you, teach one another according to the office wherewith I have appointed you;

24. And let every man esteem his brother as himself, and practise virtue and holiness before me.

D & C 88:77-78 *(Revelation to Joseph Smith — December, 1832)*

77. And I give unto you a commandment that you shall teach one another the doctrine of the kingdom.

78. Teach ye diligently and my grace shall attend you, that you may be instructed more perfectly in theory, in principle, in doctrine, in the law of the gospel, in all things that pertain unto the kingdom of God, that are expedient for you to understand;

D & C 88:118 *(Revelation to Joseph Smith — December, 1832)*

And as all have not faith, seek ye diligently and teach one another words of wisdom; yea, seek ye out of the best books words of wisdom; seek learning, even by study and also by faith.

WITHOUT THE SPIRIT WE SHALL NOT TEACH

D & C 42:14 *(Revelation to Joseph Smith — February, 1831)*

And the Spirit shall be given unto you by the prayer of faith; and if ye receive not the Spirit ye shall not teach.

LET THE STRONG IN SPIRIT STRENGTHEN THE WEAK

D & C 84:106 *(Revelation on Priesthood to Joseph Smith — September, 1832)*

And if any man among you be strong in the Spirit, let him take with him him that is weak, that he may be edified in all meekness, that he may become strong also.

EMPLES

DAVID IS COMMANDED TO BUILD A TEMPLE

2 Samuel 7:5-6 *(The Lord commands King David through Nathan, the prophet)*

5. Go and tell my servant David, Thus saith the Lord, Shalt thou build me an house for me to dwell in?

6. Whereas I have not dwelt in any house since the time that I brought up the children of Israel out of Egypt, even to this day, but have walked in a tent and in a tabernacle.

GOD DIRECTS BUILDING OF TEMPLES

Psalms 127:1 *(David's psalm to Solomon)*

Except the Lord build the house, they labour in vain that build it: except the Lord keep the city, the watchman weaketh but in vain.

HOUSE OF THE LORD IN THE MOUNTAINS

Isaiah 2:2-3 *(Isaiah tells of the last days)*

2. And it shall come to pass in the last days, that the mountain of the Lord's house shall be established in the top of the mountains, and shall be exalted above the hills; and all nations shall flow unto it.

3. And many people shall go and say, Come ye, and let us go up to the mountain of the Lord, to the house of the God of Jacob; and he will teach us of his

ways, and we will walk in his paths: for out of Zion shall go forth the law, and the word of the Lord from Jerusalem.

THE SPIRIT OF THE LORD CANNOT DWELL IN UNHOLY TEMPLES

Helaman 4:24 *(Nephi, the son of Helaman gives an account of the wickedness of the Nephites — 30 BC)*

. . .the Spirit of the Lord did no more preserve them. . .because the Spirit of the Lord doth not dwell in unholy temples.

TEMPLES ARE A HOUSE OF PRAYER, FASTING, FAITH, AND GLORY

D & C 109:16 *(Prayer offered at the dedication of the Kirtland Temple — March, 1836. This prayer was given to Joseph Smith by revelation from Jesus Christ.)*

And that this house may be a house of prayer, a house of fasting, a house of faith, a house of glory and of God, even thy house.

THE LORD'S HOUSE IS A HOUSE OF ORDER

D & C 132:8 *(Revelation on temple marriage — July, 1943)*

Behold, mine house is a house of order, saith the Lord God, and not a house of confusion.

ᴛEMPTATION

(See Sin)

COME UNTO JESUS

Matthew 11:28-30 *(Jesus Christ to the multitude)*

28. Come unto me, all ye that labour and are heavy laden, and I will give you rest.

29. Take my yoke upon you, and learn of me; for I am meek and lowly in heart: and ye shall find rest unto your souls.

30. For my yoke is easy, and my burden is light.

GET THEE BEHIND ME SATAN

Matthew 16:23 *(also Mark 8:33) (Jesus Christ rebuked Peter for tempting him not to suffer the crucifixion)*

But he turned, and said unto Peter, Get thee behind me, Satan: thou art an offence unto me: for thou savourest not the things that be of God, but those that be of men.

WATCH AND PRAY ALWAYS LEST YOU FALL INTO TEMPTATION

Mark 14:38 *(also Matthew 26:41) (Christ talks to Peter, James, and John after they fell asleep on Gethsemane)*

Watch ye and pray, lest ye enter into temptation. The spirit truly is ready, but the flesh is weak.

1 Corinthians 10:13 *(Paul to the people of Corinth)*

There hath no temptation taken you but such as is common to man: but God is faithful, who will not suffer you to be tempted above that ye are able; but will with the temptation also make a way to escape, that ye may be able to bear it.

BLESSED IS THE MAN THAT ENDURETH TEMPTATION

James 1:12 *(Epistle of James, the brother of Christ)*

Blessed is the man that endureth temptation: for when he is tried, he shall receive the crown of life, which the Lord hath promised to them that love him.

GOD WILL NOT TEMPT MAN WITH EVIL

James 1:13 *(Epistle of James, the brother of Christ)*

Let no man say when he is tempted, I am tempted of God: for God cannot be tempted with evil, neither tempteth he any man:

THERE MUST BE OPPOSITION IN ALL THINGS

2 Nephi 2:11 *(Lehi's teachings to his son, Jacob — 570 BC)*

For it must needs be, that there is an opposition in all things. . .

BEWARE OF THOSE WHO SAY; EAT, DRINK, AND BE MERRY

2 Nephi 28:7-8 *(Nephi predicts several forms of false doctrine that will be popular in the last days — 545 BC)*

7. Yea, and there shall be many which shall say: Eat, drink, and be merry, for tomorrow we die; and it shall be well with us.

8. And there shall also be many which shall say: Eat, drink, and be merry; nevertheless, fear God — he will justify in committing a little sin; yea, lie a little, take the advantage of one because of his words, dig a pit for thy neighbor; there is no harm in this; and do all these things, for tomorrow we die; and if it so be that we are guilty, God will beat us with a few stripes, and at last we shall be saved in the kingdom of God.

AFTER MUCH TRIBULATION COMES THE BLESSINGS

D & C 58:2,4 *(Revelation to Joseph Smith — August, 1831)*

2. . . .blessed is he that keepeth my commandments, whether in life or in death; and he that is faithful in tribulation, the reward of the same is greater in the kingdom of heaven.

4. For after much tribulation come the blessings. . .

ᎶESTIMONY

THE SPIRIT WILL DIRECT WORDS OF TESTIMONY

Matthew 10:19-20 *(Jesus Christ's instructions to the twelve apostles)*

19. . . .take no thought how or what ye shall speak: for it shall be given you in that same hour what ye shall speak.

20. For it is not ye that speak, but the Spirit of your Father which speaketh in you.

TESTIMONY IS BUILT BY OBEDIENCE

John 7:17 *(Jesus Christ to the Jews on the Mount of Olives)*

If any man will do his will, he shall know of the doctrine, whether it be of God, or whether I speak of myself.

THE TESTIMONY OF TWO WITNESSES SHALL BE TRUE

John 8:17 *(Jesus Christ to the Jews on the Mount of Olives)*

It is also written in your law, that the testimony of two men is true.

PAUL'S TESTIMONY TO KING AGRIPPA

Acts 26:28-29 *(Paul to King Agrippa)*

28.   Then Agrippa said unto Paul, Almost thou persuadest me to be a Christian.

29.   And Paul said, I would to God, that not only thou, but also all that hear me this day, were both almost, and altogether such as I am, except these bonds.

BE READY ALWAYS TO BEAR TESTIMONY

1 Peter 3:15 *(Epistle of Peter)*

But sanctify the Lord God in your hearts: and be ready always to give an answer to every man that asketh you a reason of the hope that is in you with meekness and fear:

IF YOU ONCE FELT THE CHANGE OF HEART, DO YOU FEEL SO NOW?

Alma 5:26-27 *(Alma the younger to the Nephites — 83 BC)*

26.   . . .if ye have experienced a change of heart, and if ye have felt to sing the song of redeeming love, I would ask, can ye feel so now?

27.   Have ye walked, keeping yourselves blameless before God? Could ye say, if ye were called to die at this time, within yourselves, that ye have been sufficiently humble? . . .

HOW DO YOU GAIN A TESTIMONY?

Alma 5:46 *(Alma teaches the people of Zarahemla — 83 BC)*

Behold, I say unto you they are made known unto me by the Holy Spirit of God. Behold, I have fasted and prayed many days that I might know these things of myself. And now I do know of myself that they are true; for the Lord God hath made them manifest unto me by his Holy Spirit; and this is the spirit of revelation which is in me.

Alma 32:27 *(Alma's discourse on faith — 74 BC)*

But behold, if ye will awake and arouse your faculties, even to an experiment upon my words, and exercise a particle of faith, yea, even if ye can no more than desire to believe, let this desire work in you, even until ye believe in a manner that ye can give place for a portion of my words.

TESTIMONIES BASED ON KNOWLEDGE OR FAITH

D & C 46:13-14 *(Revelation to Joseph Smith — March, 1831)*

13.   To some it is given by the Holy Ghost to know that Jesus Christ is the Son of God, and that he was crucified for the sins of the world.

14.   To others it is given to believe on their words, that they also might have eternal life if they continue faithful.

Ŏithing

A TENTH TO THE LORD

Genesis 28:22 *(Jacob's promise to the Lord)*

And this stone, which I have set for a pillar, shall be God's house: and of all that thou shalt give me I will surely give the tenth unto thee.

HOW A MAN ROBS GOD

Malachi 3:8-10 *(also 3 Nephi 24:8-10) (Malachi's prophecy is repeated by Jesus Christ during his visit to the Nephites — 34 AD)*

8.   Will a man rob God? Yet ye have robbed me. But ye say, Wherein have we robbed thee? In tithes and offerings.

9.   Ye are cursed with a curse; for ye have robbed me, even this whole nation.

10.   Bring ye all the tithes into the storehouse, that there may be meat in mine house, and prove me now herewith, saith the Lord of hosts, if I will not open you the windows of heaven, and pour you out a blessing, that there shall not be room enough to receive it.

THE WIDOW'S MITE

Mark 12:43-44 *(Jesus Christ to his disciples)*

43.   . . . .Verily I say unto you, That this poor widow hath cast more in, than all they which have cast into the treasury:

44.   For all they did cast in of their abundance; but she of her want did cast in all that she had, even all her living.

ABRAHAM PAID TITHES TO MELCHIZEDEK

Alma 13:15 *(Genesis 14:20) (Alma's discourse on the priesthood — 82 BC)*

And it was this same Melchizedek to whom Abraham paid tithes; yea, even our father Abraham paid tithes of one-tenth part of all he possessed.

TITHING IS A VALUABLE FIRE INSURANCE

D & C 64:23 *(Revelation to Joseph Smith — September, 1831)*

. . .he that is tithed shall not be burned at his coming.

D & C 85:3 *(Revelation to Joseph Smith — November, 1832)*

. . .he may tithe his people, to prepare them against the day of vengeance and burning. . .

TITHING IS A LAW OF THE PRIESTHOOD

D & C 119:4 *(Revelation to Joseph Smith — July, 1838)*

And after that, those who have thus been tithed shall pay one-tenth of all their interest annually; and this shall be a standing law unto them forever, for my holy priesthood, saith the Lord.

TRIBULATION

THE LORD LOVES THOSE WHOM HE CORRECTS

Proverbs 3:11-12 *(Proverb of Solomon, King of Israel)*

11.   My son, despise not the chastening of the Lord; neither be weary of his correction:

12.   For whom the Lord loveth he correcteth; even as a father the son in whom he delighteth.

AFFLICTIONS BECOME OUR GAIN

2 Nephi 2:2 *(Lehi to his son, Jacob — 570 BC)*

Nevertheless, Jacob, my firstborn in the wilderness, thou knowest the greatness of God; and he shall consecrate thine afflictions for thy gain.

BE FAITHFUL IN TRIBULATION

D & C 58:3-4 *(Revelation to Joseph Smith — August, 1831)*

3.   Ye cannot behold with your natural eyes, for the present time, the design of your God concerning those things which shall come hereafter, and the glory which shall follow after much tribulation.

4.   For after much tribulation come the blessings. Wherefore the day cometh that ye shall be crowned with much glory; the hour is not yet, but is nigh at hand.

D & C 122:5-8 *(The Lord to Joseph Smith and his companions after they had been in the Liberty jail for several months — March, 1839)*

5.   If thou art called to pass through tribulation; . . .

6.   If thou are accused with all manner of false accusations; . . .

7.   And if thou shouldst be cast into the pit, or into the hands of murderers, and the sentence of death passed upon thee; . . . know thou, my son, that all these things shall give thee experience, and shall be for thy good.

8.   The Son of Man hath descended below them all. Art thou greater than he?

TRIBULATION GIVES US EXPERIENCE

D & C 122:7 *(Revelation given to Joseph Smith while a prisoner in Liberty jail — March, 1839)*

And if thou shouldst be cast into the pit, or into the hands of murderers, and the sentence of death passed upon thee; if thou be cast into the deep; if the billowing surge conspire against thee; if fierce winds become thine enemy; if the heavens gather blackness, and all the elements combine to hedge up the way; and above all, if the very jaws of hell shall gape open the mouth wide after thee, know thou, my son, that all these things shall give thee experience, and shall be for thy good.

CRUTH

TRUTH BRINGS FREEDOM

John 8:31-32 *(Jesus Christ to the Jews who believed in him)*

31. . . .If ye continue in my word, then are ye my disciples indeed;

32. And ye shall know the truth, and the truth shall make you free.

THE SPIRIT OF TRUTH GUIDES US TO ALL TRUTH

John 16:13 *(Jesus Christ promises the Holy Ghost to his disciples)*

Howbeit when he, the Spirit of truth, is come, he will guide you into all truth: for he shall not speak of himself; but whatsoever he shall hear, that shall he speak: and he will shew you things to come.

CHRIST CAME INTO THE WORLD AS A WITNESS FOR TRUTH

John 18:37 *(Christ's answer to Pilate's question, "Art thou a King?")*

. . .Thou sayest that I am a king. To this end was I born, and for this cause came I into the world, that I should bear witness unto the truth. Every one that is of the truth heareth my voice.

PILATE QUESTIONS TRUTH

John 18:38 *(Pilate's question at the trial of Jesus Christ)*

. . .What is truth? . . .

THE RIGHTEOUS LOVE TRUTH

2 Nephi 9:40 *(Jacob's teachings to the Nephites — 545 BC)*

. . .I know that the words of truth are hard against all uncleanness; but the righteous fear them not, for they love the truth and are not shaken.

THE PROCESS FOR DETERMINING TRUTH

D & C 9:7-9 *(Revelation through Joseph Smith to Oliver Cowdery — April, 1829)*

7.   Behold, you have not understood; you have supposed that I would give it unto you, when you took no thought save it was to ask me.

8.   But, behold, I say unto you, that you must study it out in your mind; then you must ask me if it be right, and if it is right I will cause that your bosom shall burn within you; therefore, you shall feel that it is right.

9.   But if it be not right you shall have no such feelings, but you shall have a stupor of thought that shall cause you to forget the thing which is wrong; therefore, you cannot write that which is sacred save it be given you from me.

DEFINITION OF TRUTH

D & C 93:24 *(Revelation to Joseph Smith — May, 1833)*

And truth is knowledge of things as they are, and as they were, and as they are to come.

TRUTH IS LEARNED THROUGH OBEDIENCE

D & C 93:28 *(Revelation to Joseph Smith — May, 1833)*

He that keepeth his commandments receiveth truth and light, until he is glorified in truth and knoweth all things.

JOSEPH SMITH QUESTIONS WHY PEOPLE PERSECUTED HIM FOR TELLING THE TRUTH

Joseph Smith 2:22,24-25 *(Extract from History of the Church)*

22. . . . though I was an obscure boy, only between fourteen and fifteen years of age, and my circumstances in life such as to make a boy of no consequence in the world, yet men of high standing would take notice sufficient to excite the public mind against me, and create a bitter persecution; and this was common among all the sects — all united to persecute me.

24. . . . I felt much like Paul, when he made his defense before King Agrippa, and related the account of the vision he had when he saw a light, and heard a voice; but still there were but few who believed him; some said he was dishonest, others said he was mad; and he was ridiculed and reviled. But all this did not destroy the reality of his vision. He had seen a vision, he knew he had, and all the persecution under heaven could not make it otherwise. . .

25. So it was with me. I had actually seen a light, and in the midst of that light I saw two Personages, and they did in reality speak to me; and though I was hated and persecuted for saying that I had seen a vision, yet it was true; and while they were persecuting me, reviling me, and speaking all manner of evil against me falsely for so saying, I was led to say in my heart: Why persecute me for telling the truth? I have actually seen a vision; and who am I that I can withstand God, or why does the world think to make me deny what I have actually seen? For I had seen a vision; I knew it, and I knew that God knew it, and I could not deny it, neither dared I do it; at least I knew that by so doing I would offend God, and come under condemnation.

Unity

A HOUSE DIVIDED CANNOT STAND

Matthew 12:25 *(Jesus Christ to the Pharisees)*

. . .Every kingdom divided against itself is brought to desolation; and every city or house divided against itself shall not stand.

HE THAT IS NOT WITH CHRIST IS AGAINST HIM

Luke 11:23 *(also Matthew 12:30) (Jesus Christ to his disciples)*

He that is not with me is against me: and he that gathereth not with me scattereth.

NO SERVANT CAN SERVE TWO MASTERS

Luke 16:13 *(Jesus Christ to his disciples)*

No servant can serve two masters: for either he will hate the one, and love the other; or else he will hold to the one, and despise the other. Ye cannot serve God and mammon.

CHRIST PRAYS THAT WE MAY ALL BE ONE

John 17:21 *(Jesus prays to his Father)*

That they all may be one; as thou, Father, art in me, and I in thee, that they also may be one in us: that the world may believe that thou hast sent me.

CHURCH ORGANIZATION IS TO BRING A UNITY OF THE FAITH

Ephesians 4:11-14 *(Paul's epistle to the Ephesians)*

11. And he gave some, apostles; and some, prophets; and some, evangelists; and some, pastors and teachers;

12. For the perfecting of the saints, for the work of the ministry, for the edifying of the body of Christ:

13. Till we all come in the unity of the faith, and of the knowledge of the Son of God, unto a perfect man, unto the measure of the stature of the fulness of Christ:

14. That we henceforth be no more children, tossed to and fro, and carried about with every wind of doctrine, by the sleight of men, and cunning craftiness, whereby they lie in wait to deceive;

BE ONE

D & C 38:27 *(Revelation to Joseph Smith — January, 1831)*

. . .I say unto you, be one; and if ye are not one ye are not mine.

VIRTUE

(See Chastity)

WHOSO COMMITTETH ADULTERY LACKS UNDER-STANDING

Proverbs 6:32 *(Proverb of Solomon, King of Israel)*

> But whoso committeth adultery with a woman lacketh understanding: he that doeth it destroyeth his own soul.

A VIRTUOUS WOMAN IS A BLESSING TO HER HUS-BAND

Proverbs 12:4 *(Proverb of Solomon, King of Israel)*

> A virtuous woman is a crown to her husband: but she that maketh ashamed is as rottenness in his bones.

A VIRTUOUS WOMAN

Proverbs 31:10 *(Proverb of Solomon, King of Israel)*

> Who can find a virtuous woman? for her price is far above rubies.

LET VIRTUE GARNISH THY THOUGHTS

D & C 121:45 *(Prayers and prophecies of Joseph Smith while a prisoner at Liberty jail, Missouri — March, 1839)*

> . . .let virtue garnish thy thoughts unceasingly; then shall thy confidence wax strong in the presence of God.

SEEK AFTER VIRTUE

Thirteenth Article of Faith

We believe in being honest, true, chaste, benevolent, virtuous, and in doing good to all men; indeed, we may say that we follow the admonition of Paul — We believe all things, we hope all things, we have endured many things, and hope to be able to endure all things. If there is anything virtuous, lovely, or of good report or praiseworthy, we seek after these things.

ᙏᴀʀ

(See Peace)

WISDOM IS BETTER THAN WAR

Ecclesiastes 9:18 *(Advice of Ecclesiastes, the preacher, son of David)*

Wisdom is better than weapons of war: but one sinner destroyeth much good.

THEY THAT TAKE THE SWORD SHALL PERISH BY THE SWORD

Matthew 26:52 *(Jesus Christ to Peter in Gethsemane)*

. . .they that take the sword shall perish with the sword.

DEFEND YOUR FAMILIES EVEN UNTO BLOODSHED

Alma 43:45-47 *(The Lord commanded the Nephites to defend their families — 74 BC)*

45. Nevertheless, the Nephites were inspired by a better cause, for they were not fighting for monarchy nor power but they were fighting for their homes and their liberties, their wives and their children, and their all, yea, for their rites of worship and their church.

46. And they were doing that which they felt was the duty which they owed to their God; for the Lord had said unto them, and also unto their fathers, that: Inasmuch as ye are not guilty of the first offense, neither the second, ye shall not suffer yourselves to be slain by the hands of your enemies.

47. And again, the Lord has said that: Ye shall defend your families even unto bloodshed. Therefore for this cause were the Nephites contending with the Lamanites, to defend themselves, and their families, and their lands, their country, and their rights, and their religion.

GOD'S LAW REGARDING WAR

D & C 98:33-37 *(Revelation to Joseph Smith regarding the protection of saints against their enemies — August, 1833)*

33. And again, this is the law that I gave unto mine ancients, that they should not go out unto battle against any nation, kindred, tongue, or people, save I, the Lord, commanded them.

34. And if any nation, tongue, or people should proclaim war against them, they should first lift a standard of peace unto that people, nation, or tongue;

35. And if that people did not accept the offering of peace, neither the second nor the third time, they should bring these testimonies before the Lord;

36. Then I, the Lord, would give unto them a commandment, and justify them in going out to battle against that nation, tongue, or people.

37. And I, the Lord, would fight their battles, and their children's battles, and their children's children's, until they had avenged themselves on all their enemies, to the third and fourth generation.

⟨U⟩EALTH

THE LORD GIVES THE POWER TO GAIN WEALTH

Deuteronomy 8:18 *(Moses exhorts the Israelites to be obedient)*

But thou shalt remember the Lord thy God: for it is he that giveth thee power to get wealth. . .

DO NOT TRUST IN RICHES

Proverbs 11:28 *(Proverb of Solomon, King of Israel)*

He that trusteth in his riches shall fall: but the righteous shall flourish as a branch.

RICH AND POOR ARE CHILDREN OF GOD

Proverbs 22:2 *(Proverb of Solomon, King of Israel)*

The rich and poor meet together: the Lord is the maker of them all.

REDEMPTION CANNOT BE BOUGHT

Isaiah 52:3 *(Teachings of Isaiah)*

. . .Ye have sold yourselves for nought; and ye shall be redeemed without money.

WHERE YOUR TREASURE IS, THERE WILL YOUR HEART BE ALSO

Matthew 6:19-21 *(also 3 Nephi 13:19-21) (Jesus Christ in the Sermon on the Mount)*

19. Lay not up for yourselves treasures upon earth, where moth and rust doth corrupt, and where thieves break through and steal:

20. But lay up for yourselves treasures in heaven, where neither moth nor rust doth corrupt, and where thieves do not break through nor steal:

21. For where your treasure is, there will your heart be also.

FIRST SEEK THE KINGDOM OF GOD

Matthew 6:33 *(also 3 Nephi 13:33) (Jesus Christ in the Sermon on the Mount)*

But seek ye first the kingdom of God, and his righteousness; and all these things shall be added unto you.

2 Nephi 23:12 *(Nephi quotes Isaiah 13:12 — 545 BC)*

I will make a man more precious than fine gold; . . .

GIVE WHAT YOU HAVE

Acts 3:6 *(Peter heals the lame man at the temple gate)*

Then Peter said, Silver and gold have I none; but such as I have give I thee: In the name of Jesus Christ of Nazareth rise up and walk.

MONEY PERISHES

Acts 8:20 *(Peter to Simon when Simon tried to purchase the power of the priesthood)*

. . .Thy money perish with thee, because thou hast thought that the gift of God may be purchased with money.

THE LOVE OF MONEY IS EVIL

1 Timothy 6:10 *(Paul to Timothy)*

For the love of money is the root of all evil: which while some coveted after, they have erred from the faith, and pierced themselves through with many sorrows.

PAUL'S RECOMMENDATION OF WHAT THE RICH NEED TO DO TO INHERIT ETERNAL LIFE

1 Timothy 6:17-19 *(Paul to Timothy)*

17. Charge them that are rich in this world, that they be not highminded, nor trust in uncertain riches, but in the living God, who giveth us richly all things to enjoy;

18. That they do good, that they be rich in good works, ready to distribute, willing to communicate;

19. Laying up in store for themselves a good foundation against the time to come, that they may lay hold on eternal life.

SEEK RICHES TO DO GOOD

Jacob 2:18-19 *(Jacob's teachings to the Nephites — 421 BC)*

18. But before ye seek for riches, seek ye for the kingdom of God.

19. And after ye have obtained a hope in Christ ye shall obtain riches, if ye seek them; and ye will seek them for the intent to do good — to clothe the naked, and to feed the hungry, and to liberate the captive, and administer relief to the sick and the afflicted.

BE LIBERAL TO ALL

Alma 1:30 *(Alma, the younger, describes the faithfulness of the Nephite saints — 90 BC)*

. . .they were liberal to all, both old and young, both bond and free, both male and female, whether out of the church or in the church, having no respect to persons as to those who stood in need.

THE PROSPERITY OF THE RIGHTEOUS NEPHITES

Helaman 3:25 *(Writings of Nephi, son of Helaman — 45 BC)*

And so great was the prosperity of the church, and so many the blessings which were poured out upon the people, that even the high priests and the teachers were themselves astonished beyond measure.

SIN HINDERS PEOPLE FROM PROSPERING

3 Nephi 6:5 *(The wealth of the Nephites — 30 AD)*

And now there was nothing in all the land to hinder the people from prospering continually, except they should fall into transgression.

SEEK NOT RICHES BUT WISDOM

D & C 6:7 *(Revelation to Joseph Smith and Oliver Cowdery — April, 1829)*

Seek not for riches but for wisdom, and behold, the mysteries of God shall be unfolded unto you, and then shall you be made rich. Behold, he that hath eternal life is rich.

ⓦELFARE

BROTHER'S KEEPER

Genesis 4:9 *(The Lord questions Cain after he killed Abel)*

And the Lord said unto Cain, Where is Abel thy brother? And he said, I know not: Am I my brother's keeper?

MAN DOES NOT LIVE BY BREAD ALONE

Deuteronomy 8:3 *(also Matthew 4:4) (Moses exhorts the Israelites to be obedient)*

. . .man doth not live by bread only, but by every word that proceedeth out of the mouth of the Lord doth man live.

RICHES SHOULD BE USED TO DO GOOD

Jacob 2:18-19 *(Jacob's teachings to the Nephites — 421 BC)*

18. But before ye seek for riches, seek ye for the kingdom of God.

19. And after ye have obtained a hope in Christ ye shall obtain riches, if ye seek them; and ye will seek them for the intent to do good — to clothe the naked, and to feed the hungry, and to liberate the captive, and administer relief to the sick and the afflicted.

WE MUST IMPART OF OUR SUBSTANCE

Alma 34:27-29 *(Amulek's testimony — 74 BC)*

27. . . .let your hearts be full, drawn out in prayer unto him continually for your welfare, and also for the welfare of those who are around you.

28. And now behold, my beloved brethren, I say unto you, do not suppose that this is all; for after ye have done all these things, if ye turn away the needy, and the naked, and visit not the sick and afflicted, and impart of your substance, if ye have, to those who stand in need — I say unto you, if ye do not any of these things, behold, your prayer is vain, and availeth you nothing, and ye are as hypocrites who do deny the faith.

29. Therefore, if ye do not remember to be charitable, ye are as dross, which the refiners do cast out, (it being of no worth) and is trodden under foot of men.

LAW OF CONSECRATION AMONG THE NEPHITES

4 Nephi 1:2-3 *(Nephi describes the Nephites after Christ's visit — 35 to 201 AD)*

2. . . .there were no contentions and disputations among them, and every man did deal justly one with another.

3. And they had all things common among them; therefore there were not rich and poor, bond and free, but they were all made free, and partakers of the heavenly gift.

THOSE WHO GIVE TO THE POOR, GIVE TO CHRIST

D & C 42:31 *(Revelation to Joseph Smith — February, 1831)*

And inasmuch as ye impart of your substance unto the poor, ye will do it unto me; and they shall be laid before the bishop of my church and his counselors, two of the elders, or high priests, such as he shall appoint or has appointed and set apart for that purpose.

CHURCH COMMANDED TO OPEN A BISHOP'S STOREHOUSE

D & C 51:13 *(Revelation to Joseph Smith — May, 1831)*

And again, let the bishop appoint a storehouse unto this church; and let all things both in money and in meat, which are more than is needful for the wants of this people, be kept in the hands of the bishop.

A TRUE DISCIPLE WILL REMEMBER THE NEEDY

D & C 52:40 *(Revelation to Joseph Smith — June, 1831)*

And remember in all things the poor and the needy, the sick and the afflicted, for he that doeth not these things, the same is not my disciple.

THE WEALTHY AND THE POOR MUST SHARE BLESSING WITH LESS FORTUNATE

D & C 56:16-18 *(Revelation to Joseph Smith — June, 1831)*

16. Wo unto you the rich men, that will not give your substance to the poor, for your riches will canker your souls; and this shall be your lamentation

in the day of visitation, and of judgment, and of indignation: The harvest is past, the summer is ended, and my soul is not saved!

17. Wo unto you poor men, whose hearts are not broken, whose spirits are not contrite, and whose bellies are not satisfied, and whose hands are not stayed from laying hold upon other men's goods, whose eyes are full of greediness, and who will not labor with your own hands!

18. But blessed are the poor who are pure in heart, whose hearts are broken, and whose spirits are contrite, for they shall see the kingdom of God coming in power and great glory unto their deliverance; for the fatness of the earth shall be theirs.

CHILDREN SHOULD FIRST DEPEND ON PARENTS

D & C 83:4-5 *(Revelation to Joseph Smith — April, 1832)*

4. All children have claim upon their parents for their maintenance until they are of age.

5. And after that, they have claim upon the church, or in other words upon the Lord's storehouse, if their parents have not wherewith to give them inheritances.

THE STOREHOUSE SHALL PROVIDE FOR THE POOR

D & C 83:6 *(Revelation to Joseph Smith — April, 1832)*

And the storehouse shall be kept by the consecrations of the church; and widows and orphans shall be provided for, as also the poor. Amen.

ORGANIZE YOURSELVES; PREPARE EVERY NEED-FUL THING

D & C 88:119 *(Revelation to Joseph Smith — December, 1832)*

Organize yourselves; prepare every needful thing. . .

Wisdom

UNDERSTANDING COMES FROM INSPIRATION NOT AGE

Job 32:7-9 *(The young man, Elihu, speaks to his elders)*

7. I said, Days should speak, and multitude of years should teach wisdom.

8. But there is a spirit in man: and the inspiration of the Almighty giveth them understanding.

9. Great men are not always wise: neither do the aged understand judgment.

TRUST THE LORD WITH ALL YOUR HEART

Proverbs 3:5-7 *(Proverb of Solomon, King of Israel)*

5. Trust in the Lord with all thne heart; and lean not unto thine own understanding.

6. In all thy ways acknowledge him, and he shall direct thy paths.

7. Be not wise in thine own eyes: fear the Lord, and depart from evil.

HAPPY IS THE MAN THAT FINDS WISDOM

Proverbs 3:13-14 *(Proverb of Solomon, King of Israel)*

13. Happy is the man that findeth wisdom, and the man that getteth understanding.

14. For the merchandise of it is better than the merchandise of silver, and the gain thereof than fine gold.

THE WISE SHALL INHERIT GLORY

Proverbs 3:35 *(Proverb of Solomon, King of Israel)*

The wise shall inherit glory: but shame shall be the promotion of fools.

WISDOM IS THE PRINCIPLE THING

Proverbs 4:7 *(Proverb of Solomon, King of Israel)*

Wisdom is the principal thing; therefore get wisdom: and with all thy getting get understanding.

WISDOM IS BETTER THAN RUBIES

Proverbs 8:11 *(Proverb of Solomon, King of Israel)*

For wisdom is better than rubies; and all the things that may be desired are not to be compared to it.

INSTRUCTIONS WILL MAKE WISE MEN WISER

Proverbs 8:33 *(Proverb of Solomon, King of Israel)*

Hear instruction, and be wise, and refuse it not.

Proverbs 9:9 *(Proverb of Solomon, King of Israel)*

Give instruction to a wise man, and he will be yet wiser: teach a just man, and he will increase in learning.

THE WISE WILL RECEIVE GOD'S COMMANDMENTS

Proverbs 9:8 *(Proverb of Solomon, King of Israel)*

Reprove not a scorner, lest he hate thee: rebuke a wise man, and he will love thee.

LOVE OF GOD IS THE BEGINNING OF WISDOM

Proverbs 9:10 *(Proverb of Solomon, King of Israel)*

The fear of the Lord is the beginning of wisdom: and the knowledge of the holy is understanding.

WISE SON MAKES A GLAD FATHER

Proverbs 10:1 *(Proverb of Solomon, King of Israel)*

. . .A wise son maketh a glad father: but a foolish son is the heaviness of his mother.

AS A MAN THINKETH

Proverbs 23:7 *(Proverb of Solomon, King of Israel)*

For as he thinketh in his heart, so is he. . .

FOOLS WALK IN DARKNESS

Ecclesiastes 2:14 *(Teachings of Ecclesiastes, son of David)*

The wise man's eyes are in his head; but the fool walketh in darkness. . .

WISDOM SHOWS IN THE FACE

Ecclesiastes 8:1 *(Advice of Ecclesiastes, the preacher, son of David)*

. . .a man's wisdom maketh his face to shine, and the boldness of his face shall be changed.

SEEK YE FIRST THE KINGDOM OF GOD

Matthew 6:33 *(also 3 Nephi 13:33) (Jesus Christ in the Sermon on the Mount)*

But seek ye first the kingdom of God, and his righteousness; and all these things shall be added unto you.

PROFESSING TO BE WISE, PEOPLE BECAME FOOLS

Romans 1:22 *(Paul to the Romans)*

Professing themselves to be wise, they became fools.

GOD CHOOSES THE FOOLISH TO CONFOUND THE WISE

1 Corinthians 1:26-27 *(Paul to the saints at Corinth)*

26.   For ye see your calling, brethren, how that not many wise men after the flesh, not many mighty, not many noble, are called:

27.   But God hath chosen the foolish things of the world to confound the wise; and God hath chosen the weak things of the world to confound the things which are mighty;

SINNERS NEVER COME TO A KNOWLEDGE OF THE TRUTH

2 Timothy 3:7 *(Paul to Timothy)*

Ever learning, and never able to come to the knowledge of the truth.

ASK GOD FOR WISDOM

James 1:5 *(Epistle of James, the brother of Christ)*

If any of you lack wisdom, let him ask of God, that giveth to all men liberally, and upbraideth not; and it shall be given him.

TO BE LEARNED IS GOOD

2 Nephi 9:28-29 *(Jacob teaches the Nephites — 559 BC)*

28.   . . .When they are learned they think they are wise, and they hearken not unto the counsel of God,

for they set it aside, supposing they know of themselves, wherefore, their wisdom is foolishness and it profiteth them not. And they shall perish.

29. But to be learned is good if they hearken unto the counsels of God.

THE FATE OF THE WEALTHY AND WISE

2 Nephi 9:42-43 *(Teachings of Jacob — 559 BC)*

42. And whoso knocketh, to him will he open; and the wise, and the learned, and they that are rich, who are puffed up because of their learning, and their wisdom, and their riches — yea, they are they whom he despiseth; and save they shall cast these things away, and consider themselves fools before God, and come down in the depths of humility, he will not open unto them.

43. But the things of the wise and the prudent shall be hid from them forever — yea, that happiness which is prepared for the saints.

DO NOT COUNSEL THE LORD

Jacob 4:10 *(Jacob to the Nephites — 421 BC)*

Wherefore, brethren, seek not to counsel the Lord, but to take counsel from his hand. For behold, ye yourselves know that he counseleth in wisdom, and in justice, and in great mercy, over all his works.

IMPORTANCE OF WISDOM

Jacob 6:12 *(Jacob to the Nephites — 421 BC)*

O be wise; what can I say more?

LEARN WISDOM IN YOUR YOUTH

Alma 37:35 *(Alma to his son, Helaman — 73 BC)*

O, remember, my son, and learn wisdom in thy youth; yea, learn in thy youth to keep the commandments of God.

SEEK WISDOM, THEN GOD WILL REVEAL HIS MYSTERIES

D & C 6:7 *(also D & C 11:7) (Revelation to Joseph Smith and Oliver Cowdery — April, 1829)*

Seek not for riches but for wisdom, and behold, the mysteries of God shall be unfolded unto you, and then shall you be made rich. Behold, he that hath eternal life is rich.

SEEK WORDS OF WISDOM FROM THE BEST BOOKS

D & C 88:118 *(also D & C 109:7) (Revelation to Joseph Smith — December, 1832)*

And as all have not faith, seek ye diligently and teach one another words of wisdom; yea, seek ye out of the best books words of wisdom; seek learning, even by study and also by faith.

THE GLORY OF GOD IS INTELLIGENCE

D & C 93:36 *(Revelation to Joseph Smith — May, 1833)*

The glory of God is intelligence, or, in other words, light and truth.

MAN WILL RECEIVE WISDOM ONLY IF HE IS PREPARED

D & C 111:11 *(Revelation to Joseph Smith — August, 1836)*

Therefore, be ye as wise as serpents and yet without sin; and I will order all things for your good, as fast as ye are able to receive them. Amen.

GOD WILL GIVE KNOWLEDGE TO THE SAINTS

D & C 121:33 *(Prophecies of Joseph Smith while he was a prisoner in the Liberty jail — March, 1839)*

How long can rolling waters remain impure? What power shall stay the heavens? As well might man stretch forth his puny arm to stop the Missouri river in its decreed course, or to turn it up stream, as to hinder the Almighty from pouring down knowledge from heaven upon the heads of the Latter-day Saints.

KNOWLEDGE AND INTELLIGENCE WILL RISE WITH US IN THE RESURRECTION

D & C 130:18-19 *(Instructions of Joseph Smith — April, 1843)*

18. Whatever principle of intelligence we attain unto in this life, it will rise with us in the resurrection.

19. And if a person gains more knowledge and intelligence in this life through his diligence and obedience than another, he will have so much the advantage in the world to come.

IT IS IMPOSSIBLE TO BE SAVED IN IGNORANCE

D & C 131:6 *(Instructions by Joseph Smith — May, 1843)*

It is impossible for a man to be save in ignorance.

WORD OF WISDOM

PREGNANT WOMEN SHOULD NOT DRINK STRONG DRINKS NOR EAT UNCLEAN THINGS

Judges 13:3-4 *(The Angel of the Lord talks to the mother of Samson)*

3. . . .thou shalt conceive, and bear a son.

4. Now therefore beware, I pray thee, and drink not wine nor strong drink, and eat not any unclean thing:

THE USE OF ALCOHOL IS UNWISE

Proverbs 20:1 *(Proverb of Solomon, King of Israel)*

Wine is a mocker, strong drink is raging: and whosoever is deceived thereby is not wise.

THE BODY IS A TEMPLE OF GOD

1 Corinthians 3:16-17 *(Paul to the Corinthians)*

16. Know ye not that ye are the temple of God, and that the Spirit of God dwelleth in you?

17. If any man defile the temple of God, him shall God destroy; for the temple of God is holy, which temple ye are.

DO NOT RUN FASTER THAN YOU HAVE STRENGTH

Mosiah 4:27 *(King Benjamin's address, 124 BC)*

. . .it is not requisite that a man should run faster than he has strength. And again, it is expedient that he should be diligent, that thereby he might win the prize; therefore, all things must be done in order.

D & C 10:4 *(Revelation to Joseph Smith — Summer, 1828)*

Do not run faster or labor more than you have strength and means . . . but be diligent unto the end.

THE SICK SHALL USE HERBS AND MILD FOOD

D & C 42:43 *(Revelation to Joseph Smith — February, 1831)*

And whosoever among you are sick, and have not faith to be healed, but believe, shall be nourished with all tenderness, with herbs and mild food, and that not by the hand of an enemy.

RETIRE TO BED EARLY

D & C 88:124 *(Revelation to Joseph Smith — December, 1832)*

Cease to be idle; cease to be unclean; cease to find fault one with another; cease to sleep longer than is needful; retire to thy bed early, that ye may not be weary; arise early, that your bodies and your minds may be invigorated.

THE WORD OF WISDOM WAS INTENDED FOR ALL SAINTS

D & C 89:3 *(Revelation to Joseph Smith — February, 1833)*

Given for a principle with promise, adapted to the capacity of the weak and the weakest of all saints, who are or can be called saints.

PROMISE TO THOSE WHO OBEY THE WORD OF WISDOM

D & C 89:18-21 *(Revelation to Joseph Smith — February, 1833)*

18. And all saints who remember to keep and do these sayings, walking in obedience to the commandments, shall receive health in their navel and marrow to their bones;

19. And shall find wisdom and great treasures of knowledge, even hidden treasures;

20. And shall run and not be weary, and shall walk and not faint.

21. And I, the Lord, give unto them a promise, that the destroying angel shall pass by them, as the children of Israel, and not slay them. Amen.

WORK

REJOICE IN YOUR OWN WORKS

Ecclesiastes 3:22 *(Teachings of Ecclesiastes, son of David)*

. . .there is nothing better, than that a man should rejoice in his own works; for that is his portion. . .

WE REAP AS WE SOW

2 Corinthians 9:6 *(Paul to the Corinthians)*

. . .He which soweth sparingly shall reap also sparingly; and he which soweth bountifully shall reap also bountifully.

GOD IS NOT FOOLED

Galatians 6:7-8 *(Paul's epistle to the Galatians)*

7. Be not deceived; God is not mocked: for whatsoever a man soweth, that shall he also reap.

8. For he that soweth to his flesh shall of the flesh reap corruption; but he that soweth to the Spirit shall of the Spirit reap life everlasting.

FORMULA TO LEARN OF THE MYSTERIES OF GOD

Alma 26:22 *(Ammon tells his missionary experiences — 77 BC)*

Yea, he that repenteth and exerciseth faith, and bringeth forth good works, and prayeth continually without ceasing — unto such it is given to know the mysteries of God. . .

DO NOT IDLE

D & C 42:42 *(Revelation to Joseph Smith — February, 1831)*

Thou shalt not be idle; for he that is idle shall not eat the bread nor wear the garments of the laborer.

D & C 60:13 *(Revelation to Joseph Smith — August, 1831)*

. . .Thou shalt not idle away thy time, neither shalt thou bury thy talent that it may not be known.

REWARD FOR THOSE WHO DO WORKS OF RIGHT-EOUSNESS

D & C 59:23 *(Revelation to Joseph Smith — August, 1831)*

But learn that he who doeth the works of righteousness shall receive his reward, even peace in this world, and eternal life in the world to come.

EVERY MAN MUST BE DILIGENT

D & C 75:29 *(Revelation to Joseph Smith — January, 1832)*

Let every man be diligent in all things. And the idler shall not have place in the church, except he repent and mend his ways.

EVERY MAN MAY GAIN MORE TALENTS

D & C 82:18 *(Revelation to Joseph Smith — January, 1832)*

. . .every man may improve upon his talent, that every man may gain other talents, yea, even an hundred fold. . .

THE LORD HOLDS EVERY MAN ACCOUNTABLE

D & C 104:13 *(Revelation to Joseph Smith — April, 1834)*

For it is expedient that I, the Lord, should make every man accountable, as a steward over earthly blessings, which I have made and prepared for my creatures.

THE LABORER IS WORTHY OF HIS HIRE

D & C 106:3 *(Revelation to Joseph Smith — November, 1834)*

. . .the laborer is worthy of his hire.

℧OUTH

JESUS CHRIST'S YOUTH

Luke 2:40 *(Luke's account of Jesus Christ's youth)*

And the child grew, and waxed strong in spirit, filled with wisdom: and the grace of God was upon him.

Luke 2:52

And Jesus increased in wisdom and stature, and in favour with God and man.

Hebrews 5:8-9 *(Paul to the Hebrews)*

8. Though he were a Son, yet learned he obedience by the things which he suffered;

9. And being made perfect, he became the author of eternal salvation unto all them that obey him.

YOUTH PUT AWAY CHILDISH THINGS

1 Corinthians 13:11 *(Paul's epistle to the saints at Corinth)*

When I was a child, I spake as a child, I understood as a child, I thought as a child: but when I became a man, I put away childish things.

THE YOUNG DO NOT HAVE TO ACT FOOLISHLY

1 Timothy 4:12 *(Paul to Timothy)*

Let no man despise thy youth; but be thou an example of the believers, in word, in conversation, in charity, in spirit, in faith, in purity.

2 Timothy 2:22-23 *(Paul to Timothy)*

22. Flee also youthful lusts: but follow righteousness, faith, charity, peace, with them that call on the Lord out of a pure heart.

23. But foolish and unlearned questions avoid, knowing that they do gender strifes.

LEARN WISDOM WHILE YOUNG

Alma 37:35 *(Alma to his son, Helaman — 73 BC)*

O, remember, my son, and learn wisdom in thy youth; yea, learn in thy youth to keep the commandments of God.

HELAMAN DESCRIBES THE STRIPLING WARRIORS

Alma 53:20-21 *(Helaman led 2000 young Lamanite warriors to battle and to his surprise not one was killed, although more than 1000 of his regular troops died — 64 BC)*

20. . . .they were men who were true at all times in whatsoever thing they were entrusted.

21. Yea, they were men of truth and soberness, for they had been taught to keep the commandments of God and to walk uprightly before him.

FAITH OF THE 2000 STRIPLING WARRIORS

Alma 56:45-47 *(Epistle of Helaman to Moroni — 64 BC)*

45. . . .had I seen so great courage, nay, not amongst all the Nephites.

46. For as I had ever called them my sons (for they were all of them very young) even so they said unto

me: Father, behold our God is with us, and he will not suffer that we should fall; then let us go forth. . .

47.   Now they never had fought, yet they did not fear death; and they did think more upon the liberty of their fathers than they did upon their lives; yea, they had been taught by their mothers, that if they did not doubt, God would deliver them.

Alma 56:56 *(Alma writing after the battle with the army of Antipus — 64 BC)*

But behold, to my great joy, there had not one soul of them fallen to the earth; yea, and they had fought as if with the strength of God; yea, never were men known to have fought with such miraculous strength; and with such mighty power. . .

Alma 57:21,26-27 *(Epistle of Helaman to Moroni — 63 BC)*

21.   . . .even according to their faith it was done unto them; and I did remember the words which they said unto me that their mothers had taught them.

26.   And now, their preservation was astonishing to our whole army, yea, that they should be spared while there was a thousand of our brethren who were slain. And we do justly ascribe it to the miraculous power of God, because of their exceeding faith in that which they had been taught to believe — that there was a just God, and whosoever did not doubt, that they should be preserved by his marvelous power.

27.   Now this was the faith of these of whom I have spoken; they are young, and their minds are firm, and they do put their trust in God continually.

YOUNG PEOPLE MUST MAKE JESUS CHRIST THEIR FOUNDATION

Helaman 5:12 *(Helaman teaches his sons, Nephi and Lehi — 30 BC)*

And now, my sons, remember, remember that it is upon the rock of our Redeemer, who is Christ, the Son of God, that ye must build your foundation; that when the devil shall send forth high mighty winds, yea, his shafts in the whirlwind, yea, when all his hail and his mighty storm shall beat upon you, it shall have no power over you to drag you down to the gulf of misery and endless wo, because of the rock upon which ye are built, which is a sure foundation, a foundation whereon if men build they cannot fall.

ZION

LAW SHALL COME FROM ZION

Isaiah 2:2-3 *(also Micah 4:1-2) (Isaiah envisioned the last days)*

2.   And it shall come to pass in the last days, that the mountain of the Lord's house shall be established in the top of the mountains, and shall be exalted above the hills; and all nations shall flow unto it.

3.   And many people shall go and say, Come ye, and let us go up to the mountain of the Lord, to the house of the God of Jacob; and he will teach us of his ways, and we will walk in his paths: for out of Zion shall go forth the law, and the word of the Lord from Jerusalem.

GATHERING OF ISRAEL

Isaiah 11:12 *(Isaiah prophecies about the last days)*

And he shall set up an ensign for the nations, and shall assemble the outcasts of Israel, and gather together the dispersed of Judah from the four corners of the earth.

Jeremiah 3:14 *(Jeremiah prophecies about the gathering of Israel)*

Turn, O backsliding children, saith the Lord; for I am married unto you: and I will take you one of a city, and two of a family, and I will bring you to Zion:

HOW BEAUTIFUL UPON THE MOUNTAINS

Isaiah 52:7-8 *(Isaiah prophecies of the last days)*

7. How beautiful upon the mountains are the feet of him that bringeth good tidings, that publisheth peace; that bringeth good tidings of good, that publisheth salvation; that saith unto Zion, Thy God reigneth!

8. Thy watchmen shall lift up the voice; with the voice together shall they sing: for they shall see eye to eye, when the Lord shall bring again Zion.

A KINGDOM WHICH SHALL NEVER BE DESTROYED

Daniel 2:44 *(Daniel interprets Nebuchadnezzar's dream)*

And in the days of these kings shall the God of heaven set up a kingdom, which shall never be destroyed: . . . but it shall break in pieces and consume all these kingdoms, and it shall stand for ever.

THE LORD SHALL COMFORT ZION

2 Nephi 8:3 *(Jacob's teachings to the Nephites — 559 BC)*

For the Lord shall comfort Zion, he will comfort all her waste places; and he will make her wilderness like Eden, and her desert like the garden of the Lord. Joy and gladness shall be found therein, thanksgiving and the voice of melody.

LABORERS IN ZION SHALL NOT LABOR FOR MONEY

2 Nephi 26:31 *(Nephi's prediction of the last days — 545 BC)*

But the laborer in Zion shall labor for Zion; for if they labor for money they shall perish.

ZION WILL BE LULLED INTO A FALSE SECURITY BY SATAN

2 Nephi 28:21 *(Nephi's testimony — 545 BC)*

And others will he pacify, and lull them away into carnal security, that they will say: All is well in Zion; yea, Zion prospereth, all is well — and thus the devil cheateth their souls, and leadeth them away carefully down to hell.

ZION SHALL BE THE ONLY NATION NOT AT WAR

D & C 45:66,68-69,71 *(Revelation to Joseph Smith — March, 1831)*

66. And it shall be called the New Jerusalem, a land of peace, a city of refuge, a place of safety for the saints of the Most High God;

68. And it shall come to pass among the wicked, that every man that will not take his sword against his neighbor must needs flee unto Zion for safety.

69. And there shall be gathered unto it out of every nation under heaven; and it shall be the only people that shall not be at war one with another.

71. And it shall come to pass that the righteous shall be gathered out from among all nations, and shall come to Zion, singing with songs of everlasting joy.

ZION MUST INCREASE IN BEAUTY AND SIZE

D & C 82:14 *(Revelation to Joseph Smith — April, 1832)*

For Zion must increase in beauty, and in holiness; her borders must be enlarged; her stakes must be strengthened; yea, verily I say unto you, Zion must arise and put on her beautiful garments.

ZION IS THE PURE IN HEART

D & C 97:21 *(Revelation to Joseph Smith — August, 1833)*

. . .this is Zion — THE PURE IN HEART. . .

ZION CANNOT BE BUILT EXCEPT UPON CELESTIAL PRINCIPLES

D & C 105:5 *(Revelation to Joseph Smith — June, 1834)*

And Zion cannot be built up unless it is by the principles of the law of the celestial kingdom; otherwise I cannot receive her unto myself.

THE PEOPLE OF ZION WILL BE OF ONE HEART AND ONE MIND

Moses 7:18 *(The writing of Moses as revealed to Joseph Smith — December, 1830)*

And the Lord called his people Zion, because they were of one heart and one mind, and dwelt in righteousness; and there was no poor among them.

ZION WILL BE BUILT UPON THE AMERICAN CONTINENT

Tenth Article of Faith

We believe in the literal gathering of Israel and in the restoration of the Ten Tribes; that Zion (the New Jerusalem) will be built upon the American continent; that Christ will reign personally upon the earth; and, that the earth will be renewed and receive its paradisiacal glory.

100 Most Quoted Scriptures

Number	Scripture	Gospel Topic
1.	Moses 1:39	God, Eternal Life
2.	Revelation 14:6-7	Missionary Work
3.	John 17:3	Eternal Life, Jesus Christ: Resurrection
4.	Joseph Smith 2:17	God
5.	Mark 16:15-16	Missionary Work
6.	Matthew 16:13, 16-17	Jesus Christ: Mortal Ministry, Revelation
7.	John 3:3-5	Baptism
8.	James 1:5	Wisdom
9.	Matthew 22:36-40	Love
10.	John 7:16-17	Obedience, Testimony
11.	Matthew 5:48	Eternal Life, Fathers, God
12.	II Nephi 2:25	Happiness, Sin
13.	Matthew 6:33	Wealth, Wisdom
14.	Moroni 10:4-5	Book of Mormon, Holy Ghost
15.	Isaiah 2:2-3	Temples, Zion
16.	John 11:25-26	Funeral Messages, Resurrection
17.	Acts 3:20-21	Apostasy
18.	Acts 2:37-38	Baptism
19.	Ephesians 4:11-14	Unity
20.	D & C 13	Priesthood
21.	Luke 23:34	Forgiveness
22.	D & C 130:20-21	Obedience
23.	John 14:15	Love
24.	John 3:16	Love

Number	Scripture	Gospel Topic
25.	Matthew 6:9-13	Prayer
26.	Malachi 4:5-6	Genealogy
27.	Genesis 1:27	Creation, God
28.	Job 19:25-27	Resurrection
29.	Matthew 25:40	Service
30.	Matthew 28:19-20	Missionary Work
31.	Daniel 2:44	Zion
32.	I Peter 4:6	Jesus Christ: Resurrection
33.	Amos 3:7	Prophets, Revelation
34.	Romans 1:16	Courage, Jesus Christ: Mortal Ministry
35.	Isaiah 29:13	Pride
36.	I Peter 3:18-19	Jesus Christ: Resurrection
37.	Matthew 11:28-30	Jesus Christ: Mortal Ministry, Temptation
38.	Matthew 7:21	Obedience
39.	I Corinthians 15:22	Atonement
40.	D & C 76:22-24	Jesus Christ: Resurrection, Resurrection
41.	John 14:1-4	Eternal Life, Funeral Messages, Preparation
42.	D & C 84:33	Priesthood
43.	D & C 121:46	Holy Ghost
44.	D & C 82:10	Covenants, Obedience
45.	John 14:6	Jesus Christ: Mortal Ministry
46.	John 1:1-5	Creation, Jesus Christ: Pre-mortal
47.	D & C 93:36	Wisdom
48.	Mark 16:17-18	Gifts, Missionary Work
49.	Matthew 24:14	Last Days, Missionary Work
50.	Acts 4:12	Jesus Christ: Resurrection
51.	I Corinthians 2:9	Love
52.	II Peter 1:21	Prophets, Scriptures
53.	I Corinthians 15:29	Baptism
54.	D & C 1:38	Missionary Work, Prophet
55.	D & C 130:22	Fathers, God
56.	Joshua 24:15	Service

Number	Scripture	Gospel Topic
57.	Malachi 3:8-10	Honesty, Tithing
58.	Moses 4:1-4	Satan
59.	Matthew 7:7-8	Prayer
60.	Acts 1:11	Jesus Christ: Second Coming
61.	I Peter 2:9	Priesthood
62.	Job 38:4,7	Praise
63.	D & C 121:45	Profanity, Virtue
64.	Genesis 3:19	Death
65.	I John 3:1-3	Resurrection
66.	Matthew 5:16	Example, Service
67.	Exodus 20:8-10	Commandments, Sabbath Day
68.	D & C 4:2	Missionary Work
69.	D & C 18:10	Missionary Work
70.	Matthew 5:44,46	Love
71.	Matthew 7:13-14	Eternal Life
72.	Revelation 20:12	Judgment
73.	John 8:31-32	Truth
74.	D & C 121:34-37	Priesthood
75.	D & C 107:99-100	Priesthood
76.	D & C 68:25, 27-28	Children, Family
77.	John 20:17	Fathers, Jesus Christ: Resurrection
78.	D & C 130:18-19	Wisdom
79.	Jeremiah 3:14	Zion
80.	II Timothy 3:1-7	Last Days
81.	John 5:39	Scriptures
82.	Exodus 20:12	Commandments, Family, Father, Mother
83.	II Nephi 28:21	Satan, Zion
84.	III Nephi 27:19-20	Judgment
85.	D & C 89:18-21	Word of Wisdom
86.	John 10:17-18	Love, Jesus Christ: Mortal Ministry
87.	Genesis 1:28	Family
88.	Isaiah 24:5	Sin
89.	D & C 131:6	Wisdom
90.	D & C 93:33-34	Happiness, Resurrection

Number	Scripture	Gospel Topic
91.	Ether 2:9,12	America, Obedience, Patriotism
92.	John 5:28-29	Resurrection
93.	Luke 2:13-14	Jesus Christ: Mortal Ministry, Peace, Praise
94.	D & C 1:35	God
95.	D & C 14:7	Obedience
96.	D & C 88:118	Teaching, Wisdom
97.	D & C 93:1	Repentance
98.	I Nephi 3:7	Commandments
99.	Thirteenth Article of Faith	Honesty, Virtue
100.	Matthew 25:21	Faith

Topical Index by Book

OLD TESTAMENT

Genesis

1:1	Creation
1:26-27	Creation
1:27	God
1:28	Family
2:18, 24	Family, Marriage
2:24	Fathers
3:19	Death
3:20	Mothers
4:7	Attitude, Sin
4:9	Welfare
5:1	Creation
12:2-3	Covenants
14:20*	Tithing
18:14	Commandments
22:17-18	Covenants
28:22	Tithing

Exodus

4:10-12	Speaking
16:8	Gossip
18:13-21	Delegation
19:5-6	Covenants
20:3, 6	God
20:3-17	Commandments
20:7	Profanity
20:8-10	Sabbath Day
20:12	Family, Fathers, Mothers,
20:14	Chastity
20:15	Honesty
20:16	Gossip, Honesty
20:17	Pride
32:26	Obedience
33:11	God

II Kings
    6:16   Fear

Job

5:17	Happiness
19:25-27	Resurrection
32:7-9	Wisdom
38:4, 7	Praise

Psalms

8:4-6	Creation
19:1	Creation
23:1-6	Funeral Message
23:4	Fear
24:1	Jesus Christ: Pre-Mortal
24:3-4	Obedience
127:1	Temples

Proverbs

1:5	Listening
1:8	Fathers, Mothers
1:10	Obedience, Sin
3:5-7	Obedience, Wisdom
3:11-12	Discipline, Family, God, Tribulation
3:13-14	Happiness, Wisdom
3:19	Creation
3:35	Wisdom
4:7	Wisdom
6:16-19	God, Pride
6:20	Fathers
6:20-22	Children, Family
6:32	Chastity, Virtue
8:11	Wisdom
8:27-30	Premortal Life
8:33	Wisdom
9:8	Wisdom
9:9	Wisdom
9:10	Wisdom

Proverbs (continued)

10:1	Children, Family, Fathers, Mothers, Wisdom
10:8	Commandments
10:21	Gossip
11:28	Wealth
12:4	Virtue
12:22	Gossip
13:1	Children, Family, Fathers
16:32	Anger
17:17	Friendship
18:24	Friendship
20:1	Word of Wisdom
22:1	Family
22:2	Wealth
22:6	Children, Discipline, Family
22:24	Friendship
23:7	Attitude, Wisdom
23:13-14	Discipline
23:22	Fathers, Mothers
24:9	Sin
25:25	Missionary Work
27:17	Friendship
29:18	Happiness, Obedience, Prophets
31:10	Virtue
31:10-31	Mothers
31:30	Pride

Ecclesiastes

2:14	Wisdom
3:1, 7	Gossip
3:22	Work
4:9-10	Marriage, Missionary Work
5:2-3	Gossip
5:4-5	Covenants, Honesty
8:1	Wisdom
9:9	Marriage
9:18	War

Ecclesiastes (continued)

12:7	Resurrection
12:13-14	Judgment, Obedience

Isaiah

1:16,18	Forgiveness
2:2-3	Temples, Zion
7:14	Jesus Christ: Mortal Ministry
9:6	Jesus Christ: Mortal Ministry
11:5-9	Millennium
11:12	Zion
12:4-5	Praise
13:12*	Wealth
14:12-15	Satan
24:5	Sin
28:9-10	Teaching
29:13	Pride
35:1-2	Millennium
40:3	Preparation
52:3	Wealth
52:7-8	Zion
52:7	Peace
55:6	Procrastination
55:8-9	God
65:19	Millennium

Jeremiah

1:5	Premortal Life
2:11	Obedience
2:32	Pride
3:14	Zion
5:25	Sin
6:14	Peace
31:34	Forgiveness

Ezekiel

37:16-17	Book of Mormon

NEW TESTAMENT

Matthew

3:11	Holy Ghost
3:13-17	Baptism
4:4	Scriptures
4:10	God
4:18-20	Stewardship
5:3-12	Obedience
5:9	Peace
5:14-16	Example
5:16	Service
5:19	Obedience, Teaching
5:22	Anger
5:23-24	Gifts
5:27-28	Attitude, Chastity
5:34-35	Profanity
5:38-39	Anger
5:41	Service
5:44, 46	Love
5:48	Eternal Life, Fathers, God
6:7	Prayer
6:9-13	Prayer
6:14-15	Forgiveness
6:16-18	Fasting
6:19-21	Wealth
6:21	Attitude, Pride
6:33	Wealth, Wisdom
7:1-2	Judgment
7:7-8	Prayer
7:12	Service
7:13-14	Eternal Life
7:15	Prophets
7:20	Example
7:21	Obedience
7:21-23	Priesthood
8:26	Fear
8:31-32	Truth
9:2	Forgiveness

Matthew (continued)

9:12-13	Repentance
9:24	Jesus Christ: Mortal Ministry
10:8	Charity
10:19-20	Testimony
10:28	Death, Fear, Sin
10:39*	Service
11:28-30	Jesus Christ: Mortal Ministry, Temptation
12:8, 12	Sabbath Day
12:25	Unity
12:30*	Unity
12:31-32	Holy Ghost
12:36-37	Profanity
12:39	Miracles
13:15	Listening
13:55-56	Jesus Christ: Mortal Ministry
13:57	Prophet
14:31	Faith
15:8-9	Commandments
15:11	Profanity
15:14	Example
15:28	Faith
16:4	Miracles
16:13, 16-17	Jesus Christ: Mortal Ministry, Revelation
16:17	Fathers
16:19	Priesthood
16:23	Temptation
16:25-26	Service
17:20	Faith
17:21	Fasting
18:1-6	Children
18:12-13	Missionary Work
18:20	Jesus Christ: Resurrection, Missionary Work
18:21-22	Forgiveness
19:13-14	Children

Matthew (continued)

19:16-22	Eternal Life
19:26	Commandments
19:30	Judgment
20:16	Judgment, Priesthood
20:27*	Service
21:22	Prayer
22:14	Priesthood
22:36-40	Love
23:11	Service
23:12	Humility
24:7,16,21,29*	Last Days
24:12-13	Discipline, Love
24:13	Discipline, Obedience
24:14	Last Days, Missionary Work
24:24	Apostasy, Last Days, Prophets
24:27	Jesus Christ: Second Coming
24:36	Jesus Christ: Second Coming
24:44	Procrastination
25:21	Faith
25:34	Eternal Life
25:34-40	Service
26:26-28*	Sacrament
26:30	Music
26:39	Obedience
26:41*	Temptation
26:52	War
27:52-53	Resurrection
28:19-20	Missionary Work

Mark

2:27-29	Sabbath Day
4:22-24	Listening, Revelation
6:4*	Prophets
8:33*	Temptation
12:43-44	Tithing
14:38	Temptation

Mark (continued)

16:15-16	Missionary Work
16:17-18	Gifts, Missionary Work

Luke

1:27-30, 37-38	Mothers
1:30	Fear
1:37	Commandments
2:4-14	Jesus Christ: Mortal Ministry
2:13-14	Praise
2:14	Peace
2:40	Youth
2:49	Obedience
2:52	Youth
6:27, 35*	Love
6:31*	Service
6:37	Judgment
6:38	Gifts, Service
6:39	Example
6:46	Obedience
7:23	Humility
10:1	Missionary Work
11:13	Gifts
11:23	Unity
12:34*	Attitude
16:13	Unity
16:31	Scriptures
18:27	God
22:19-20	Sacrament
22:32	Service, Teaching
22:42*	Obedience
23:34	Forgiveness
24:1-7	Resurrection
24:36, 38-39	Jesus Christ: Mortal Ministry, Resurrection

John

1:1-5	Creation, Jesus Christ: Premortal
3:3-5	Baptism
3:16	Love

John (continued)

3:19	Sin
4:13-14	Eternal Life
5:28-29	Resurrection
5:39	Scriptures
6:26-27	Miracles
7:16-17	Obedience
7:17	Testimony
7:24	Judgment
8:7	Sin
8:12	Jesus Christ: Mortal Ministry
8:17	Testimony
8:31-32	Truth
8:34	Sin
10:4-5	Teaching
10:16	Book of Mormon
10:17	Love
10:17-18	Jesus Christ: Mortal Ministry
11:25-26	Funeral Messages, Resurrection
11:41	Listening
13:34-35	Friendship, Love
14:1-4	Eternal Life, Funeral Messages, Preparation
14:6	Jesus Christ: Mortal Ministry
14:15	Love
14:16-17, 26	Holy Ghost
14:27-28	Fear
14:27	Peace
14:28	God
15:13	Friendship, Love
15:16	Prayer, Priesthood
15:26	Holy Ghost
16:13	Holy Ghost, Truth
16:33	Happiness, Patience, Peace
17:3	Eternal Life, Jesus Christ: Resurrection
17:21	Unity
18:37	Truth

John (continued)

18:38	Truth
19:26-27	Mothers
20:17	Fathers, Jesus Christ: Resurrection
20:21	Peace
20:31	Bible
21:15-17	Teaching
21:24-25	Bible

Acts

1:11	Jesus Christ: Second Coming
2:37-38	Baptism
3:6	Gifts, Wealth
3:19	Repentance
3:20-21	Apostasy
4:12	Jesus Christ: Resurrection
7:55-56	God
8:20	Wealth
10:34-35	God
17:23, 27-29	God
20:30	Apostasy
20:35	Gifts
24:16	Honesty
26:28-29	Testimony

Romans

1:16	Courage, Jesus Christ: Mortal Ministry
1:22	Wisdom
5:3-5	Patience
6:3-5*	Baptism
6:9-10	Atonement
6:23	Eternal Life, Sin
8:16-17	Eternal Life
8:31	God
10:17	Faith, Listening
12:21	Obedience
13:8	Debt, Love
13:9-10	Love

I Corinthians

1:26-27	Wisdom
2:1-4	Speaking
2:5	Faith
2:9	Love
3:16-17	Word of Wisdom
9:14	Example, Teaching
9:16	Missionary Work
10:13	Temptation
11:11-12	Marriage
11:23-30*	Sacrament
12:14-29*	Stewardship
13:3-8, 13	Charity
13:11	Youth
14:8-9	Teaching
14:8	Example
14:15	Music
14:19	Teaching
14:19,33	Missionary Work
14:33	God, Peace
15:22	Atonement
15:29	Baptism
15:40-42	Eternal Life
15:55, 57	Atonement, Death, Funeral Messages
15:56	Sin

II Corinthians

3:17	Free Agency, Patriotism
7:10	Repentance
9:6	Work
9:7	Gifts

Galatians

5:1	Free Agency
5:19-22	Chastity
6:7-8	Work

Ephesians

1:4	Premortal Life
2:19-20	Jesus Christ: Mortal Ministry
3:9	Creation, Jesus Christ: Premortal
3:17-19	Love
4:11-14	Unity
5:31	Marriage
5:33	Marriage
6:1-3	Children
6:1-4	Children, Discipline, Family, Fathers
6:11-12*	Courage

Philippians

4:8	Honesty
4:11	Contentment

Colossians

3:14	Charity
3:16	Music
3:20-21	Children, Discipline, Family

I Timothy

1:15	Jesus Christ: Mortal Ministry
2:5-6	Jesus Christ: Mortal Ministry
3:5	Family
4:7	Gossip
4:12	Example, Youth
4:14	Gifts
5:8	Family
6:6	Contentment
6:7	Death
6:10	Wealth
6:12	Faith
6:17-19	Wealth

II Timothy

1:7	Fear
2:16	Gossip
2:22-23	Youth
3:1-7	Last Days
3:7	Wisdom
3:16-17	Scriptures
4:7-8	Faith, Funeral Messages

Hebrews

5:8-9	Youth
11:1	Faith
11:40	Genealogy
12:1	Patience
12:2	Faith
12:9	Discipline, Obedience

James

1:2-4	Patience
1:5-6	Prayer
1:5	Wisdom
1:12	Temptation
1:13	Temptation
1:15	Sin
1:22	Listening
1:26	Profanity
2:8*	Love
2:14, 17-18, 20, 26	Faith
2:23	Friendship
4:11	Gossip
4:17	Sin
5:14-15	Priesthood
5:16	Prayer

I Peter

2:9	Priesthood
3:15	Testimony
3:18-19	Jesus Christ: Resurrection

BOOK OF MORMON

Title Page	Book of Mormon
I Nephi	
1:1	Family
2:20	America
3:7	Commandments
4:13	Book of Mormon
6:4	Book of Mormon
10:17	Holy Ghost
11:20-21	Jesus Christ: Mortal Ministry
13:10-12	America
13:17-19	America
13:28	Apostasy
17:45	Procrastination, Sin
19:23	Scriptures
22:15	Millennium
22:22	Fear
22:23	Apostasy
22:25-26	Millennium
II Nephi	
1:5	America
1:7	Patriotism
1:7, 9	America
1:15	Love
1:23	Courage
2:2	Tribulation
2:6-7	Atonement
2:11	Temptation
2:22-25	Sin
2:25	Happiness
2:27	Free Agency, Satan
3:15	Prophets
4:15	Scriptures
4:28	Sin
4:31	Sin
8:3	Zion
9:4	Death

II Nephi (continued)

9:6-9	Atonement
9:10-13	Death
9:16	Resurrection
9:28-29	Wisdom
9:40	Fear, Truth
9:41	Jesus Christ: Resurrection, Judgment
9:42, 43	Wisdom
10:11-14	America
10:16	Obedience
10:23	Free Agency
11:5	Covenants
22:2, 5	Music
23:12	Wealth
25:23	Jesus Christ: Resurrection
25:26	Book of Mormon
26:10	Pride
26:29	Priesthood
26:30	Charity
26:31	Zion
26:33	God
28:7-8	Temptation
28:21	Satan, Zion
29:3, 4, 10	Bible
30:11-15*	Millennium
31:5	Baptism
31:17, 19-20	Eternal Life
32:5	Holy Ghost
32:8	Prayer
33:1	Holy Ghost, Speaking

Jacob

2:16	Pride
2:18-19	Wealth, Welfare
2:28	Chastity
2:35	Example, Family
3:10	Example, Family

Jacob (continued

4:10	Jesus Christ: Mortal Ministry, Wisdom
6:12	Wisdom
7:11	Prophet

Enos

:10	Diligence
:27	Funeral Messages

Jarom

:9	Obedience

Omni

:6	Obedience

Mosiah

2:17	Service
2:28	Funeral Messages, Music
2:38	Judgment
2:41	Happiness
3:5-8	Jesus Christ: Mortal Ministry
3:17-19	Atonement
3:18-19	Humility
4:10	Repentance
4:14-15	Family
4:19, 28	Debt
4:28	Debt
4:27	Diligence, Discipline, Stewardship, Word of Wisdom
5:7	Covenants
8:16-17	Prophets
8:18	Miracles
13:16-19*	Sabbath Day
13:15*	Profanity
13:20*	Family, Fathers, Mothers
13:22*	Honesty
13:23*	Gossip, Honesty

Mosiah (continued)

13:24*	Pride
23:15*	Love
18:8-10	Baptism
27:3-4	Pride
29:26-27	Patriotism

Alma

1:27	Fashion
1:30	Wealth
4:10	Apostasy, Example
5:16-19	Judgment
5:26-27	Testimony
5:28	Pride
5:40	God
5:46	Testimony
5:57-58	Records
7:14	Baptism
10:25	Satan
11:37	Sin
11:41-43	Judgment
12:9-11	Humility
12:16	Death
12:24	Purpose of Life
13:15	Tithing
13:18-19	Priesthood
17:2-3	Fasting
24:30	Apostasy
26:22	Work
26:37	Missionary Work
29:1-3, 6-7, 9	Missionary Work
30:53	Satan
30:60	Satan
31:5	Missionary Work
31:24, 28	Fashion
32:16	Humility
32:19	Sin
32:21	Faith

Alma (continued)

32:23	Prophets
32:27	Faith, Testimony
32:28	Faith
33:14	Scriptures
34:27-29	Prayer, Welfare
34:32-33	Procrastination
34:32	Preparation, Purpose of Life
34:34-35	Procrastination, Repentance
37:33-35	Missionary Work
37:35	Family, Youth, Wisdom
37:37	Prayer
39:5	Chastity
39:8	Sin
40:11-12	Funeral Message
40:23	Resurrection
41:10	Sin
42:25	Judgment, Repentance
43:45-47	War
45:16	Patriotism, Sin
48:11, 17	Example
53:20-21	Courage, Youth
56:45-47	Courage, Youth
56:47	Faith, Fear
56:47-48	Family, Mothers
56:56	Youth
57:21, 26-27	Youth
60:23	Repentance
62:40	Prayer

Helaman

3:25	Wealth
4:24	Temples
5:12	Youth
5:17	Repentance
5:32	Repentance
6:30	Satan
7:28	Patriotism
12:4	Sin

III Nephi

1:13	Jesus Christ: Mortal Ministry
6:5	Wealth
9:15	Creation
9:19-20	Sacrifice
9:22	Children
11:3	Speaking
11:1, 3, 7-8, 10-11	Jesus Christ: Resurrection
11:29	Anger
12:3-12*	Obedience, Peace
12:15-16*	Example
12:22*	Anger
12:24*	Gifts
12:27-28*	Attitude
12:38-39*	Anger
12:44*	Love
13:16-18*	Fasting
13:21*	Attitude
13:33*	Wealth
14:1-2*	Judgment
14:15*	Prophets
15:21, 24	Book of Mormon
17:21	Children
18:21	Family, Prayer
18:29	Sacrament
23:7-13	Records
24:8-10*	Honesty
26:6	Scriptures
27:3, 5, 8	Priesthood
27:19-20	Judgment
27:21, 27	Jesus Christ: Mortal Ministry
27:25-26	Judgment, Records
27:27	Example

IV Nephi

1:2-3	Welfare
1:15-16	Happiness

Mormon

9:31	Book of Mormon, Scriptures

Ether

2:7	America
2:9,12	America, Patriotism
3:9	Faith
3:15-16	Jesus Christ: Premortal
12:6	Faith
12:12	Miracles

Moroni

4:1-3*	Sacrament
5:1-3	Sacrament
6:8	Repentance, Satan
7:12, 17	Repentance
7:16	Jesus Christ: Resurrection
7:26	Prayer
7:46-48	Charity
7:47	Love
7:48	Resurrection
8:9-12	Baptism
8:16	Fear
9:9	Chastity
10:4-5	Book of Mormon
10:5	Holy Ghost
10:18, 30	Gifts

DOCTRINE AND COVENANTS

1:2	Prophet
1:12	Preparation
1:14	Listening
1:16	God
1:17	Prophets
1:23	Missionary Work
1:28	Humility
1:31	Obedience, Sin
1:32-33	Repentance
1:32	Forgiveness
1:35	God
1:37	Commandments
1:38	Missionary Work, Prophets
2:1-2	Fathers
2:1-3*	Genealogy
3:19-20	Book of Mormon
4:1-7	Missionary Work
4:2	Missionary Work
4:6	Patience
6:7	Eternal Life, Wealth, Wisdom
6:12	Gossip
6:13	Gifts
6:16	God
6:20	Love, Obedience
6:29-30	Missionary Work
6:32*	Missionary Work
6:33, 36	Fear
8:2	Holy Ghost
9:7-9	Truth
10:4	Word of Wisdom
10:5	Satan
10:28	Honesty
11:7*	Wisdom
11:21	Teaching
12:8	Humility
13	Priesthood
14:7	Obedience

Doctrine and Covenants (continued)

18:10, 13, 15-16	Missionary Work, Repentance
18:23	Jesus Christ: Resurrection
19:4, 16-18	Repentance
19:23	Listening
20:37	Baptism
20:73	Baptism
20:77	Sacrament
20:79	Sacrament
21:1	Records
21:5	Prophets
25:12	Music, Praise
27:2-3	Sacrament
27:11	Fathers
27:15-18	Courage
29:11	Jesus Christ: Second Coming
29:34	God
29:46	Death
29:46-47	Baptism, Children
31:12	Prayer
38:23-24	Teaching
38:24-25	Friendship
38:27	Unity
38:30	Fear, Preparation
38:39	Pride
41:5	Obedience
42:6	Missionary Work
42:11	Missionary Work
42:12	Book of Mormon
42:14	Teaching
42:22, 25	Chastity
42:29	Love, Service
42:31	Welfare
42:38	Service
42:42	Work
42:43	Word of Wisdom
42:44, 46, 48	Death
42:44,46	Funeral Message

Doctrine and Covenants (continued)

Doctrine and Covenants (continued)

58:47	Missionary Work	
58:64	Missionary Work	
59:6*	Love	
59:9-13	Sabbath Day	
59:14-16	Fasting	
59:23	Eternal Life, Peace, Work	
60:2	Fear	
60:2-3	Missionary Work	
60:13	Work	
61:36-39	Funeral Message	
62:6	Honesty	
63:50-51	Millennium	
63:61-62	Profanity	
64:7	Forgiveness	
64:8-9	Forgiveness	
64:10	Forgiveness	
64:23	Tithing	
64:29	Priesthood	
64:29-30	Delegation	
64:33	Diligence	
65:2	Missionary Work	
65:3-4	Missionary Work	
68:4	Scriptures	
68:6	Courage	
68:25, 27-28	Children	
68:25, 28	Family	
70:3-4	Stewardship	
72:3-4	Judgment	
74:7	Death	
75:10	Holy Ghost	
75:28	Fathers	
75:29	Diligence, Work	
76:22-24	Jesus Christ: Resurrection, Resurrection	
76:25-31*	Satan	
76:41	Jesus Christ: Mortal Ministry	
76:73*	Jesus Christ: Resurrection	

Doctrine and Covenants (continued)

78:7	Preparation
78:13-15	Preparation
82:3	Delegation, Sin, Stewardship
82:7	Sin
82:10	Covenants, Obedience
82:14	Zion
82:18	Work
83:4-5	Welfare
83:6	Welfare
84:26-27	Priesthood
84:33-40	Priesthood
84:43-44	Diligence
84:45-46	Jesus Christ: Resurrection
84:77	Friendship
84:106	Teaching
84:107-108	Stewardship
84:109-110	Stewardship
85:3	Tithing
87:1-3	America
88:15-16	Resurrection
88:22	Judgment
88:77-78	Teaching
88:81-82	Missionary Work, Sin
88:110	Millennium
88:110-114	Millennium
88:118	Teaching, Wisdom
88:119	Family, Welfare
88:124	Word of Wisdom
89:3	Word of Wisdom
89:18-21	Word of Wisdom
90:11	Missionary Work
90:24	Covenants
93:1	Repentance
93:24	Truth
93:28	Truth
93:29	Creation
93:33-34	Happiness, Resurrection

Doctrine and Covenants (continued)

93:36	Wisdom
93:40	Family
93:45	Friendship
93:49	Prayer
95:1	Repentance
97:21	Zion
98:4-10	America
98:8	Free Agency
98:15	Covenants
98:33-37	War
101:28-31	Millennium
101:80	America, Patriotism
104:11-13	Stewardship
104:13	Work
104:18	Charity
104:78	Debt
105:5	Zion
106:3	Work
107:2-4	Priesthood
107:5, 8	Priesthood
107:13-14	Priesthood
107:68	Priesthood
107:99-100	Priesthood
108:7	Gossip
109:7*	Wisdom
109:16	Temples
110:4	Jesus Christ: Resurrection
110:13-16	Genealogy
111:11	Revelation, Wisdom
112:10	Humility
115:4	Priesthood
119:4	Tithing
121:7-10	Friendship
121:33	Wisdom
121:34-37	Priesthood
121:39-40	Priesthood
121:41-43	Priesthood

Doctrine and Covenants (continued)

121:43	Discipline
121:45	Profanity, Virtue
121:46	Holy Ghost
122:5-8	Tribulation
122:7	Tribulation
122:7-8	Sacrifice
127:4	Diligence, Patience
128:8	Records
128:12	Baptism
128:15	Genealogy
128:18	Genealogy
130:18-19	Wisdom
130:20-21	Obedience
130:22	Fathers, God
131:1-3	Covenants
131:1-4	Marriage
131:6	Wisdom
132:8	Temples
132:15-17	Marriage
132:19-20	Marriage
133:5	Repentance
133:10	Procrastination
133:37	Missionary Work
134:1-2	Patriotism
135:3	Prophets
136:28	Praise
138:29-30	Delegation

PEARL OF GREAT PRICE

Moses

1:11	God
1:33	Creation, Jesus Christ: Premortal
1:39	Eternal Life, God
3:3	Sabbath Day
3:5, 7	Creation
3:18*	Marriage
3:24*	Marriage
4:1-4	Satan
5:5-9	Sacrifice
5:10, 11	Sin
5:13	Satan
6:46	Genealogy
6:57	Family
6:53, 59-60	Baptism
6:64-65	Baptism
7:18	Zion
7:64-65	Millennium

Abraham

2:9-11	Covenants
2:10	Fathers
3:22-23	Premortal Life
3:24	Creation
3:25-26	Purpose of Life

Joseph Smith

2:12	Scripture
2:17	God
2:19	Pride
2:22, 24-25	Truth
2:32	Resurrection

Articles of Faith

1	God
2	Sin
3	Atonement

Articles of Faith (continued)

4	Baptism, Faith, Holy Ghost, Repentance
5	Missionary Work
6	Priesthood
7	Gifts
8	Bible, Book of Mormon
9	Revelation
10	Zion
11	Free Agency
12	Patriotism
13	Honesty, Virtue

Refers to scriptures quoted regularly that have more than one scriptural reference and are therefore included by reference only, not the entire text.

My Own Favorite Scriptures

_____

_____

_____

_____

_____

_____

_____

_____

_____

_____

_____

_____

_____

_____